INSIDE THE CULT

OXFORD STUDIES IN SOCIAL
AND CULTURAL ANTHROPOLOGY

Oxford Studies in Social and Cultural Anthropology represents the work of authors, new and established, which will set the criteria of excellence in ethnographic description and innovation in analysis. The series serves as an essential source of information about the world and the discipline.

INSIDE THE CULT

RELIGIOUS INNOVATION AND TRANSMISSION IN PAPUA NEW GUINEA

HARVEY WHITEHOUSE

CLARENDON PRESS · OXFORD
1995

Oxford University Press, Walton Street, Oxford OX2 6DP
Oxford New York
Athens Auckland Bangkok Bombay
Calcutta Cape Town Dar es Salaam Delhi
Florence Hong Kong Istanbul Karachi
Kuala Lumpur Madras Madrid Melbourne
Mexico City Nairobi Paris Singapore
Taipei Tokyo Toronto
and associated companies in
Berlin Ibadan

Oxford is a trade mark of Oxford University Press

Published in the United States
by Oxford University Press Inc., New York

© Harvey Whitehouse 1995

British Library Cataloguing in Publication Data
Data available

Library of Congress Cataloging-in-Publication Data
Whitehouse, Harvey.
Inside the cult : religious innovations and transmission in Papua
New Guinea / Harvey Whitehouse.
— (Oxford studies in social and cultural
anthropology)
Based on the author's thesis (doctoral)—University of Cambridge,
1990.
Includes bibliographical references and index.
1. Cargo cults—Papua New Guinea.   2. Baining (Papua New Guinea
people)—Religion.   3. Papua New Guinea—Religion—20th century.
I. Title.   II. Series.
GN671.N5155   1995   299'.92—dc20   94–45751
ISBN 0–19–827981–7
ISBN 0–19–828051–3(Pbk.)

1 3 5 7 9 10 8 6 4 2

Typeset by Graphicraft Typesetters Ltd., Hong Kong
Printed in Great Britain
on acid-free paper by
Biddles Ltd, Guildford and King's Lynn

Dedicated to
my parents

ACKNOWLEDGEMENTS

THIS book is based on my doctoral research at the University of Cambridge (1986–90), funded by an ESRC Student Competition Award. A grant from the Smuts Memorial Fund covered the costs of audio-visual equipment used in the field. A Research Fellowship at Trinity Hall, Cambridge (1990–3) enabled me to develop my thesis for publication. I will always be grateful to my erstwhile teachers, fellow students, and colleagues at Cambridge for their stimulation and encouragement.

I am particularly indebted to my former supervisors, Gilbert Lewis and Ernest Gellner, and examiners, Alfred Gell and Stephen Hugh-Jones, for their constructive criticisms of my work. I have similarly benefited from incisive comments on earlier drafts from Simon Harrison and Eric Hirsch. A visit to Paris in 1994, funded by the CNRS, provided me with an opportunity to discuss my research in detail with Carlo Severi, Michael Houseman, and Pascal Boyer. Their valuable comments and criticisms spurred me to make a number of last-minute changes to the typescript. The insights of these nine people have been indispensable, and I hope that they will not be too disappointed by the finished product.

I should like to express my deepest thanks to the people of Dadul, Maranagi, and Sunam for their time, energy, and generous hospitality. In this study, I have used pseudonyms or titles for many of my close friends and 'informants' in the field, but out of the context of the events described below I shall dispense with this subterfuge and acknowledge my particular gratitude to: Tomay, Raphael, Michael, Vitalis, Blasias, Stanis, Elisa, Tade, Tarsisias, Pious, Konrad, Andrew, Lucas, Brusias, Nelson, Dakala, Daniel, Elizabeth, and ToMaibe. I should also like to express my deep appreciation to Kolman and Francis for their openness and hospitality. In Rabaul the staff of the United Church Community Hostel were more than generous and I will always remember them with affection.

Finally, I should like to thank my wife, Karen, for her companionship and optimism in the field, despite the many hazards that we faced. I am indebted to both Karen and my son Danny for putting up with my hermit-like behaviour when writing up. Danny will not remember Papua New Guinea, where he was born, but I hope this book will provide a vivid record of the events in which we were all once embroiled.

CONTENTS

FIGURES

MAPS

TABLES

INTRODUCTION

We look back because we are lost in the world of the whiteman's knowledge. Recalling our ancestors, Adam and Eve, we see that their lives were good in Paradise. But they sinned, and now we must all toil and suffer. So we ask ourselves in our confusion today: 'Where are we to go? Where is our home?' All the whiteman's knowledge has blinded us to what we once possessed. Today, the mission tells us that Jesus will come in sight of all of us—those of us who are alive, and those who have died. So we ask ourselves: 'Who will bring back our ancestors? Many people seek knowledge but we—the Baining peoples—are the last to receive it. So, who will transform the old world into a new world?'

(The First Orator in the Kivung community of Dadul)

THE Pidgin word *kivung* means a 'meeting' or 'to meet'. For thousands of people living in East New Britain, Papua New Guinea, the word also refers to a religious movement, based around a mixture of millenarian, Christian, nationalist, and 'cargo cult' ideas. In spite of Christian influences, the attitudes of Kivung supporters are basically anti-missionary. The movement's full title, the 'Pomio Kivung', associates it with the 'Pomio' peoples, living within a radius of some forty miles of a coastal settlement called Pomio in the south-west of East New Britain. There is no language called 'Pomio'—the term has simply become a way of referring to the many indigenous groups of the area speaking a number of languages.

The Pomio Kivung is a larger phenomenon than its name suggests. In addition to its many Pomio supporters, it has loyal followers to the north, extending deeply among the Mali Baining, who live on the borders of a wealthy, cosmopolitan region in the north-east. This region, the centre of modern industry and government in the province, is occupied by the Tolai, whose relations with their poor neighbours, the Baining, have always been basically exploitative. The Tolai have abundant capital, education, and technology, but an extreme shortage of land. Their territory, encompassing some of the richest volcanic soils in Papua New Guinea, was seized from the Baining in the late eighteenth century, when the Tolai's ancestors migrated from nearby New Ireland. The Baining were driven into the less fertile mountains and coastal areas to the south and west. Following pacification by Germany in the late nineteenth and early twentieth centuries, the Tolai threat of enslavement, cannibalism, and raiding was gradually replaced by the threat of encroachment, through covert sorcery, trickery, and European complicity. Australian administration, between 1919 and 1975 (notwithstanding the devastating period of Japanese occupation during the Second World War), accelerated the pace of development among the Tolai, establishing some of the highest rates of education, population growth, and white-collar employment in the country. The Tolai rapidly became an indigenous élite in Papua and New Guinea, and accomplices in the colonization and missionization of the country. Following independence in 1975, the Tolai naturally dominated the administration of East New Britain, having an inexhaustible supply of sophisticated politicians and bureaucrats to run the provincial government.

The peoples known as Pomio and Baining, along with other rural populations, have witnessed all this with some frustration. Comparing themselves with the Tolai, they see that they are poor, uneducated, and politically under-represented. The Baining see their land diminished with every passing year as the Tolai spread further into the mountains and along the coasts. The Pomio Kivung sees itself as the champion of these rural peoples. Its followers oppose the sale of land to the Tolai, and repudiate all Tolai customs and overtures of friendship. Prior to the spread of the Pomio Kivung, some rural groups, under the influence of Tolai missionaries, had adopted shell money in certain transactions, and had learned the magic, language, and other ways of the Tolai. Pomio Kivung members reject all this, along with the chewing of betel-nut, a practice for which the Tolai are renowned. They avoid dealings with the provincial government and its varied personnel: they raise their own 'taxes', use their own legal apparatus, and look forward eagerly to political autonomy. This latter aspiration is pursued by pragmatic means, in that Pomio Kivung leaders have long campaigned in central government for their own province, separate from the Tolai region. For most supporters, however, it is a supernatural intervention that will deliver them from Tolai domination. Their ancestors will return with white skin, bearing all the wealth and technology of the whiteman. The non-Tolai region will be transformed into a vast metropolis, a sort of urban paradise, in which all goods known to man will be freely available. The rural peoples will have their own government. This government is said to exist already in the 'other world', the world of the dead. All those ancestors who are expected to return are members of the ghostly assembly, and are referred to collectively as the 'Village Government'.

This study focuses initially on the Pomio Kivung movement as a whole: its ideas, organization, external relations, and history. The central part of the study, however, is concerned with a small splinter group among the Mali Baining that temporarily broke away from the mainstream movement in a unilateral attempt to bring back the ancestors. The splinter group engaged in extraordinary new rituals, involving the 'reinvention' of traditional cultural materials, the receiving of messages from the dead, and much dancing, singing, and feasting. This culminated in a period when all subsistence activity was abandoned, and the group devoted its energies to all-night vigils in readiness for a supernatural transformation. Eventually, health problems and external pressure forced group members to return to their daily lives, and they were accepted back into the mainstream Pomio Kivung.

I witnessed these events from start to finish, and my description of them is organized more or less chronologically, in a form which at times resembles a diary or novel. But the material is intended to illuminate a particular theoretical problem, namely, the relationship between the way religious ideas are codified and transmitted, and the sociological dimensions of Kivung activity.

The Problem

The central problem of this book is the relationship between two contrasting politico-religious regimes which coexist within the Pomio Kivung. These two regimes comprise the mainstream movement described in Chapters 2 and 3, and the splinter group described in Chapters 4 to 6.

The mainstream movement encompasses a large religious community, spread out across several language groups. Every Kivung village has its own orators and other officials who play leading roles in the rituals. The leaders of the movement, operating from their imposing headquarters in the Pomio region, continually dispatch 'supervisors' to patrol among supporters, ensuring that the mainstream institutions are uniformly observed. Any village which deviates, either doctrinally or in the performance of rituals, may have its membership revoked. The policies of the leaders are held to be incontrovertible because they are received directly from the ancestors. In the course of the book, I show that there is a complex relationship between these features of uniformity, hierarchy, and scale, on the one hand, and the way Kivung ideology is logically organized, verbalized, disseminated, and remembered, on the other. The emphasis on repetitive practices is linked to specific aspects of cognition which underpin the emergence of an 'imagined community', and the articulation of a nationalist vision.

These general features of the mainstream movement contrast starkly with those of the splinter group. The latter was a very small-scale phenomenon, encompassing a population of closely related kinsmen. The distinctive ideas of the splinter group did not take the form of a complex, logically integrated body of doctrine, but were codified in concrete metaphors, principally the metaphor of a ring. The ring took many forms: it was a circle of house posts, of buried bottles, and of wild vines, but most prominently it was formed by a circle of human bodies, on certain occasions naked and motionless and on others dramatically decorated and animated. The metaphor of the ring had many guises, but its transmission was more than a symbolic 'statement' of the group's unity; it created, enacted, and expressed that unity. Through such rituals, the community evoked powerful emotions, sensations, and revelations which, entailing both extraordinary and unique experiences, were encoded in episodic memory. The sense of solidarity and inspiration stimulated by the splinter group was radically different from the experience of oratory and routinized ritual in the mainstream movement. Differences in the cognitive, affective, and transmissive dimensions of mainstream and splinter-group activities are shown, in the course of this book, to produce divergent political regimes: the one large-scale, standardized, enduring, verbally transmitted, logically integrated, centralized, hierarchical, transportable, routinized; the other small-scale, innovative, temporary, non-verbally transmitted, focused around analogic imagery, difficult to spread, emotional, climactic, and sporadic.

These are just some aspects of the divergence which will unfold in the ensuing pages. Nevertheless, the mainstream movement and the splinter group are part of a single ideological system. Moreover, the differences between them are only superficially about opposition and 'breaking away'. It is shown that splinter groups are a widespread feature of the Pomio Kivung, and that their supporters almost always return to the fold when the ancestors fail to arrive. I therefore seek to establish what, if anything, splinter-group activity contributes to the Pomio Kivung movement as a whole. I argue that it supplies a dimension to religious experience which is lacking in the humdrum routines of orthodox ritual, and that it renews commitment to Kivung aspirations. If so, this is certainly an unintended consequence of climactic ritual, and it does not imply some kind of 'functionalist' interpretation. It is rather an attempt to understand how people handle religious experience cognitively, how this affects their commitment to the Pomio Kivung, and why, every so often, they are willing to risk their health and even their lives by breaking away from the safe routines of daily life.

This subject matter recalls numerous attempts in the sociology of religion to grapple with an ethnographically pervasive divergence in religious thought and behaviour. One thinks immediately of Max Weber's distinction between 'routinized' and 'charismatic' authority, of Ernest Gellner's 'pendulum swing theory of Islam', of Victor Turner's distinction between 'structure' and '*communitas*', and of other theories in a dichotomous mould. The theoretical arguments of this book have much in common with all these approaches, as well as with less obvious ones, such as Jack Goody's discussion of the divergent implications of literacy and orality. At the end of this study, however, it will become clear that I am not merely proposing 'yet another' dichotomy to add to the list, but one which aims to tie certain aspects of them together, by recasting the problem in the light of recent findings in cognitive psychology.

In Chapter 1 I sketch the culture and history of the region where I worked, while Chapter 2 provides an introduction to the Pomio Kivung movement, which became the focus of my research. Chapter 3 explores the principal features of the mainstream movement and some of the crucial links between language-based codification, routinization, structure, and scale.

Chapter 4 describes the emergence of a Kivung splinter group in two Mali Baining villages, a process inspired by the dramatic and unexpected possession of a young man, called Tanotka. Support for Tanotka was covertly developed by his 'brother', Baninge. Gradually, and through a complex series of behind-the-scenes machinations, the two men consolidated a core of loyal followers. The distinctive ideas and ritual practices of a local cult began to emerge. In contrast with the humdrum, repetitive practices of the mainstream movement, the 'new' activities led by Baninge and Tanotka were highly evocative of emotions and sensations, ranging from euphoria to shameful eroticism. In Chapter 5 I describe the climactic rituals of the splinter group, in which a break from mainstream institutions became increasingly pronounced. A tendency towards non-verbal transmission, analogic communication, and emotionality found full expression in a period of vigils held to welcome the ancestors back from the dead. The sermonizing and routinized rituals of Kivung orthodoxy were replaced by an enthusiastic exploration of more ecstatic forms of religiosity. In both these chapters, I explore the sociological implications of a fundamental shift in the mode of religiosity. Chapter 6 then describes the

aftermath of these dramatic events. My account of this period is tied in
to the theoretical design of the study, but it also serves to complete a story
about the lives of real people with whom I hope the reader will, by this
stage, have come to empathize.

    Chapter 7 attempts to explain the popularity of the Pomio Kivung in
its various guises in a way that is linked to my discussion of divergent
modes of religiosity. Chapter 8 draws together the arguments of the book,
and its principal implications for the anthropology of religion. First, it is
argued that the relationship between millenarism and nationalism is not,
as is widely supposed, related to the content of ideology, but more fundamentally to its mode of transmission. Secondly, it is argued that the
limitations of existing dichotomous representations of religion lie in their
failure to theorize adequately the connections between psychological and
sociological dimensions of religious life. In seeking to remedy this situation, I come to my third and final claim, namely that the theory adopted
here crosses the boundaries between intellectualist, psychological, and
sociological perspectives on religion, and fuses elements of each into a
new and portentous unity.

Orientation

I was 'in the field' with my wife for twenty months, between October
1987 and June 1989. During the first year we lived in Dadul, a village of
about seventy Mali Baining people, virtually all of whom were members
of the Pomio Kivung. Our arrival in the village is described in Chapter 4,
because it forms part of the story of the splinter group which began there.
Initially, there was a widespread feeling that we were ancestors, who had
been sent by the Village Government as a sign that it would soon materialize on earth. People also tended to think that we were trying to find
out who could be trusted, and who might tell lies. This information, it
was assumed, would be used on the Day of Judgement. Ideas about my
wife and me crystallized along these lines as time passed, partly in response to developments already occurring within the community, and
partly in response to our own behaviour. It was soon realized that I was
interested primarily in the Kivung, and worked mainly with men and
boys, whereas my wife spent most of her time with the women, investi-
gating their techniques of child care, gardening, and domestic work, their
experiences of marriage and patterns of interaction within the family.
When my wife became pregnant in 1988, and delivered our son in April
1989, this curiously did not disprove speculation about our other-worldly
origins. One man confided in me that it had come as a shock, not because

it meant we were 'human' but because it meant that ancestors could, after all, produce children. But I never discovered in detail how views on the matter evolved, because by the time the pregnancy was visible we had moved to the village of Sunam, several miles down the road, and, in spite of making visits to Dadul, my knowledge of rumours and discussion there was less intimate than before, particularly when it came to such personal topics.

The move to Sunam was partly a response to the pregnancy, and the desire to be within easy reach of a hospital, should problems arise. The move coincided, however, with a period of intense opposition towards the people of Dadul on the part of the government, mission, and local communities. According to these onlookers, the people of Dadul had become 'cargo cult' fanatics, bent on severing all customary relations with the outside world, violating the law, and risking their own health and economic resources. This climate of criticism inevitably extended to me, since I had been very visibly a part of the Dadul community, a prominent bystander, and even a participant during the most controversial developments. I made every effort, with considerable soul-searching, to ensure that I had as little influence as possible on the splinter group. Nevertheless, for the sake of personal security and good public relations, the move to Sunam, which was 'outside' the Pomio Kivung, seemed at the time to be a necessary precaution. The people there, especially the Community Court Magistrate and Chairman, were extremely hospitable, in spite of probable reservations about the nature of my work. For their part, the people of Dadul expressed no resentment at our removal, and considerable concern about our welfare. That it must have been a source of disappointment to them was inevitable, but their continued co-operation with my research is a striking testimony to the generosity of the people there and (I feel) to the friendship which existed between us.

In view of the highly controversial nature of many events described in this book, I have changed the names of all participants except politicians, whose actions and views have already been subjected to public scrutiny. My main concern is that, should any readers of this book come into contact with the Mali Baining, they respect the secrecy surrounding the *awan* and other male cult activities, and that discussion of Kivung religion is handled sensitively and sympathetically. Among the many 'Westernized' people of Papua New Guinea, there is widespread prejudice towards so-called 'cargo cults'. As far as I can see, the highly intelligent individuals who helped me to comprehend the Pomio Kivung stand to gain nothing from this publication, but I hope readers will view their predicament and efforts with respect and compassion.

1

The Cultural and Historical Setting

EAST New Britain Province is best known in economic and political anthropology as the home of the Tolai, whose 'primitive capitalism' (T. S. Epstein 1968) has brought them academic fame and whose successful manipulation of Western resources and institutions has made their region a political and economic powerhouse in Papua New Guinea (see especially A. L. Epstein 1969, 1978; Salisbury 1970; Neumann 1992). Yet the Tolai occupy only a small area of the province, albeit the choicest region from the viewpoint of commercial exploitation (largely due to the rich volcanic soil, flat topography, and mercantile opportunities afforded by the natural harbour at Rabaul). The mountainous area of rainforest covering the rest of the province is sparsely populated by a variety of other groups, whose languages contrast very starkly with the Melanesian vernacular of the Tolai.

Beyond the terrestrial boundaries of the Tolai region lie the populations collectively known as 'Baining', who speak non-Austronesian languages. The roughly square head of land at the eastern reaches of New Britain island is called the Gazelle Peninsula. Apart from the north-eastern sector (Tolai region), this peninsula is occupied exclusively by the Baining. South-west of the neck of land separating Open Bay to the west and Wide Bay to the east lie a number of other groups (Panoff 1969), most of which are subsumed under the collective label 'Pomio'. Of the Pomio peoples, the Maenge who live around Malmal at Jacquinot Bay figure most highly in my account.

This book is primarily concerned with certain Baining communities. The first thing to note about the Baining is that they do not constitute a homogeneous population, but may be divided into at least five extant groups. The north-west quarter of the Gazelle Peninsula is occupied by the Kaket Baining (see Bateson 1931/2, Pool 1984, and Fajans 1985) who are geographically isolated by uninhabited mountains and rainforest from all other Baining peoples. The southern half of the Gazelle Peninsula is occupied by the four remaining Baining groups: the Uramot, Kairak,

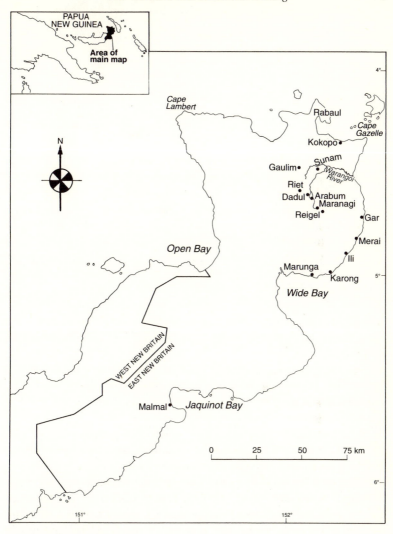

East New Britain Province

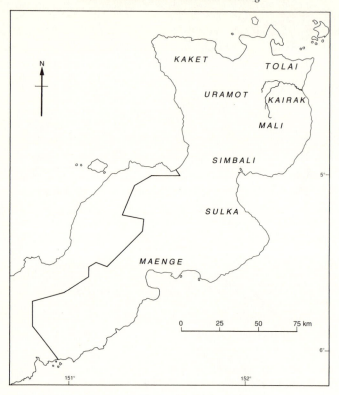

Distribution of Baining, Tolai, Sulka, and Maenge groups

Mali, and Simbali. All five groups have distinct languages (of which there may be several dialects) and cultural traditions.

Kaket (and its dialects) is the only Baining language to have been described (Parker and Parker 1974), but it is more distantly related to the other four Baining languages than the latter are related to each other. The Uramot and Kairak tongues are particularly closely related and this is explained locally by a myth in which ('long ago') an Uramot man in a state of delirium mispronounced his language and was copied by his kinsmen, thereby founding the Kairak tongue. Likewise, the Mali and Simbali languages have clear phonological affinities.

I conducted all my interviews in Pidgin, a language that everybody in Dadul and Sunam spoke fluently. I struggled continuously to learn Mali, but never advanced beyond the ability to understand the gist of simple conversations. My attempts to speak Mali were faltering and invariably riddled with errors. I relied heavily on informants for the translation of public oratory. I do not consider this to have been a crippling disadvantage when it came to understanding Kivung ideas. These were originally transmitted to the Mali Baining in the medium of Pidgin, and this is also the language through which the Maenge leadership, and its representatives, communicated with Baining supporters. Moreover, all the Mali phrases (including euphemisms) for Kivung rituals, buildings, equipment, and doctrines are literal, direct translations from the Pidgin. For this reason, when discussing institutions prevailing in the movement as a whole, I refer only to Pidgin terms.

The five Baining groups which I have mentioned each occupy a bounded region of land to which they enjoy exclusive rights of 'customary ownership' recognized by the government legal apparatus. Such land is owned by the group as a whole. In general, Baining groups have an abundance of land and any Baining person enjoys the right to cultivate any unused land associated with speakers of the same mother tongue. Unused land includes not just virgin forest but also tracts which have been cultivated in the past but are no longer bearing. When unused land is sold to outsiders, the money ideally belongs to the language group (e.g. Mali) or part of it (e.g. coastal Mali villages) as a whole (e.g. it may be split between all the Mali households in all the relevant Mali villages). Membership of these large land-holding groups is passed on through the mother. Neither the idea of collective land ownership, nor the inheritance of rights over land, are traditional Baining customs but were introduced as a result of colonization. The precise origins of the inheritance rule are unclear, but one advantage (which must have been apparent to all concerned) was that it obviated disputes regarding paternity.

Although Baining peoples are distinguishable into separate groups, they have a keen sense of their relatedness. The name 'Baining' appears to be a Tolai word meaning 'inland people' with the pejorative connotation of 'bush person', but it is the name which Baining people have come to use for themselves when dealing with all non-Baining persons (see Fajans 1985: 58). Among Mali, Simbali, Uramot, and Kairak speaking groups, it is usual for people to use the term 'Baining' even among themselves as the standard referent for their ethnic identity. For example, if an elder is castigating an audience for being lazy in some context, he is likely to say: 'We Baining people are notoriously lazy', even though he may be referring only to the reputation of certain Uramot villages. On the other hand, of course, it is occasionally necessary to use the names of distinct Baining groups, for example, when there is a dispute over the boundary between Mali and Uramot customary land or when attention is being drawn to some difference in ritual practices.

Habitual reliance on the term 'Baining' is not necessarily demoralizing. Whatever derisive connotations the term might convey in the Tolai language, these are not universally recognized among the Baining themselves. Meanwhile, the breadth of application for the term 'Baining' provides a basis for large-scale ethnic solidarity in the face of 'foreign' domination. This principle is extended by the compound term 'Pomio-Baining', which nowadays tends to convey the common interests of rural groups in East New Britain in the face of the much wealthier and more powerful Tolai. Moreover, those who recognize that the Tolai word 'Baining' connotes 'backwardness' or 'underdevelopment', sometimes claim that its usage contributes to a critique of iniquities in the region, so that the persistence of a pejorative label is to some extent turned to political advantage.

In spite of the widespread recognition of common Baining identity, Baining groups occasionally repudiate the term, either in pursuit of a more dignified and indigenous catch-all term for 'Baining peoples', or for the purposes of redefining the range over which ethnic identity is acknowledged. The latter process was discernible in the course of my fieldwork in the Mali Baining village of Dadul. Links with other Baining groups were repudiated, and the Uramot Baining in particular were classified along with the Tolai as foreigners whose customary practices were potentially contaminating. At that time the referent for ethnic identity in Dadul was the term 'Mali', and the term 'Baining' was consciously avoided. This innovation was part of an attempt to effect sweeping transformations in the memories and identity of a small population near the borders of the Tolai region, a process which I focus upon in Chapters 4 to 6. As with other cultural innovations at that time, the new emphasis on Mali identity was constructed in opposition to a common stock of ideas about Baining ethnicity, which were transformed rather than diminished by a repudiation of the term itself. Moreover, this repudiation of the Baining label was short-lived, and the conventional terminological practices, outlined above, were reinstated.

In view of the importance and malleability of indigenous conceptions of group identity, it is difficult to find a satisfactory method of labelling populations in the region for the purposes of this study. Nevertheless, in the interests of clarity and consistency, I shall depart from conventional local practice by referring to speakers of the Mali language at all times by the specific terms 'Mali' or 'Mali Baining', and only use the label 'Baining' on its own to refer nonspecifically to members of Kaket, Uramot, Kairak, Mali, and Simbali groups (or some combination of them).

Baining Dances

The Baining are probably best known, among Melanesianists, for their extraordinary daytime and night-time dance cycles, and the elaborate costumes worn by participants. These traditions are all the more striking because they contrast with the simplicity and even drabness of everyday material culture among the Baining. The Baining do not transact feathers, shells, or other artefacts, as occurs elsewhere in Papua New Guinea. Prior to contact, the height of Baining architectural achievements were their temples—round, undecorated houses with thatched roofs of blade grass.[1] But these were small and unimpressive in comparison with, for example, the awesome *haus tambaran* architecture of the Sepik (e.g. Forge 1966). Domestic dwellings, moreover, were little more than lean-to shelters. Since colonization, and the formation of permanent Baining villages, rectangular houses came to be constructed (sometimes raised on stilts) in the style favoured by government patrol officers. The Baining have no tradition of carving, no bows and arrows, and no elaborate musical instruments. Occasionally, however, the men construct complex, beautifully decorated costumes for the purpose of dances which, having been used, are carefully destroyed. European impressions of this state of affairs were succinctly expressed by the pioneering anthropologist Gregory Bateson (1931/2: 338), who lived among the Baining for several months in 1927:

The material culture of this people is among the most miserable in the world, and yet it has blossomed out into the strange extravagance of these patterned head-dresses. In his idle hours, when another native might ornament or carve some object, the Baining man will pick a piece of charcoal out of the fire and begin to draw geometrical patterns, rehearsing those he has seen before, or experimenting to discover new designs.

There is considerable variation among Baining groups with regard to their dances and costumes. Corbin (1979: 159–60) divides them into three broad traditions: the North-west Baining (Kaket, composed of several dialectally distinguished groups); the Central Baining (Kairak, Uramot, and the now extinct Vir); the South-east Baining (Mali, Simbali, and the now extinct Kachin and acculturated Mokolkol). These divisions are based on Corbin's assessments of stylistic variation, but precise information on the sociological differences between dance traditions is not available. According to Corbin, all Baining dances, regardless of stylistic differences, incorporate a 'daytime/night-time, male/female, and village/bush series of dualisms' (1979: 179). These binary oppositions are apparent throughout the region, but it is doubtful whether they are conceptually organized in Baining thought in a 'structuralist' fashion, such that, for example, day dance is to night dance as female is to male, as village is to bush. Certainly, none of my Baining informants provided evidence of this type of digital codification with regard to dances (cf. Barth 1975: 223–331).

In keeping with the tentative nature of Corbin's statements about the organizing themes of Baining dances is a general confusion and vagueness in the literature regarding their overt purposes. Baining dances have been associated, among other things, with male initiation, the celebration of harvests, and mourning the dead. Corbin, however, associated male initiation only with the night dance (1979: 168) and fertility/funereal celebrations with the day dance (1979: 160). Other commentators hedge the question. Hesse, for example, in a passage on Baining dances entitled 'Fertility Cult or Initiation Rite?' (1982: 41–2), argues that Baining celebrations are:

moments to break the monotony of one's everyday ordinary life. . . . For some younger people this particular feast will gain special importance, because they will participate for the first time in the making of a mask, or in performing a spear dance, or maybe because they will find a companion for the years ahead. It would be undue exaggeration though to reduce the Baining dances to initiation ceremonies or to a fertility cult.

This quotation contains Hesse's only reference to 'initiation', and the matter is dropped. Bateson observed that the difficulty in resolving such issues lay in the reluctance of the Baining 'to talk about their religion'. He lamented: 'I could never collect any general statement either that the ceremonies were good for the crops or that they referred to ghosts or ancestors' (1931/2: 337). Exegesis for dances may well be absent for all Baining groups, although some older Mali Baining men claim that the ancestors sustained an elaborate exegetical tradition which has now been lost.[2] Nevertheless, this should not obstruct interpretation, as Gell's classic analysis of the Umeda Ida (1975), in the absence of extensive indigenous commentaries, amply demonstrates (although see Juillerat 1992).

A rather more serious problem facing the contemporary investigator is that some Baining groups, such as the inland Mali and certain Kaket populations, abandoned many of their dance traditions in the wake of missionization. Fajans (1985: 86) explained:

I was unable to elicit information about how dances were traditionally initiated. At present the occasions for dances all seem to be stimulated by external influences. The missionaries call for dances at the dedication of a new church, school, or health centre. Teachers initiate dances to celebrate the end of term.

Among the Mali, I was able to collect some basic details of the former religion, which are now presented in summary form. The dances I describe were only dimly remembered in my fieldwork area, but an attempt to restore part of the tradition occurred in 1988 (see Chapter 4). In this section, I will also discuss the role of Uramot dances among the inland Mali Baining which, having survived the censure of missionaries, nowadays provide an important dimension of the relations between Kivung members and 'outsiders' (discussed further in Chapter 2).

The Mali Baining traditionally had two main categories of dance, the *awan* and the *mendas*. The *awan* was performed to mark important occasions, such as the death of a family man, an extraordinary or portentous occurrence, a successful raid against enemy groups, or merely to celebrate and consume an abundant harvest. The costumed figures that appeared at the *awan* were called *awanga*. Their costumes were constructed by men at a secret location in the bush, a few days before the dance. The most elaborate part of the costume was the head-dress, assembled around a conical wooden frame and covered with strands of a certain species of wood, which I have been unable to identify. When stripped of bark and beaten, the wood breaks into its constituent fibres, resembling a brush. The base of the stick was inserted at the apex of the conical frame and the strands bent back so that they draped down around the cone, like thick, straight hair. The strands, which are naturally white, were then coloured by 'spitting' a yellow dye over them, using a technique of blowing through pursed lips (see Fig. 4). It required some skill to achieve the proper spraying effect. The body was covered from head to toe by wild palm fronds. The palm was split and the stem bent into a circular band so that the fronds draped downwards. One band was worn at the waist, its fronds covering the dancers legs. Two were worn diagonally from shoulder to hip, so that they crossed at the chest. A fourth was worn like a giant necklace. The body thereby seemed enlarged by the mass of foliage. The yellow headdress was secured by a chin strap, and the face covered by an oval mat of woven string, at the centre of which, resembling a nose, was a fragment of white shell, obtained on excursions to the coast. The identity of the dancers, when fully attired, was impossible to discern even at close quarters (see Fig. 1). Although this masked figure was known as *awanga*, certain other words were used, metonymically, to refer to it: *bunangga* (meaning 'yellow'), *angguron* (the name of the yellow dye), and *agasogi* (the name of the head-dress).

The *awanga* always danced in the daytime. Their arrival was announced by the scream of bullroarers, called *angarega*, handled by the *awanga* themselves, or the undecorated elders who sometimes accompanied ('guided') them (see Fig. 2). In addition, simple reed instruments, known as *kelarega*, were sounded. These were fashioned from a folded strip of vine, encasing a blade of grass (see Fig. 3). The sounds were enough to send women and children scurrying for cover. The *awanga*, brandishing heavy clubs, were liable to beat anybody foolish enough to cross their path. They would proceed to a clearing, such as a hamlet where a man had recently died, and dance frenetically to the accompaniment of songs. These were sung by a male choir, simultaneously beating rhythms with lengths of bamboo on planks of wild palm.[3] The *awan* was invariably followed by a feast.

The *awanga* were greatly feared by women and children. Physical contact with them carried terrible supernatural sanctions ranging from severe illnesses to death. If a pregnant woman were even inadvertently to pass close to a site in the bush where *awanga* were being constructed, her foetus would be horribly deformed. For these reasons, any man who revealed the secrets of *awanga* production would be killed. The *awanga* themselves would undertake this kind of homicide, by bludgeoning the transgressor with their clubs. Moreover, they punished almost any kind of serious offence in the same manner—stealing, adultery, or unprovoked violence. The *awanga* meted out the most extreme, organized, coercive sanctions available in the traditional society. Since the men who donned the costumes invariably slipped away from their fellows unnoticed, nobody (except the *awanga* themselves) could know who carried out the death sentence, and retaliation against participants in these executions was impossible.

After the *awanga* had performed, their costumes and instruments were utterly destroyed and buried in the bush beneath felled trees and other foliage. Only two small items were retained for future performances. The first was the sound-producing part of the bullroarer, a small, pointed piece of wood with a hole in it which functioned rather like a whistle. Its name, *angarega*, meant 'large tooth', and it was thus of a size which made it easy to secrete. The other type of item was the face mask, which was

FIG. 1. The *awanga* wears a woven face mask with a white shell over the nose.

FIG. 2. Sounding the bullroarer (*angarega*).

FIG. 3. Playing the reed instrument (*kelarega*).

F IG. 4. Spitting yellow dye (*angguron*) on the head-dress (*agasogi*) of an *awanga*.

obtained by each man in the course of his initiation rites, which I now describe in summary form.

Initiation rites were performed as part of the most dramatic ceremonial complex of the Mali Baining, known as the *mendas*. Many types of masks and head-dresses were constructed for the *mendas*, and preparations began months in advance of the public performance. A large shelter was constructed by men at a secret location in the bush, at which the various materials for costume production were gradually accumulated. Approximately two weeks before the celebration, all uninitiated boys from the area, aged between about 10 and 17, were brought to the shelter and shown the masks in a state of near completion. Each boy had his own instructor, ideally a maternal uncle, who, over the ensuing fortnight, revealed the names of different masks (*awilinigal*, *ladirura*, *aiumegi*, *unggwarumgi*, *walwal*, etc.). Instructors were also required to produce an *awanga* face mask for the novice in their care, which would belong to the boy thereafter, enabling him to participate in a future *awan*.

The tuition given by instructors was largely of a technical nature—where materials for dance costumes should be collected, how they are utilized, what different designs are called, and in what order the costumed dancers appear at the *mendas*. The principal taboo which the boys were required to observe was that they should not have contact with women during their seclusion. Above all, they were required to abstain from any sexual relations and to avoid being seen by their mothers. During the course of the fortnight, one or more wild pigs were very slowly cooked in a ground oven and if one of the boys were to break the taboo on inter-sexual contact, the pork would 'stink' and the transgressor would be slain. Moreover, the boy's personal instructor would have to submit to a severe or fatal beating at the hands of the novice's enraged father.

By all accounts, no substantial corpus of myths or exegetical commentaries was transmitted to novices, but two secrets were revealed, considered to be of the utmost importance. The first concerned the origins of the world, a single myth relating the creation of humans and the natural environment, and the seizure by men of the *angarega* from primordial women. The second concerned the technique of producing red colouration on the dance masks of the *mendas*. This was achieved by cutting the tongue with the sharp edge of a folded leaf (a species of Ficus, according to Bateson 1931/2: 335), and spitting blood directly onto the mask before it was used for dancing. This tongue-bleeding was thought to purge the skin of toxic material believed to accumulate as a direct result of coitus. If blood were not drawn and expelled in this way, sexually active men would have fallen sick. Novices were therefore required to learn the technique. The only other ordeal required of novices arose from the technique of attaching the phallocrypt worn by costumed dancers at the *mendas*. The phallocrypt, consisting of a barkcloth tube mushrooming into a disk at the end, was sewn into the pubic hair and its strap secured at the back (passing between the buttocks) by a 'pin' (sharpened bone) inserted through the skin at the base of the spine.

A few days prior to the *mendas*, girls aged between about 10 and 16 underwent initiation rites of their own, co-ordinated by a female elder. These rites were comparatively simple, involving the construction of costumes consisting entirely of foliage (i.e. without complex head-dresses). A dance was learned by the girls in which they moved in a tight, shuffling crowd and threw small pieces of uncooked taro on the ground. No exegesis for these activities was available to me. The initiations were performed at a secret location in the bush, scrupulously avoided by men who believed that contact with the women's costumes would cause them to grow breasts and suffer crippling diseases.

The *mendas* itself began at dawn, accompanied by the beating of slit-gongs by the women, with the dance of a particular male costumed figure called *alawopka* (the figure, however, represented a female principle and its name derives from the Mali word for 'woman', *lawopki*). This dance was followed by a specific sequence of other dancers, in a manner which (from the verbal descriptions I collected) recalls the general form of Ida or Yangis in the Sepik Border Mountains (Gell 1975, Juillerat 1992). The daytime celebrations culminated in a dance by the female novices, who were described as 'cooling down' the ground. This was followed, some hours later, by a night dance, to the sounds of a male orchestra (singing accompanied by the rhythmic beating of lengths of bamboo), illuminated by a huge fire in the centre of the dancing ground.

This summary of Mali Baining dances is necessarily brief and superficial. The *mendas* had not been performed by the people I lived with for a very long time. Although more distant Mali Baining groups were said to have preserved the knowledge of *mendas*, I collected information on this topic mainly from the old men in my fieldwork area, who bemoaned the loss of these traditions locally, the censure of early missionaries who caused the *mendas* to be abolished, and the consequent unreliability of their own knowledge. The *mendas*, however, and the initiation rites connected with it, do not impinge directly on the subject of this book, and I shall not dwell further on the subject. The *awan*, as we shall see, is of greater relevance to my account of the Kivung splinter group (especially in Chapter 4), and further reference will be made to its central figures, the *awanga*. Before moving on, something must be said about the Uramot dance traditions, because they are an important feature of contemporary life among the Mali Baining with whom I lived, and affect relations between Kivung members and 'outsiders'.

The Mali Baining people of Dadul and Sunam live in close proximity to Uramot populations, clustered principally around the settlements of Riet and Arabum. Indeed, Dadul and Sunam are appreciably closer to Uramot villages than they are to each other, or to any other Mali settlements. All Uramot Baining, with the exception of some who have married into the Mali population, are 'outside' the Pomio Kivung, and are mostly members of the United (formerly Methodist) Church. This difference of religious affiliation, as between Dadul and Uramot villages, produces somewhat antipathetic relations. The Uramot privately express contempt for Kivung practices, and the people of Dadul regard their Uramot neighbours as 'sinners' (drunken, promiscuous, deceitful, etc.). Uramot children deride and ridicule Kivung children, who are in any case discouraged from mixing with the Uramot for fear that they will imitate their 'evil' ways. The people of Sunam, by contrast, mix easily with their Uramot neighbours, and are much more inclined to intermarry with them. The United Church is well established in Sunam, as is trenchant opposition to the Pomio Kivung. Moreover, the people of Sunam, like their Uramot neighbours but unlike Kivung members, indulge in the chewing of betel-nut, which they see as a pre-eminently sociable activity. Nevertheless, all these villages 'put on' a publicly harmonious exterior by contributing to each other's major celebrations. If, one year, the people of Riet celebrate the completion of a major project, such as the erection of a church building, they can rely on material assistance from Sunam, Dadul, and other villages. Similarly, if the people of Sunam celebrate the departure of a pastor, or a major Christian festival, they can bank on support from Uramot and Mali neighbours alike, regardless of their religious affiliations. This kind of inter-village co-operation has a long history in the area, having been nurtured by missions and colonial administrations, and encouraged by the Pomio Kivung leadership in the name of good public relations.

Most commonly, celebrations of this type take the form of Uramot night dances, or what are known throughout East New Britain as 'fire dances'. Knowledge of how to make the costumes and perform fire dances in the Uramot tradition is common to all Mali Baining villages in the vicinity, and the tradition is said to resemble what is remembered of the nocturnal dance at the *mendas*. In common with the *mendas*, all preparations for the Uramot fire dance take place at a secret location in the bush, out of the sight and earshot of women and children. Adult males of any ethnic group may visit the secret site and assist in preparations, although they are sometimes required to undergo a simple initiation ceremony for which payment in cash is demanded. This 'initiation' appears to be a recent invention, modelled on the rules for entry into the *tubuan* cult of the neighbouring Tolai. The red markings of fire dance masks are created with red paint, purchased in shops, rather than blood extracted from the tongue, and the phallocrypts of dancers are secured with waist straps rather than the agonizing procedure of pinning. Participants have nothing to say about the links between fire dances and traditional cosmology, but stress only the beauty and joy of these occasions, appropriate to Christian celebration.

I attended several fire dances, which were indeed very spectacular occasions. They begin at dusk, with the lighting of a massive bonfire in the centre of the dancing ground. Some twenty yards from the fire is a male choir, equipped with lengths of bamboo and seated in rows among planks of wild palm, upon which they beat a succession of rhythms. Singing occurs intermittently during the first few hours of the evening, while anybody who feels like it (but mostly children) dance aimlessly around the fire, pausing occasionally to pile on additional fuel. Later, perhaps after midnight, the volume of the singing increases. Elaborate costumed figures suddenly appear, one by one, in the dancing arena, which is now enclosed by a ring of excited onlookers. These figures are invariably of three main types, arriving in the following order. First, there is a series of dancers described as the *lingan*. They are identified by conical head-dresses constructed of bark and painted red. Second to appear are the *kavat*, whose head pieces consist of large masks with protruding, open mouths and large, staring eyes. These are constructed around large frames covered with barkcloth. They come in many shapes and sizes, and are painted with a wide variety of black and red designs. The last figures are always of the *vungvung* type, a huge, rectangular frame also decorated with red and black designs. Inside the frame, a man blows on a large, barkcloth-covered bamboo trumpet, producing an effect like a distant foghorn.

Kavat are the most vigorous dancers, occasionally veering threateningly towards spectators and even lashing out at them with sticks. They also intermittently run into the fire, with the result that the legs of *kavat* dancers may be severely burned. The true *vungvung* (as opposed to other costumes of its type) is markedly gentle and slow-moving. The hand of the man inside grips the head of a live python, while an undecorated man, walking alongside, holds the tail of the snake and appears to guide the *vungvung* around the arena. Occasionally, women bring their sick babies to the *vungvung* and thrust them inside its mask. The trumpet is sounded and the child may be expected to recover. The dancing and singing continues until dawn, amidst much drunkenness and sometimes violence. At first light, food may be distributed among guests from other villages, and the gathering breaks up. Guests may be dissatisfied with the meagre provisions of their hosts, and may lament the passing of a time when people knew how to put on a feast, but if, at this stage, they are not in a drunken stupor, their ears ring with music, their eyes blink with colour and drama, and their minds swim in anticipation of sleep and dreaming.

Mali Baining History

There are many published accounts of the history of the Gazelle Peninsula, from the establishment of the Methodist Mission in 1875 (e.g. Brown 1908) to the much-televised campaign for independence in the early 1970s (e.g. A. L. Epstein 1978). But the antagonists in these historical dramas are rarely Baining people. This is understandable. Many Baining did not experience sustained contact with missionaries and government personnel until the 1950s, at a time when many of their Tolai neighbours had become successful businessmen, or white-collar workers, and had long since gained a sophisticated understanding of Christianity.

Even today, there are Baining people who live very much as their ancestors did before the arrival of Europeans. Their day-to-day social organization is, and seems to have been, remarkably simple. Pool (1984: 229) observed that:

in the Melanesian context, the Baining represent an extreme in the direction of minimizing the importance of social ties. Whereas most societies described in the anthropological literature are seen as having family-type units which are functional but dependent sub-groups of larger, more independent units (e.g. lineages, clans, extended families), Baining families are best seen as the independent units which combine to form larger, but dependent units (households, hamlets, and transient inter-family relationships).

The absence, traditionally, of corporate groups, and of genealogies extending beyond the grandparental generation, distinguish the Baining from their matrilineal neighbours. Affinal relations are similarly undeveloped. Among the Kaket, Pool claimed that 'no importance is placed on the relationship between two families whose children marry' and correspondingly 'little importance is placed on the identity of these families in the arrangement of a marriage' (1984: 230). This is also generally true of the Mali Baining. Christian weddings, where they occur, are far more complex and large-scale affairs than the indigenous marriage ceremony, which consisted of a simple sharing of taro under the supervision of a few close family members. Nevertheless, regardless of how the marriage is ceremonially formed, few material goods flow between the families of the bride and groom, and no enduring obligations are established between them.[4] The Mali Baining, unlike the Kaket, used to favour the 'exchange' of sisters between families, but this seems to have been more an ideal than a statistical pattern. Nowadays it is not even an ideal and young people more or less enjoy freedom of choice with regard to marriage partners. Moreover, the traditional obligation of a wife-receiving family to reciprocate in the fullness of time, was probably in most cases a pretext rather than a motivation for inter-family violence. This took the form of nocturnal raids conducted by two or three 'brothers' against a family in the vicinity. The only occasions for wider co-operation were the sporadic *awan* and even more infrequent *mendas*.

T A B L E 1. *Census data collected in Dadul and Sunam, 1987*

	Dadul		Sunam	
Age group	Males	Females	Males	Females
0–5	5	6	9	8
6–17	16	13	12	15
18–45	11	12	17	12
Over 46	5	2	2	3
Total	37	33	40	38
Total population		70		78

T A B L E 2. *Census Data from Rural Community Register, ENBP, Jan. 1983*

Village	Land Owners	Official Church Affiliation	Population
Riet	Uramot	United Church (Methodist)	185
Arabum	Uramot	Catholic	269
Maranagi	Mali	Catholic	91
Reigel	Mali	Catholic	143
Kiligia	Mali	Catholic	29
Sinbum	Mali	United Church (Methodist)	121

The people who figure most prominently in this study have had a longer experience of external influence than many other Baining populations. They came under the influence of German and Tolai missionaries between the two World Wars, and were rapidly forced to abandon many of their more violent traditional practices. Mali converts were sought by the Catholic and Methodist Churches, both of which were established on the Gazelle in the nineteenth century. Lively competition between the two missions has been apparent in the region from the outset, and some people alive today, for example the older people of Dadul, have been baptized by both. In the remaining pages of this chapter, I provide an historical orientation towards the villages in my fieldwork area, paying particular attention to Dadul and Sunam. Some basic demographic information on the latter is given in Table 1, while some more general data on other villages in the vicinity is given in Table 2. It will be noted that Arabum is listed as an Uramot village, but it also contains a small Kairak population and an even smaller Mali one.

Neither Dadul nor Sunam is located on Mali land. Both were sited on territory which the colonial authorities came to recognize as the 'customary land' of the Uramot group. The colonial divisions of Baining territory did not correspond to any indigenous 'custom', as the term 'customary land' would seem to suggest. The oral histories which I collected indicate that all pre-contact Baining groups, including the Kaket Baining (Pool 1984: 224), did not have any concept of collective rights in land. Such rights as existed concerned the ownership of gardens by the individuals or families responsible for their cultivation. These rights, however, pertained only to crops and not to the soil itself. Thus, when an old garden was abandoned, all rights held by the cultivator (i.e. in the things that grew there) were accordingly forfeited.

During the inter-war years, Western missionaries and administrators encouraged a number of Baining, regardless of their linguistic and cultural differences, to live together in substantial settlements or villages. This was seen as a necessary development because small, shifting hamlets or households scattered through the forest were difficult to govern, let alone to inculcate with Christian and Western morality. The sites of Sunam, Dadul, and Arabum were chosen for the establishment of settlements, partly because of their relative proximity to the administrative centre of New Britain in the north-east (Tolai) region. It so happened that all three of these sites were located on land which had formerly been occupied exclusively by members of the Uramot group.

Since the Baining traditionally had no concept of land ownership, they did not regard the land on which Sunam, Dadul, and Arabum were established as belonging to Uramot speakers. This idea was introduced in the course of colonization. Using information on the distribution of Baining languages prior to contact, the authorities established the territorial boundaries of Mali speakers, Uramot speakers, and so on. These are the group boundaries recognized today.

Having established that the sites of Sunam, Dadul, and Arabum were located on Uramot land, the right of non-Uramot groups to reside at these settlements was questioned by Australian administrators in the years leading up to the Second World War. It was observed in particular that the population at Dadul was predominantly composed of Mali speakers. It was therefore decided that the Mali group should 'purchase' the Uramot land in and around Dadul for the sum of £A10. In the eyes of the Administration, this transaction accorded to the Mali settlers at Dadul (including their relatives and descendants) the right to cultivate and reside on the land indefinitely. From the Baining viewpoint, however, the ritual of exchanging money for land was not clearly understood. Patrol reports indicate that well into the post-war period, there was a poor understanding in the region of the function of money. Moreover, oral histories suggest that the transaction between Mali and Uramot groups in relation to the land at Dadul was undertaken in obedience to unintelligible foreign morality. At Sunam and Arabum, however, at least three linguistic groups (Mali, Uramot, and Kairak) were mixed together and so no pressure was exerted on the Uramot group to sell these lands to the non-Uramot villagers living there. Such a sale would have been unworkable because Uramot and other groups' gardens and houses could not be separated even into approximately distinct geographical zones.

Aside from the Mali families at Dadul, Sunam, and Arabum (many of which had been drawn originally from the Maranagi area and were closely linked by kinship to the people still living there), the rest of the inland Mali people were living on Mali customary land (except for a small Mali settlement at Laup, a short distance to the north of Sunam, also located on Uramot territory). The inland Mali settlements on Mali land included Maranagi, Reigel (which was then called Lemingi), and Aringi (which was later to fuse with Maranagi and, on a smaller scale, with Lemingi). But these large settlements did not contain the whole inland Mali population because many domestic groups continued to live in the pre-contact style, isolated from regular community life and scattered in the forest. Some such households resided together in permanent or semi-permanent hamlets, but others maintained their independence, forever moving from one garden to the next and sleeping in makeshift shelters.

Between 1942 and 1946, the effects of modern warfare on the Mali people were devastating (see Klemensen 1965: 162; Fajans 1985: 26–30). Intense bombing of the region claimed many victims, but other effects of the Japanese occupation were even more damaging to the settled communities. Oral histories reveal that the continuous Japanese advance through the region meant that Mali gardens were requisitioned on a long-term basis and the villagers murdered or forced to flee into the forest where their main source of subsistence was wild foods. The Japanese rounded up many of the younger Mali men and used them as carriers and guides. Those who fled to the hills managed to supplement a hunter-gatherer diet with tubers 'stolen' from their own gardens during the hours of darkness. Yet most available foods had to be cooked (in order to be edible) and the light or smoke from fires made the refugees popular targets during air raids. In consequence, many groups were forced to live in natural caves which were damp and contributed to the spread of disease. Nearly four years later, patrol officers recorded that the populations of all Mali settlements were 'greatly depleted by illness and ill-treatment during the Japanese occupation' (Lang 1950).

During the immediate post-war period, the settlements at Dadul and Sunam were not substantially re-established. Many households roamed between old dilapidated gardens, planting new crops before moving on. Those who did return to village settlements made an effort to re-establish their gardens and livestock, but disease continued to claim many lives (particularly those of women and the elderly). By 1950 it had become clear that there was a severe shortage of women. There is no conclusive explanation of the high rate of female mortality after the war, but the demographic facts do not seem to be in doubt (Lang 1950). According to patrol officers and Baining oral histories, the need to marry off surviving women and thereby stimulate population growth informed a new drive to fuse Mali populations into larger settlements. As things stood in the late 1940s, marriages within settlements like Sunam would have had to involve incestuous couplings. Therefore, Laup's population uprooted and settled in Sunam along with many of the households which had, up until this time, still been scattered in the bush. Moreover, the settlement at Dadul was not re-established and most of the surviving pre-war residents of Dadul also gathered at Sunam. The same processes meanwhile occurred elsewhere (e.g. the Aringi population merged with that of Maranagi and, to a lesser degree, with that of Lemingi).

Between 1950 and 1962 Dadul continued to lie derelict and the old village site was reclaimed by the forest. The quality of life in Sunam apparently improved as many new domestic groups were formed by marriage and increasing land was brought under cultivation. Sunam benefited from some government assistance, being the nearest of the inland Mali settlements to the developed north-east region of the province. In the early 1950s agricultural officers assisted the people of Sunam with the planting of more varied subsistence crops (in addition to the established species such as taro, sweet potato, and sugar cane). There was even a drive to plant copra and the beginnings of cocoa production. But the introduction of Sunam to the cash economy really began with the sale of vegetable crops at small Tolai markets north of the Warangoi River. The people of Sunam soon learned that it was worth engaging in such small-scale commercial activity in order to obtain knives, kerosene, nails, cloth, and similar materials. The planting of cocoa and copra in the 1950s, however, had less to do with commercial aspirations than with the desire to comply with the inscrutable dictates of colonial officials.

As early as 1951 colonial authorities and businessmen were beginning to give some thought to the commercial potential of the land around Sunam (cf. Boro 1951). But an outright purchase of the land in and around Sunam did not occur until 21 June 1955. The land was purchased by the Australian Administration along with a number of other large areas in the vicinity of the Warangoi River. In fact, the land which passed to the Administration was so extensive that it encompassed territory belonging to a number of ethnic groups besides the Uramot. A proportion (if not all) of the money accruing to the people of Sunam as a result of the land purchase was held in trust by the Administration.

Meanwhile, a few individuals in Sunam were, by the late 1950s, showing signs of adopting a more 'progressive' outlook with regard to cash cropping. This surprised patrol officers whose stereotypes of the Baining were expressed in the frequent use of adjectives like 'apathetic' and 'backward' in official reports. Cash-cropping activities were optimistically interpreted as an attempt by Baining individuals 'to bring their economic standard to the same high level as their Tolai neighbours' (Fayle 1959). It was added, however, that although such individuals 'have shown greater interest than shown before in the possibilities of cash cropping, as previously stated the progress made is negligible' (Fayle 1959). Indeed, in Sunam, there were only two domestic units which owned more than 30 cocoa or coconut trees (oral testimony). All the same, with 932 coconut palms in all (Fayle 1959), Sunam was showing much more commitment to the idea of cash cropping than any other inland Mali village (although the absence of roads in the area meant that there was, as yet, little opportunity for the sale of crops).

In the early 1960s a combination of local efforts and government assistance resulted in the completion of a dirt road to Sunam. Part of the money for the Warangoi land sale, formerly held in trust by the Administration, was now released to fund the development of cash crops in Sunam and other villages and to provide a truck for the transportation of crops. The government lent assistance by establishing resident agricultural officers near to Sunam, whose station also provided an outlet for cash crops.

The marking out of portions of land within the large areas obtained by the Administration was undertaken in 1960. Many large portions of land were subsequently made available to expatriate settlers to develop plantations. A total of 121 much smaller areas or 'blocks' (roughly 10–15 acres each) were leased to native settlers. Most of the latter were Tolai individuals, reflecting the Administration's concern to relieve existing and potential land pressures among the Tolai. The Vunamami Council was allocated 34 blocks (each of 10–12 acres) which it was permitted to sublease to two individuals from each of the 17 Tolai villages in the Council area. These 33 blocks, which were adjacent to Sunam, came to be known collectively as Vunamami Blok. Further details of the Vunamami Council's resettlement schemes have been recorded by Salisbury (1970: 97–103) and Fingleton (1985: 256–73). Meanwhile, 69 blocks of land were allocated to other native settlers (mostly, but not quite exclusively, Tolai individuals). The remaining 18 blocks were supposed to have been made available to the Mali families living at Sunam (in keeping with the Administration's promise during the Warangoi purchase). In practice, however, only 4 of the 18 blocks were allocated to the Mali families at Sunam. The rest went almost exclusively to Tolai settlers.

Mali and Tolai informants alike, who had been living in the Warangoi region during the early 1960s, told me that it was primarily fear which had prevented most Baining families from claiming the blocks of land set aside for them by the Administration. The first Tolai settlers to arrive on Vunamami Blok and other portions of land were considered in Sunam to be sorcerers. Some Baining families fled at once to more remote areas, one of these domestic units returning alone to the old site of Dadul. In due course, a few of the more respected Baining elders in Sunam became better acquainted with their Tolai neighbours. On their visits to Vunamami Blok, however, these elders heard that extortionate taxes would soon be levied by the Administration. In response to the tax scare, several more Baining families fled to Dadul to join the one family now re-established there. The settlers at Vunamami Blok meanwhile spread onto Sunam's land and refused either to budge or to pay agreed compensation in coconuts to the remaining Baining families. The regular waves of migration out of Sunam by anxious Baining families ended around 1971. By that time, 14 out of the 18 blocks originally set aside for Baining farmers had been overtaken by Tolai settlers. The four remaining households were befriended by neighbouring Tolai families who persuaded the Baining heads-of-household to register themselves as leaseholders on blocks set aside for the Sunam villagers. This core of Baining families took over the crops left behind by those who had fled to Dadul.

By the early 1970s the four Baining families remaining in Sunam had put aside former tensions with the Vunamami settlers and had become closely allied to them in the context of a secular, anti-colonial movement, called the Mataungan Association. Meanwhile, in Dadul, the same period marked the arrival of a popular religious movement called the Pomio Kivung. The early and mid-1970s were a fertile time for social movements, not just among the Mali Baining but in Papua New Guinea generally. People all around the country knew that 'national independence' was on the horizon, but what this would entail was a matter for the

most diverse speculation. Many persuasive visions of the future emerged
at this time, from the nationalistic to the cataclysmic, and from the
pessimistic to the utopian (see McDowell 1988: 130). It is undoubtedly
the case that the ending of colonial rule in Papua New Guinea as a whole
deeply affected the nature and aims of social movements which found
support in Dadul and Sunam. Nevertheless, the Pomio Kivung and, in a
less overt way, the Mataungan Association, have continued to dominate
people's lives in the region up to the present day, more than 15 years after
independence.

The Mataungan Association was a large-scale, secular, protest movement, founded in 1969 among the Tolai of East New Britain. The movement strenuously opposed the Australian Administration and advocated
an alternative form of government which would be more responsive to
Tolai interests. It attempted to achieve its goals, not through the performance of rituals in pursuit of supernatural intervention, but exclusively
through the implementation of a pragmatic programme for action. This
programme had three main elements.

The first was concerned with exerting pressure on the Australian
Administration to accede to various Mataungan demands. The principal
method was the organization of mass demonstrations and meetings to
which the colonial regime responded with the deployment of a costly and
politically embarrassing concentration of law enforcement agencies. But
in spite of the perceived threat of rioting, these mass demonstrations were
remarkably well-organized and peaceful, contributing to the projection of
a positive image of Mataunganism in the mass media. On Australian
television especially, the articulate and reasonable demands of the movement's leaders contrasted favourably with the initial insensitivity of the
Administration, dramatically conveyed by media images of riot police and
helicopters. Secondly, the movement established an alternative system of
Tolai regional government known as the 'Warkurai Nigunan'. And thirdly,
the Mataungan Association was closely associated with the setting up of
a collective commercial endeavour known as the 'New Guinea Development Corporation'. These three fields of organization, along with the
ideological framework of the Mataungan Association, constituted its institutional substance and legacy.

The ideology of the Mataungan Association proceeded from the
assumption that every country has the right to govern its own affairs.
The validity of this assumption was self-evident, not only to Mataungans
but also to the Australian Administration, and areas of conflict tended
to focus on means rather than on ends. Given that independence was

an indisputably legitimate goal, which the Mataungans pursued and the Administration withheld (with or without good reason), the movement campaigned from a platform of moral strength. It rapidly won the argument in spirit and the opposition occupied a defensive position. Other aspects of Mataungan ideology were similarly difficult for the Administration and its supporters to contest. The movement's leaders emphasized the merits of hard work and sound investment, of harmony and co-operation in family life, the rejection of 'cargo cult' ideas, moderation in alcohol consumption, and other principles which the Administration had long advocated (T. S. Epstein 1969: 11). Thus, Mataungan ideology was founded upon a sophisticated understanding and broad acceptance of Western morality.

On the face of it, the Mataungan Association addressed itself to specifically Tolai grievances, and used the sentiments associated with Tolai ethnicity as a basis for unification in the face of 'foreign' domination. As Grosart (1982: 149) explains, however, there was:

an element of Mataunganism which was relevant to all Papua New Guineans. This is the central paradox of the Mataungan Association: an aggressively local, even ethnic movement flaunting the *tubuan* figure as its symbol but nevertheless recognized as having meaning for other Papua New Guineans who had no knowledge of the *tubuan*.[5]

It is possible that the 'cosmopolitan' leadership of the Mataungan Association was primarily motivated by a nationalist vision, and somewhat reluctantly obliged to pander to Tolai chauvinism, as their ideals proved difficult to spread among other ethnic groups. Considerable effort was certainly made to disseminate Mataungan ideology widely among Baining neighbours. Nowhere were these efforts rewarded more enthusiastically than in Sunam, situated just beyond the boundaries of Tolai territory, where a large Tolai presence had become established on land purchased from the Baining by the Administration and leased to Tolai and expatriate farmers.

By the late 1960s those Baining families in Sunam who had determined not to join the exodus to more remote settlements like Dadul were establishing increasingly close ties with their Tolai neighbours. As the Tolai settlements around Sunam joined the Mataungan Association and became established as political units within the emergent Warkurai Nigunan, the people of Sunam experienced strong incentives to follow suit. Several of the senior men in Sunam recalled a fervent desire to participate in the Mataungan Association and to reap the rewards of development and political power which independence seemed to promise. Some of these men were persuaded to undertake patrols to more remote Baining settlements, gathering opinion and attempting to cultivate support for the Mataungan Association and to disseminate its propaganda. The Sunam men who went on these patrols recalled the indifference with which their message was greeted in the inland, subsistence-oriented villages. Along the coast, where interest in cash cropping was rapidly developing, the messengers from Sunam were more enthusiastically received, but the impact of Mataunganism did not endure.

For the people of Sunam, two strands of Mataungan ideology seemed at the time to be especially radical and exciting. The first was that the indigenous peoples possessed the practical means and moral right to regain lands occupied by expatriate farmers. According to Mataungan leaders, white plantation owners pursued personal gain and profit, and did not appreciate the moral need to enter into relations of reciprocity with the traditional land owners ('true fathers' of the land). Mataungan supporters were therefore entitled to exert whatever pressure they could to induce the whiteman to sell up and leave the country. Sunam villagers were inspired by the example of Tolai acquaintances who had raised money from cash cropping to buy back land, and who had even allegedly resorted to threats and vandalism in an attempt to dislodge the expatriate settlers.

Secondly, the Mataungans argued that government should not be the instrument of colonial domination, but the 'servant' of the indigenous peoples. This was expressed in the oft-quoted slogan of the time: 'we are the government.' Although not an entirely alien idea for many Tolai, the people of Sunam regarded this principle as especially radical. Several Baining men were persuaded to 'prove' that the government was their 'servant' by seeking advice from a Tolai government official (an agricultural officer) on the technicalities of cocoa production. Having discovered that assistance was indeed forthcoming, and that independence would result in even more generous and approachable government agencies, the people of Sunam recall that they were deeply impressed.

During the early 1970s the involvement of the Sunam villagers in the Mataungan Association was intense. Sunam was defined as a village unit within the framework of the Warkurai Nigunan, and elected its own representative to the area council. Sunam itself became established as the venue for quarterly council meetings. The people of Sunam contributed their views to these quarterly debates and, on one occasion, requested that their contribution to the financing of the movement be reduced to an annual 50c head tax. The significance of this request was not that the commitment of Sunam villagers was on the wane (for, at that time, 50c per head was not proposed as a derisory sum), but rather that they had gained the confidence to assert their views within a movement composed of comparatively wealthy and highly educated Tolai, whose sophistication in public affairs had formerly intimidated them.

In addition to the large-scale quarterly meetings, the people of Sunam participated in more regular gatherings (approximately three times a month), for the purposes of which they combined with the Tolai settlers at Vunamami Blok. At these meetings appointed speakers from Sunam and the Blok urged members of the movement to work hard in the production of cash crops and to lend full support to other Mataungan policies. Although this involved preaching to the converted, the persuasive arguments of the orators served to renew and intensify people's commitment to the movement's ideology, and to sustain their familiarity with the issues involved. The day-to-day running of the two communities was also discussed on these occasions. Disputes were debated and settled, and task forces appointed for the performance of various duties connected with sanitation or beautification within settlements. Thus, at the village level, the Warkurai Nigunan took over the functions of colonial government, and removed the need for statutory bodies.

In addition, the Sunam villagers frequently travelled to Rabaul and other parts of the Gazelle Peninsula to participate in the mass demonstrations of the Mataungan Association. They were therefore fully aware of the scale of the movement as a whole, and its collective strength in the face of the Administration. The people of Sunam today maintain that the Mataungan Association drove out the Australians by sheer force and against their will. However impressive the coercive apparatuses of the state may have seemed in the past, the Mataungan Association was seen as being more powerful still, because of the previously unimaginable size of its congregations.

Although, in the conditions surrounding the achievement of independence, mass demonstrations became less common, and the Mataungan Association ceased to be a viable protest movement, certain elements of Mataunganism have continued to play a central role in the political organization of Sunam. The Warkurai Nigunan failed to form the governmental structure of East New Britain, but at the local community level it had an enduring impact, as Grosart (1982: 161) explains:

In some places area councils did (and still do) function most effectively as enabling and implementing bodies, deciding how their particular community would respond to actual legislation. Their intended second function of debating, thrashing out, and preparing new legislation was clearly inhibited by the Warkurai's failure to embrace all of the Tolai and to secure statutory recognition. The spirit of the Warkurai has clearly been influential, on East New Britain and beyond, in the current statutory approaches to community government and village courts.

Sunam rapidly became an administrative centre for the Warangoi region with the establishment of a village court, at which one of the three elected magistrates was a Baining man. Following his death in 1977, another Baining magistrate was installed and has remained in office until the present time. The other magistrates, both originally Tolai men, were likewise former Mataungans and their behaviour in court (notwithstanding the observance of new statutory procedures) was seen as being continuous with that exhibited in the settlement of disputes at community meetings within the Warkurai Nigunan. Meanwhile, the general character and flexible definition of village units established in the Warkurai system is reflected in the structure of community government. The idea of an area council has likewise been preserved, with the election of regional representatives or 'councillors' who meet regularly at the community government headquarters. Although the community government presides over a smaller area than the Warkurai provincial assembly once did, the former is manifestly modelled on the latter. Thus, although the Warkurai Nigunan was forced out of provincial politics, it has been extensively preserved at the community level of administration. From the viewpoint of the Baining villagers at Sunam, the community government system and the Warkurai Nigunan are not clearly distinguishable. Both are associated strongly with the Mataungan cause; it is mainly the terminology which has changed.

Mataungan ideology has continued to affect the people of Sunam in other ways. The impassioned advocacy of family values and hard work continues in regular village or court meetings, and in general moral discourse. Moreover, the preoccupation with hygiene and neatness in the village is associated with the Warkurai Nigunan. These sentiments are not peculiar to Mataunganism but the movement presented them in a new and persuasive way. Sunam villagers acknowledge that the colonial authorities promoted cash cropping, general tidiness, and sanitary practices, but they did so coercively, often against the inclinations of the Baining. It is commonly said in Sunam that the Mataungan Association enabled people to take charge of their own affairs, and to perform community tasks voluntarily and in the manner of their own choosing. The work was then undertaken more efficiently, in an atmosphere of fraternity rather than fear. Thus, Mataunganism continues to be embodied in the sentiments and attitudes surrounding the performance of community tasks.

In addition, Mataungan ideology is preserved in more sporadic activities, focused around elections and temporary development projects instigated by local leaders. Typically, these activities are pursued in concert with the settlers at Vunamami Blok, with whom the villagers meet to conduct debates and formulate policies. In the case of elections, still larger gatherings are organized and these are highly reminiscent of the quarterly area council meetings of the Warkurai Nigunan. On such occasions, references are frequently made to the pressing political issues of the early 1970s. Concerns over Australian domination, and expatriate land ownership in particular, are earnestly raised in discussion, sometimes for the purposes of the most specious analogies with current events. These are issues which many orators, still bewitched by the intense anticipation of the pre-independence years and the former glory of the Mataungan Association, can never entirely relinquish.

Around the time that Mataungan ideas became popular in Sunam, the people of Dadul, in common with many other Mali Baining villages (especially along the coast) were persuaded to join the Pomio Kivung. A coastal villager, selected by the Pomio Kivung leadership as one of its first Mali Baining 'supervisors', patrolled inland areas to muster support for Kivung ideas. In the late 1960s the founder of the movement visited the inland Baining region and delivered a series of impressive speeches, setting out his vision of the future for Pomio-Baining peoples. His central message was that people should obey his version of the Ten Commandments, for their obedience would be rewarded by a 'new life'. Images of the new life focused around the arrival of a 'government' for the indigenous, non-Tolai peoples of East New Britain. Although these ideas were ambiguously expressed, it was widely understood that the 'government' which would come was not of this earth. Rumours spread that the Pomio-Baining ancestors would return with white skin, and that the living would be 'made white' also, and together they would run the new government, which would be called the 'Village Government'. The mountains would be levelled and a thriving city would emerge. Here, the Pomio-Baining peoples would live a life of ease and luxury, with access to every kind of modern technology. The Tolai would be comparatively 'backward', thus reversing the historical trajectory. Efforts in Dadul to bring about this desirable state of affairs began in the late 1960s with the institution of meetings, and the payment of fines for violations of the 'Ten Laws'. In the 1970s more complex Kivung rituals were adopted, in line with Pomio teachings, and this required the construction of various kinds of temple. A detailed description of the ideas and practices which became established in Dadul is presented in the next two chapters.

The Pomio Kivung emerged as a clearly anti-Tolai movement, campaigning for Pomio-Baining interests, whereas the Mataungan Association was essentially concerned with Tolai advancement. Inevitably, the two movements were deeply opposed, creating a rift between the people of Dadul and Sunam. For Mali Baining people, there seemed to be two paths to 'development' and a better way of life. The Mataungan path entailed ostensibly pragmatic and secular action—cash cropping, astute investment, demonstrations, and other ventures. The Pomio Kivung path advocated ritual action and 'spiritual' transformation, leading to supernatural intervention. There is a risk, however, of misunderstanding this divergence as a contrast between capitalist aspirations, on the one hand, and a 'Melanesian' conception of reciprocity with other-worldly beings, on the other. Such a contrast articulates easily with the entrenched dichotomy in Western history between nationalism and millenarism. Yet there was an element of 'nationalism' in both Mataungan and Kivung movements, in so far as both united large populations in pursuit of political autonomy from the colonial regime. The 'millenarian' component of Mataunganism, at least as far as Sunam villagers were concerned, is harder to flesh out, but it has to do with the way material goods are construed in Papua New Guinea.[6]

It is clear that Mataungan ideology emphasized the importance of cash cropping and other kinds of business enterprise. This aspect of the movement found expression particularly in the activities of the New Guinea Development Corporation. It might be argued that both small-scale and collective commercial enterprise in the movement was pursued on the understanding that profit-making, reinvestment, and economic advancement were desirable goals in their own right, and not merely (or even necessarily) techniques of cultivating dependence, prestige, and other bases for traditional authority. Crops (or other products) were converted into money which, functioning as capital, facilitated further production in the celebrated model: M→C→M' (Sahlins 1972: 83). Products were alienable, being impersonally quantified, valued, and transacted as mere objects, rather than as the 'carriers' of social relations. The attribution of such a 'capitalistic' orientation to what was after all a Melanesian movement, is lent some credence by T. S. Epstein's interpretations of the traditional Tolai economy as a system of 'primitive capitalism' (1968).

Prior to contact with the West, the Tolai allegedly possessed an 'all-purpose currency' (shell-money or *tabu*), principles of banking, pornbroking, rational investment, and some conception of waged labour. In this view, Mataungans were no strangers to the principles of a commodity economy.

In the case of the Pomio Kivung, it is clear that production and exchange are undertaken in the model of the gift economy. The objects presented to the ancestors in temples, and the money channelled into the movement by other means, are seen as embodying the spiritual aspects of both the producers and the donors, and are intended to cultivate bonds with ancestors and other agencies (see Chapter 2). Goods are inalienable, setting up enduring obligations between donors and recipients.

This contrast between Mataungan and Kivung orientations is overly simplistic, however. The extent to which both the traditional Tolai economy and the commercial activities of Mataungans were continuous with the principles of capitalism is easily exaggerated. The accumulation of wealth among the pre-contact Tolai was concerned with securing brides and with the pursuit of prestige posthumously conferred through the scale and glory of one's funeral (T. S. Epstein 1968: 30–1). Whatever the status of T. S. Epstein's claim that, in the traditional Tolai society, almost everything had its price (1968: 24), during the colonial era Tolai shell-money (*tabu*) seems to have functioned as a special-purpose money, in the sense that it was widely regarded as the only legitimate currency for the payment of brideprice, cash being suitable strictly for the purchase of subsistence goods and luxuries (Salisbury 1970: 278):

The Tolai themselves avoid European scorn by concealing most *tabu* transactions. . . . They encourage people to acquire cash to buy material comforts, but they all recognize that only *tabu* can maintain the fabric of social relationships. Only *tabu* can give people power. *Tabu* is a 'strong thing'.

The use of shell-money, at least, has to be understood in terms of gift exchange rather than the commodity model. Moreover, Mataunganism particularly appealed to those sectors of Tolai society who deplored the destructive effects of capitalism on the system of bridewealth and the prestige economy generally. The extent to which Mataunganism was seen as the champion of capitalism is therefore called into question.

The resolution of this paradox arises partly from the observation that many Mataungans understood the pursuit of profit, through hard work and sound investment, to be part of a struggle for the restoration of traditional political and moral principles. A central concern for many Tolai, during the 1960s, was the intense pressure on land, and the erosion of traditional authority consequent upon it. One of the grounds for Mataungan protest against the colonial regime was that the 'Tolai land' occupied by Westerners was morally inalienable, and this motivated the drive to accumulate the necessary funds to reclaim expatriate landholdings. The production of commodities had to do with the reinstitution of the social fabric of a gift economy, in which elders could once again discharge their obligations to supply shell-money finance and matrilineage land, and the dependence and respect of the younger generation might be restored. Thus, for at least some Mataungans, capitalism was the means to a 'traditional' end, rather than an end in itself.

For the Mali Baining people at Sunam, there was probably an even more direct and compelling resonance between commercial activity and the logic of reciprocity. One of the most exciting messages of Mataunganism was that the *gavman* ('government') should not be regarded as a remote, powerful, dangerous, and capricious agency, but as a valuable resource to be harnessed and controlled for the benefit of all. Recalling their attitudes towards the Australian Administration, some people in Sunam emphasized feelings of awe, fear, and vulnerability—the same gamut of emotions stimulated by encounters with supernatural agencies dwelling in the forest. The activities of colonial authorities, like those of powerful spirits, were at turns harmful and beneficial, but ultimately inscrutable. Dealings with both *gavman* and *masalai* (spirits) were guided by the desire to avoid causing offence, primarily through the performance of only partially intelligible rituals. Thus, the cutting of grass under the stern gaze of the patrol officer and policeman reverberated with the idea of propitiation under the invisible eyes of capricious spirits.

But Mataunganism promoted a more attractive vision of the *gavman*. Through the mediation of the movement's leaders, and indigenous agents of the Administration, new relations between 'the people' and 'the government' were being cultivated. The people of Sunam still talk of these relations in the idiom of reciprocity. When Mataungan leaders urged them to start building a road, the *gavman* 'saw' the commitment of the Sunam villagers and provided resources to assist them; when the people planted cash crops, the *gavman* provided technical advice and expertise. In Sunam the prospect of such relations between themselves and the government had the character of a major revelation, and it seemed to foreshadow an era of escalating prosperity in which a new kind of *gavman*, the 'independent state', would be obliged to unleash ever more extravagant assistance to the people as their efforts to advance became increasingly ambitious.

There were thus fundamental similarities between the 'Village Government' envisaged in Dadul and the 'independent government' anticipated in Sunam. The role of both in the establishment of new kinds of material prosperity and social harmony was seen as the culmination of reciprocity between 'the people' and 'the government'. The 'work' of presenting offerings in temples and raising cash crops both sought to establish enduring social bonds with the agencies of modernization. This fundamental affinity between cargoism and commerce has been widely documented in Papua New Guinea.

David and Dorothy Counts have compared the ideologies of two communities among the Kaliai of West New Britain. One, celebrating the 'Rule of Money', was oriented to commercial enterprise and national independence, like the Mataungans in Sunam. The other, advocating the 'Law of the Story', was primarily concerned with the production of a miracle, like Kivung supporters in Dadul. Yet the common assumption of both ideologies was that collective efforts, whether these were invested in agriculture or ritual, would confer upon powerful external agencies an obligation to repay this commitment with an appropriate share of their bountiful resources. The morality of gift exchange is therefore applied in many Melanesian societies, not only to relations with transcendental beings, but to dealings with remote governments and world markets, which are perceived in much the same way. Thus, Counts and Counts (1976: 301) write:

There seem to be no basic philosophical differences between those who joined the Story and those who did not. . . . The Story teaches that the new order will come suddenly and totally; the snow will fall and when it melts the millennium will have arrived. Progressives seem to assume that the stroke of the pen marking independence will likewise institute a new order for which they must prepare themselves.

In addition to the study of Counts and Counts, McDowell cites numerous publications in which it is argued that the assumptions, conceptual categories, and even the goals associated with 'cargo ritual' and commercial enterprise are difficult to disentangle (1988: 128–9). And her list could readily be extended (see, for example, Gerritson 1975, May 1975, Calvert 1976, and Gesch 1990, all of whom stress the covariation and interrelatedness of 'cargo cults' and development associations). In the following pages, I focus on the 'path' selected in Dadul. Although heading roughly in the same direction as the Mataungan Association, the Pomio Kivung has undoubtedly provided a more undulating, complex, and scenic route.

Notes

1. Only the oldest men in my fieldwork area could remember what these temples looked like. The Mali Baining recognized a single god, whose relics (human bones, wrapped in a tight bundle of barkcloth) were kept in the round temple. In some areas, the name of this god was Kanungga (meaning 'sun'), who was believed occasionally to take a human form, specifically the form of a small boy with shocks of white hair. In other areas, the god was construed as female, and known as Morki (meaning 'big one', but with the feminine marker 'i'). These names were closely guarded secrets, as were the names of god in other Baining language groups (e.g. Klemensen 1965: 173). Each Mali Baining region, at least, had its own name for god, its own relics, and its own temple. Only senior men were permitted to conduct temple rituals, for I was told that terrible disasters (e.g. earthquakes) would have befallen the population if women, children, or ignorant men had set eyes upon the bones of god, or had committed some other sacrilege. A team of German Catholic missionaries, often described in native accounts as 'brothers', removed the relics from all Mali Baining temples during the 1930s, and it is locally believed that the relics were then shipped to Europe. The temples fell into a state of disrepair, and very little is now known of what went on in them.
2. Jeremy Pool (1984: 232), however, who worked among the Kaket, was sceptical about Baining claims that their ancestors possessed extensive religious knowledge.
3. For further details, see Whitehouse, forthcoming *b*.
4. Some Mali Baining marriages, under Tolai influence, have entailed a nominal payment of brideprice, but this practice, where it has occurred, does not imply any fundamental change in social organization.
5. The word *tubuan* refers to the Tolai masked figure (see Salisbury 1970: 300–7).
6. The modern classic on this subject is M. Strathern's *The Gender of the Gift* (1988).

2

The Pomio Kivung Movement

We would like to see Pomio–Baining people look after their own
affairs, become their own masters, you see? . . . But we cannot do
anything unless we unite ourselves and we become a force to be
reckoned with. . . . So I see Kivung as a force . . . It promotes the
spirit of fighting together.

(Francis Koimanrea, Pomio Kivung Supervisor)

T o recapitulate, the Pomio Kivung is a large-scale, centralized movement among the Pomio–Baining peoples of East New Britain in Papua
New Guinea.[1] On one level it is concerned with the acquisition of Western technology through the performance of ritual and a Christian-syncretic
vision of eternal 'heaven on earth'. In these respects it forms part of a
tradition of millenarian and 'cargo cult' activity in the Pomio and Baining
regions. But the movement also pursues political goals by parliamentary
and other secular means. The founder of the movement, Michael Koriam
Urekit (generally known as 'Koriam'), held continuous office in the House
of Assembly (national parliament) at Port Moresby from 1964 until his
death in 1978. But in the eyes of his followers, Koriam was more than a
worldly politician: he was an embodiment of God (Trompf 1990a: 65;
Tovalele 1977: 124), whose spirit resided among the ancestors. Koriam's
associate, Bernard Balatape (known as 'Bernard'), and subsequently his
successor Kolman Kintape Molu (known as 'Kolman'), were likewise
deified and considered to reside at a spiritual level in the world of the
ancestors. In this chapter, I seek to provide a general introduction to the
ideas, rituals, political structure, scale, and external relations of the Pomio
Kivung movement.

The Pomio Kivung was first established at Malmal in the south-east
region of East New Britain. According to Trompf (1984: 38; 1990a: 64),
the Pomio Kivung dates back to 1963, when Bernard of Kraiton village
proclaimed some of the basic tenets of the movement and prophesied the
arrival of its divine leader, Koriam of Ablingi village in West New Britain. Nevertheless, it is 1964, the year of Koriam's election to the Pomio-

Kandrian seat in the House of Assembly, which Pomio Kivung supporters regard as the authoritative date for the foundation of their movement
(see Koimanrea and Baloenakia 1983 and Tovalele 1977). What is clear is
that the Pomio Kivung has been in existence for more than a quarter of
a century and has retained a substantial following up to the present day.
By 1983 representatives of the movement were laying claim to a membership of over 30,000 (Koimanrea and Baleonakia 1983: 171), encompassing
a wide area around Malmal, extending especially to the northern (Sulka
and Baining) regions. Even the more conservative missionary figures of
the mid-1970s placed Pomio Kivung membership at over 8,000 in the
Pomio sub-district alone and revealed that 28 out of 37 major Maenge
villages were affected by the movement (Trompf 1990*a*: 68). The popularity of the Pomio Kivung has from the outset provided a reliable electoral base from which to seek representation at all levels of government.
For fourteen years Koriam retained his seat in the House of Assembly
and, following his death in office, Pomio Kivung leaders have continuously occupied this national seat until the present time (from 1979 on-
wards, the sitting member has been the tough, outspoken, and widely
respected Alois Koki). The movement has also maintained long-term
representation in provincial and community government. In addition to
its remarkable longevity and political record, the financial achievements
of the Pomio Kivung are impressive. The gradual accumulation of fees,
donations, and fines paid by members have resulted in a massive collective investment which in the mid-1980s was equivalent to more than a
quarter of a million pounds.

The goals of the Pomio Kivung are often expressed in secular terms.
Among the most well-known political aims of the movement have been
the promotion of law and order in village life and the establishment of a
separate province for the Pomio-Baining peoples to liberate them from
perceived Tolai domination and to provide them with the prerequisites
for Western-style development. The ostensible reason for saving money
in a collective fund has been to attract foreign technology and investment
after self-government is achieved. In the meantime, portions of the collective fund have been used for a variety of projects, including the establishment of a high school, the extension of health care services, and the
provision of aid for disaster victims at home and abroad (see Koimanrea
and Bailoenakia 1983: 177–185).

The stated goals of the movement's political leaders, their policies in
government, and the uses to which they put (or have proposed to put)
collective resources, are invariably subject to religious interpretations

among Pomio Kivung members. The anticipated arrival of self-government has always been construed as an essentially supernatural event. The 'government' itself is said to exist already on a transcendental plane. In the early days of the movement it seems that this government was referred to as the 'Ancestral Council' (*Kaunsel Tumbuna*)[2], but by the time of my fieldwork in the 1980s it was generally known as the 'Village Government' (*Vilij Gavman*). This government is composed of God and a large number of ancestors who have received forgiveness from Him for whatever sins they committed during their lifetimes.[3] Since the foundation of the movement, followers have anticipated the return of these ancestors and the consequent establishment of political autonomy for Pomio-Baining peoples. The return of the ancestors is commonly described as the 'breaking of the fence' dividing the living and the dead. Sometimes this fence is said to contain a door which will be opened. More rarely, the arrival of ancestors is described simply as the 'miracle' (using the English word).

In addition to setting up a separate state (or in some versions a separate province), it is maintained that the returning ancestors will convey a great volume of technological knowledge and resources to the living and will establish urban settlement and a vast industrial base for the production of Western goods. Followers of the movement maintain that their collective fund will be used as a contribution to the financing of such activities, as a means of 'buying shares' in the new companies. Indeed, the anticipated transformation is described throughout the Pomio Kivung as the 'Period of the Companies' (*Taim Bilong Kampani*). It is held that the reason for Koriam referring to the ancestors as 'foreign investors' or 'Western scientists and industrialists' is that they will be disguised as such, having white skins and European appearance and bearing no resemblance to their former earthly selves.

The arrival of the Village Government is contingent upon various kinds of moral improvement on the part of the living, and the cultivation of bonds with the ancestors based on solidarity and reciprocity. Koriam's vigorous promotion of law and order, and the uses to which Pomio Kivung resources have been put in the past, are both widely interpreted in terms of these religious understandings. Koriam's policies on law and order were based upon a deep reverence for the Old Testament Ten Commandments. The first thing a newcomer notices when entering a Pomio Kivung village is a decorous post, prominently positioned, bearing the Roman numerals I to X (see Fig. 5). Moreover, Pomio Kivung members typically cite the Decalogue as the corner-stone of the movement's

FIG. 5. Every Kivung
village has a post at the
entrance, on which are
inscribed the roman
numerals I–X
(representing the Ten
Laws).

rituals and ideology. Koriam modified and interpreted the Commandments to produce an elaborate and encompassing morality. Referred to as
the 'Ten Laws' (*Tenpela Lo*), they are essential to an understanding of
daily ritual in the Pomio Kivung, and they inform most areas of social life
in general.[4]

Just as the pursuit of political autonomy and collective investment turn
out to have a non-secular dimension, so Koriam's advocacy of law and
order forms part of the religious agenda. Obedience to Koriam's Ten
Laws has never been simply a matter of promoting a peaceful and harmonious society as an end in itself, nor merely of the expectation of rewards
in the next life. The observance of these rules has an essentially 'activist'
character (Worsley 1957: 12), in so far as it is directed towards an imminent

transformation in 'this world' which will replace an old oppressive order with a new, liberating, and enriching one. Moral improvement, measured in terms of obedience to the Ten Laws, is explicitly construed as a precondition for the fulfilment of the millenarian prophesy.

Even the practical uses which have been made in the past of Pomio Kivung finances have been understood in terms of the guiding religious schema. For example, in 1974 the Pomio Kivung contributed K4,000 to an Australian relief fund, intended to assist victims of a cyclone in Queensland. As representatives of the movement later explained (Koimanrea and Bailoenakia 1983: 180):

This was a way of showing our gratitude for the fact that it was their tax money which had brought Papua New Guinea to independence and had enabled a lot of development. The Kivung gave this aid in the spirit of love for those in need.

On one level, this was an act of reciprocity in the same idiom as that employed in relations between the living and the Village Government. In addition to being an expression of gratitude, the relief money maintained an ongoing relationship between whites and indigenous New Guineans, at a time when Pomio Kivung members feared that independence would sever the relationship. Meanwhile, the unquestionably generous donation, like the observance of the Ten Laws, was believed to effect moral improvement and to expedite the Period of the Companies.

These examples of the ambiguous nature of Pomio Kivung political rhetoric are a familiar feature of new religious movements in Melanesia. In his excellent analysis of 'cargo movements' in the Madang area of north-east New Guinea, Lawrence recorded how Yali and his followers erected a 'political cover behind which the ritual could be safely performed' (1971: 211). Lawrence described this capacity to express millenarian aspirations in the 'politically correct' discourse of colonial Administration as a kind of 'double-talk', and certainly one reason why Pomio Kivung ideas have always been expressed to outsiders in the form of political 'policies' and 'financial' or 'development' goals is to allay criticism from the state, missions, and surrounding communities.

But the idea of double-talk introduces certain limitations or biases into the interpretation of Pomio Kivung statements. For example, it might imply that the movement's secular or 'worldly' goals are, or have been, less than sincere. The reality, however, is that Pomio Kivung leaders *have* consistently lobbied for a separate Pomio-Baining province by parliamentary means; they *have* given serious consideration to the release of collective funds for the purposes of large-scale commercial enterprise

(such as logging, mining, and fishing) with the backing of foreign investment, skills, and technology; they *have* drawn national and international
attention to the uneven distribution of development in East New Britain
and *have* succeeded in securing substantial funds from central government to identify and remedy the problems of rural underdevelopment;
they *have* a longstanding and sincere interest in establishing a peaceful,
harmonious society 'in the here and now', complying with the laws of the
land.

The catalogue of tangible achievements of the movement testifies to
the fact that it possesses a sincere programme for improving 'this world'
through practical intervention. Although Pomio Kivung supporters are
pursuing a miracle, they recognize and value the secular purposes and
achievements of the movement and do not dismiss them as merely an
exercise in public relations. The movement's pragmatic programmes have
valuable rewards, and the silencing of critics is only one of them. What
can be said is that these pragmatic activities also contribute to a goal
which Pomio Kivung members regard as more important (materially,
politically, and spiritually) and that is the creation of a new order in
which the living and the dead are reunited on earth.

Recent studies of religious movements in Papua New Guinea have
increasingly stressed the interrelatedness of millenarian and secular aspirations (see McDowell 1988: 128–9 for a summary of this literature). In
the Pomio Kivung, secular and supernatural goals are combined, but they
are not conflated. For example, the accumulation of a collective fund is
intended to serve purposes which are premised upon secular *and* supernatural interventions, and these are conceptually distinguished. The fact
that members of the movement explain the existence of their collective
fund in terms of a desire to attract Western technology and investment
does not necessarily indicate a conflation on their part of Westerners and
ancestors. Nor do they confuse the practical pursuit of foreign assistance
in some development programme with the return of the dead. It is simply
that the discourse used to talk about the former is also used to talk about
the latter. The meanings of this discourse are 'layered'. Pomio Kivung
members are quite explicit about this. In fact, they use a vertical spatial
metaphor to convey this understanding: the millenarian aspirations are
described as the 'deep' or 'underlying' (*ananit*) meanings of political
discourse. Although this is logically implied, I have never heard the
secular goals of the Pomio Kivung described by members as 'superficial'
or 'surface things'. Nevertheless, the greater importance of the religious
dimension is clearly conveyed by other metaphors in which 'this worldly'

pursuits are denigrated as 'bodily' in contrast with ritual activities which attend to 'spiritual' needs.

This distinction makes proper sense when it is appreciated that the Period of the Companies is not first and foremost a material and political achievement, but a spiritual one. It is held to be a temporary phase of temptation (*traim*), during which the living will be presented with ample opportunities for all kinds of physical indulgence (*hamamsim skin*). Those who are impervious to the seductions of the flesh and who channel their wealth, knowledge, and power back into the movement in pursuit of absolution (see below), will share in the millennium. This is construed as a period of eternal bliss on earth, often described as 'Paradise' or, more commonly the 'Period of the Government (*Taim Bilong Gavman*). What characterizes this period is the absence of suffering, death, reproduction, labour, and conflict. Moreover, the living will shed their brown skin (a process described as analogous to removing their shirts) to reveal white skin beneath, unblemished by sores and other afflictions. All Pomio Kivung members cite these transformations, although some also mention idiosyncratic fantasies which they acknowledge to be speculative (*tingting bilong mi tasol*). A point on which everyone agrees is that people who abuse their new-found wealth during the Period of the Companies, through personal indulgence and hedonism, will not enter the millennium, but will be dispatched to hell (*kalibus*—also the word for 'gaol').

In summary, the Pomio Kivung is simultaneously concerned with pragmatic and millenarian activities, and uses a form of discourse normally appropriate only to the former to talk about both. This is markedly the case in interactions with outsiders. But although references to cargoist and millenarian themes are more explicit among Pomio Kivung members, the ambiguous discourse is generally pervasive, and euphemisms for sacred beings or principles are regularly employed.[5]

Institutional Framework of the Pomio Kivung

Pomio Kivung members describe the political structure of the movement as a three-tier hierarchy with the religious and political leaders at the top, exercising authority from their headquarters at Malmal in the Maenge-speaking region. The middle tier is composed of so-called 'supervisors', who convey the messages and instructions of the leadership to all the villages affected by the movement. At the village level, the most prominent official is referred to as the *komiti*, which has been translated by Pomio Kivung representatives to mean 'community leader' (Koimanrea and Bailoenakia 1983: 175). Since this study involves a detailed analysis of different kinds of local leadership, I prefer to avoid the general label 'community leader' for the *komiti*, and propose instead to use the term 'orator' since their main role is to make speeches. Thus, Pomio Kivung followers represent authoritative information as flowing from the Village Government, via the supreme leaders, down to the supervisors, then to the orators, and so to the rank and file members. In practice, during their visits to member villages, supervisors often address supporters directly and do not rely entirely on the orators as intermediaries. Moreover, ordinary Pomio Kivung members (especially men) travel to the movement's headquarters from time to time and thereby receive information directly from the overall leaders. Conversely, the leaders may occasionally undertake patrols to outlying member villages but this is usually in their role of professional politicians. When Koriam was alive, he did a certain amount of patrolling, indeed he was under some pressure to do so as a Member of the House of Assembly. Bernard, Koriam's right-hand man, was not a politician and showed contrastingly little inclination to travel extensively in the region. Bernard died in 1976, and since Koriam's death in 1978 supreme religious authority has been exercised by Kolman. Like Bernard, however, Kolman is not a politician and he rarely undertakes patrols. Indeed, he has never visited some of the more distant strongholds of the movement in his capacity as a Pomio Kivung leader.

Communications radiate from the centre of the Pomio Kivung with particular intensity around the time of elections. In the build up to elections, it is not merely the supervisors and other activists who undertake patrols in order to disseminate current policies and (most importantly) instructions as to how supporters should vote, but the candidates themselves. In some cases, supervisors stand for election to positions in community or provincial governments. But the national seat is conceptually associated with a higher level of authority in the movement. Koriam was both the supreme religious authority and also the highest-ranking politician in the movement. Since his death, however, overall religious leadership has devolved entirely upon Kolman, and Alois Koki has assumed responsibility for the movement's political activities; Koriam's original role has thus been divided up between Kolman and Koki. Koki is correspondingly much more mobile than Kolman. As a political representative he regularly visits villages across a wide region, seeking support and lending advice and assistance even in villages which repudiate the Pomio Kivung.

Supporters of the movement do not expect Koki to make explicit references to religious matters. His words are often interpreted as having 'deeper' meanings but the millenarian undertones in his discourse are not as pronounced as Koriam's were reported to be. Like Koriam, but unlike Koki, Kolman frequently makes highly ambiguous, suggestive, or mystical statements and, when addressing exclusively sympathetic audiences (typically at the movement's headquarters), he is known to refer most explicitly to the religious dimensions of the Pomio Kivung. I was privileged to have lengthy conversations with Kolman before an audience of supporters in which he spoke candidly about the deeper spiritual themes of the movement and, on one occasion, permitted me to conduct an extended interview with his wife in a state of mediumship and, through her, with the spirit of Koriam.

Koki's political discourse, like all such discourse in the Pomio Kivung, is undoubtedly subject to religious interpretations by followers. But his responsibilities are construed as fundamentally secular: his principal task is to protect the movement and its members from domination by hostile forces in 'this world' (stereotypically the provincial government and the Tolai, as I explain below). Koki carries clout in the world of men, and people in the movement speak of his protective strength with gratitude, pride, and respect. To a lesser extent, Koki is valued by Pomio Kivung supporters for his achievements in attracting national government resources to the Pomio-Baining region. Nevertheless, religious authority is valued above all else, and if there is a paramount living leader in the movement it is undoubtedly Kolman.

Thus, it is possible to identify two sorts of information flowing from a centralized seat of authority in the Pomio Kivung, and by rather different channels of dissemination. On the one hand, there is information on the secular policies of the movement, its strategies in dealing with external threats or obstacles and for improving the worldly existence of supporters through practical intervention. This kind of information is disseminated by patrolling candidates and activists, who go to the people in order to influence their voting behaviour or to advise, assist, or direct them in other ways. The movement's political policies are formulated in meetings of high ranking officials at a central location where the most influential voice in the planning of secular strategies is that of Alois Koki. Meanwhile, there is also a high degree of centralized control over the religious ideas and practices of the movement. Like Koriam and Bernard before him, Kolman is believed to be a representative of the Village Government on earth. He is physically in 'this world' but his soul resides with the ancestors. Kolman is therefore able to express the will of God and his instructions are at all times to be obeyed. If Kolman orders some change in the rituals of the movement, then the new requirements are rapidly transmitted to all member villages by a team of supervisors.

The task of announcing that the miracle of returning ancestors is finally due to occur also falls to Kolman. For this reason, he is often referred to as the 'holder of the key' to a spiritual gate or fence (*banis*) dividing the living and the dead. Kolman cannot cause the miracle (use the key when he pleases) for this is the responsibility of the people collectively who must entice the ancestors by satisfying certain conditions. But Kolman will enable the people to prepare for it, and will ceremonially preside over its occurrence. Any messages concerning changes in the institutions of the movement, or in the proximity of the miracle, are transmitted from Kolman to his supporters by his official representatives. Alternatively, he may send word that the orators from member villages should come to his headquarters so that he can speak to them directly. Patrolling appears to be incompatible with Kolman's religious role and his detachment from the world of party politics and elections. In part, travelling would seem undignified and is avoided on that account. To some extent, Koriam was able to combine mobility and regality by being carried around on a stretcher. But a more compelling explanation is that Kolman would be subjected to considerable external criticism if he were to proselytize too openly, spreading *kago kalt* to large gatherings, and stimulating 'unrest'. Koriam edged further in that direction under the guise of his work for the Administration, but no such justification is available to Kolman.

A remaining basis for regular contact between the central authorities of the movement and its member villages is essentially financial. Supervisors are sent at regular intervals to all member villages to collect money for the movement's collective fund. I shall presently describe how money is raised at the village level, but at this point suffice to say that all Pomio Kivung members seek moral improvement through monetary donations under two broad headings: absolution donations (concerned with purification) and catharsis donations (concerned with the renewal of spiritual strength and the elimination of shame). These donations accumulate in every Pomio Kivung community and combine to form a so-called 'District Fund' which is passed on to representatives from Malmal and deposited in a collective bank account, held in the name of the Pomio Kivung.

In the light of the foregoing summary, a number of broad similarities are evident in the overall structure of the Pomio Kivung and of Yali's mature movement in north-east New Guinea, described by Morauta (1972, 1974). Contrasting Yali's movement with a number of much smaller 'cults' in the Madang region, Morauta commented on the relationship between the scale of movements and the types and channels of communication which they utilized. The small cults relied heavily on traditional or pre-existing inter-personal ties between villages for the dissemination of ideas and practices. By contrast, the institutions of Yali's movement spread along wider, non-traditional channels accessible to Yali through his work for the Administration (Morauta 1972: 435). This has also been the pattern of spread in the Pomio Kivung. Like Yali, Koriam disseminated his ideas through his election campaigns and patrols, and by means of his many public speeches as a member of the House of Assembly. And since both leaders addressed themselves to large and linguistically diverse populations, they conveyed their messages in the common medium of Pidgin, unlike the leaders of small-scale cults whose ideas tended to be confined to local language groups. Moreover, Yali's movement, like Koriam's, was centrally regulated and employed 'a hierarchy of leaders who are in touch with one another over a wide area' (Morauta 1972: 435). Morauta contrasted this situation with the organizational pattern of small cults whose leaders did not maintain regular contacts, or owe allegiance to a central authority from which messages were conveyed or before which they were expected to convene. A further similarity between Yali's movement and the Pomio Kivung, differentiating both from many smaller cults, might be the way in which religious materials are codified and transmitted. Yali's and Koriam's revelations were extensively codified in language, facilitating their transportation over a wide area. It is possible that smaller cults, however, cultivated religious insights mainly through collective ritual performances, rather than through verbally transmitted ideology, and were therefore much more difficult to transport (Whitehouse 1992*b*: 792–3; Barth 1990: 646–7).

One major respect in which the overall organization of Yali's movement differs quite markedly from that of the Pomio Kivung is at the level of the village. Morauta has stressed how support for Yali cut across village membership (as well as membership of other 'traditional' social units such as the clan and family). But in the Pomio Kivung, the most elaborate forms of political organization take the village settlement as their conceptual unit. Villages may be divided in their loyalties to the Pomio Kivung, and indeed Trompf states (1990*a*: 68) that in 1975 roughly one-third of pro-Kivung Maenge villages had mixed allegiances, although the remaining majority of villages were united in their support for the movement. But even where villages are divided, Pomio Kivung members act as a collective unit in the form of a body of people who reside together, forming a sort of 'village within a village'. For the sake of clarity, I shall refer to village-level organization in the movement as the 'community'. I now turn to a summary of the institutional system of the Pomio Kivung community.

Every Pomio Kivung community incorporates a similar structure of officials and groups responsible for the performance of uniform rituals and other duties. Most positions of an official nature are allocated by popular decree to post-pubescent males, and the positions of highest rank to married men. The offices available in a given community include (typically) three 'orators' (*komiti*), three 'witnesses' (*kuskus*) who perform special duties in temple rituals, a 'lawyer' (*loea*), a 'magistrate' (*ministret*), and an assortment of offices associated with the performance of special duties in the communal temples, sacred gardens, or meetings. Women and children are involved as audiences in many rituals, and are also employed in teams and task-forces concerned with diverse activities such as the daily preparation of offerings to the ancestors or the weeding of the cemetery or sacred gardens.

In order to gain a coherent impression of community life in the Pomio Kivung, it is first necessary to appreciate that all activities at this level of organization are explicitly directed towards the satisfaction of certain conditions for the return of the ancestors. Each community seeks to satisfy these conditions by the same methods, employed independently as self-contained units. Nevertheless, the central authorities maintain that the occurrence of the miracle cannot be brought about by any single community, but will result from their simultaneous efforts, as each community pulls in the same direction.

The conditions which must be met by each community are threefold: (1) the establishment of bonds with the ancestors based on kinship solidarity and a kind of divine reciprocity which transcends it; (2) the pursuit of moral strength so that the community will not fail the test which the Period of the Companies ostensibly represents; (3) the endurance of God's punishment for original sin. I now examine these in turn.

Bonds with the ancestors are cultivated most prominently in the performance of temple rituals, which entail the presentation of food and monetary offerings to the ancestors. There are three kinds of temple in every Pomio Kivung community, the highest of them being the 'Cemetery Temple' (*Haus Matmat*). Every day, lengthy ritual procedures are undertaken by a large specialist work-force to produce and present offerings to

FIG. 6. Family Temples in Dadul.

the Village Government which meets there in the afternoons. The rituals of the Cemetery Temple are rather elaborate but the basic idea is that they express the reciprocal relationship between humans and God in which humans offer devotion, respect, and moral strength to the Village Government (which is the spirit of the offerings, as opposed to their material substance) and receive in return atonement (*marimari*). Although the term *marimari* is used in the region to refer to the Christian conception of reconciliation between God and worshipper (atonement), and is used in the Pomio Kivung to denote the same kind of transaction between the dead and the living, it also carries the connotation of pity or sympathy as might be felt for any vicitm of misfortune. In addition, similar ritual presentations (also on behalf of the community as a whole) are made at another big temple twice a week, dedicated to Koriam's associate Bernard (this temple is known as the *Haus Bilong Bernard*). There are also numerous small temples ministered by and on behalf of individuals and dedicated to specific dead relatives. These are known as 'Family Temples' (*Haus Famili*—see Fig. 6). When ancestors receive offerings in Family Temples, it is not in the role of remote, godly beings but in the capacity of kinsmen. The main point is that all temple ritual seeks to establish bonds with the ancestors either in the idiom of kinship (based on the sharing of food, affection, and ties of common interest) or in a more

Christian idiom of atonement and mercy. It is thought that the ancestors will not leave their perfect transcendental world to be reunited with their descendants unless there are strong affective bonds between the living and the dead.

The cultivation of bonds with the ancestors is also to be seen in abstention from productive labour on Sundays (in keeping with the Third Law) and on Thursdays. There is some disagreement as to whether Koriam or Bernard was the original advocate of the Thursday prohibitions (Trompf 1990*a*: 78–9). Nevertheless, cult activities in the Pomio area which predate the Pomio Kivung are known to have attributed considerable significance to Thursday, and it has been linked to plantation-worker practices in the mid-1950s (Trompf 1990*a*: 63). In the current movement, at any rate, the special sanctity of Thursday is attributed to the fact that Koriam received the Ten Laws from God on a Thursday. Abstention from work on Sundays celebrates the divinity which unites God and humanity, because symbolically humans behave like God: just as God rested on Sunday after the work of creation, so humans rest on that day. But Sunday and Thursday prohibitions are particularly efficacious in so far as they presage the conditions of Paradise. Moreover, lethargy, seniority, white skin, and ancestors are all strongly associated with moral fortitude and the Period of the Government. These characteristics are equally strongly contrasted with physical desire, energy, juniority, disobedience, and moral weakness. Thus, abstention from (and particularly a lack of will to perform) work can be indicative of moral fortitude, and so Sunday and Thursday prohibitions on work are an expression of the community's solidarity with God and the ancestors, and their desire to join them in Paradise. As with rituals in the Cemetery Temple, such abstentions cultivate bonds of likeness and common purpose in the idiom of solidarity.

The pursuit of moral strength obviously overlaps with the search for deeper spiritual bonds with the ancestors. These are really two aspects of the same thing. Nevertheless, there are certain kinds of ritual activity in the Pomio Kivung which are concerned more with combating sinfulness than with expressing reciprocity or solidarity with the ancestors. The Pidgin word for sin (*pekato*), used frequently by Pomio Kivung members, has a specifically religious meaning (deriving, of course, from missionary teaching) and is construed as a kind of invisible mark, often described as 'dirt', staining the spirits of those who violate the Ten Laws. Sin is essentially a human problem, for the Village Government is by definition untainted by it. A principal forum for the struggle against evil (a concept usually personified as 'Satan' or 'Satan's work') is provided by the public meetings held in the communal 'Meeting House' (*Haus Kivung*) twice a week. At these meetings, attended by all local supporters of the movement, the orators deliver powerful sermons urging the congregation to renounce the pleasures of the flesh and to seek absolution for their sins. The orators stir up a deep horror of evil spirits (*masalai*) and of the Devil (*Setan*), employing grisly metaphors to convey the miseries of damnation. Moreover, orators may single out people at the meeting who should change their ways lest they offend the ancestors and obstruct the miracle. If specific violations of the Laws have come to the attention of the community, offenders are tried and punished by the legal officials (mentioned earlier), with the assistance of the orators. Punishment takes the form of fines and shaming, followed by public reconciliation.

Temple rituals are also concerned to some extent with the elimination of sin. It is assumed that not all violations of the Laws are detected by the community and therefore it is necessary to rely in some degree on revelations from the ancestors themselves with regard to the moral condition of the living. The Cemetery Temple provides a mechanism for the transmission of such revelations. A 'witness' (*kuskus*) is seated every day within the temple while offerings are laid out. During his lengthy vigil, the witness either perceives signs of ancestral visitation or he does not. If not, this is taken as an indication that the living have caused offence and there follows a public investigation into the source of the trouble. Such investigations may be assisted by dreams, voluntary admissions of guilt, or accusations. Nevertheless, acrimony is ideally kept to a minimum and harmony ritually restored through hand-shaking and the exchange of fines. On these occasions, a collective donation of money is made in pursuit of absolution to which every person (even the smallest infant) contributes.

Pomio Kivung members are required to seek absolution for their sins as soon as possible after committing them. They do this by placing money in a special receptacle known as the *Glas Bilong Sek* ('Glass for Checking Up [on oneself]') or the *Glas Bilong Stretim Lo* ('Glass for Straightening/Correcting [violations of] the Law'). A penniless sinner can obtain absolution simply by placing the palm of his or her hand over the glass. Sin, as I have pointed out, is seen as an incorporeal substance, likened to dirt, which attaches to a person's spirit when he or she has violated one of the Ten Laws. Absolution is accordingly described as a laundering process, whereby donations of money serve to wash away the dirt leaving the spirit purified. The term commonly used for absolution is, as far as I know, peculiar to the Pomio Kivung, and means literally 'to pay for [violations of] the Law' (*Baim Lo*). The rituals of absolution are undertaken individually in an atmosphere of profound contrition and reverence (otherwise they are not effective). Afterwards, the sinner must also put money in (or place a palm over) a catharsis receptacle, which eliminates residual shame and guilt. This receptacle is known as the *Glas Bilong Rausim Sem* ('the Glass for Casting out Shame'). Catharsis donations are also regularly undertaken to express goodwill towards the ancestors and obtain protection from illness and other misfortunes. As such, they are concerned with the ongoing renewel of bonds with the Village Government based around reciprocity. People memorize their absolution donations and declare the total to the community 'bookkeeper' on a ceremonial occasion at the end of each month. Catharsis donations are reported rather more frequently to the bookkeeper and in more informal circumstances. Thus, each person's donations into the District Fund are recorded, and these donations will be taken into account on the Day of Judgement following the Period of the Companies, and directly preceding the Period of the Government.

In addition, collective absolution donations are performed on the last Thursday of every calendar month. The aim of this ritual is to gain absolution for the souls of all (anonymous) people who have died but who have not yet entered the Village Government. In so far as these monthly donations are altruistic, they once again express the desire of the living to cultivate their 'most moral' aspects and become 'like the ancestors'. It is assumed that these monthly donations are responsible for the continuous release of souls from a kind of purgatory or limbo into the Village Government.

The institutional arrangements I have highlighted constitute examples of the methods used by Pomio Kivung communities to expedite the Period of the Companies. But none of these practices entails the endurance of God's punishment for original sin. According to Pomio Kivung cosmology, the story of creation in the Old Testament is held to be broadly correct. Nevertheless, it is asserted that original sin had nothing to do with the eating of a forbidden fruit but consisted instead of sexual intercourse between Adam and Eve (Adam having been tempted by Satan to commit this sin). When God saw what his human creations had done, He put it into Adam's head to send Eve up a betel palm to fetch him some betel-nut. While Eve was at the top, God caused Adam to lodge a piece of flint in the tree trunk so that, as Eve slithered down, the flint cut into her vagina producing a strong flow of menstrual blood. This blood was imbued with supernatural energy, causing Eve to grow breasts and enabling her to bear children. But the blood was dangerous to Adam and he was prohibited from coming into contact with it when it flowed every month thereafter.

In effect, this story parallels the biblical idea that child-bearing was part of God's punishment to Eve for original sin (Gen. 3: 16). But the Pomio Kivung story introduces an additional punishment for Eve, namely the menstruation prohibitions. Menstruating women are prohibited from participating in Pomio Kivung rituals because their blood is held to be polluting. A further concomitant of the story of original sin is that there is a total ban on the chewing of betel-nut, because the red substance which this produces is similar to menstrual blood. One of the idiosyncratic features of Pomio Kivung villages is that their members do not chew betel, although they are permitted to sell it in modest quantities to persons outside the movement, as long as the money accrued in this way is not used in sacred donations. Abstention from chewing betel is upheld as a considerable sacrifice on the part of Pomio Kivung members and as evidence of their will-power, commitment, and moral superiority over non-Kivung (betel-chewing) neighbours.

Apart from the prohibitions surrounding betel and menstruation, Pomio Kivung members acknowledge a similar list of punishments for original sin as those cited in Genesis 3: 19. Humans, they say, should work hard, endure suffering, live frugally, and produce children. In general, the pursuit of these miseries is somewhat automatic but the ideology succeeds in making necessary suffering and toil appear to be the voluntary renunciation of wealth and luxury. The pursuit of Western goods and an easy life are seen as immoral, whereas the attempt to live as much like the ancestors as possible, toiling and suffering, is virtuous. This idea finds full symbolic expression in the two communal gardens of every Pomio Kivung community, especially the one which is called 'Paradise'. Without at this stage going into the cosmological significance of these gardens and the rituals performed there, it is necessary to note that when the whole community works together in Paradise every fortnight, it is held to be enacting God's punishment for original sin.

This then completes my summary of the institutional structure of the Pomio Kivung, its religious, political, and economic goals, patterns of leadership and dissemination, and organization at the level of the local community. I have highlighted the corner-stones of the movement and its most enduring themes by focusing on contemporary institutions, as I came to understand them in the course of my fieldwork. A few of the practices I have described are subject to variation across time and space, but most of the basic ideas and rituals of the Pomio Kivung are uniformly observed and have undergone relatively little modification since its foundation. A critical question which remains to be addressed is where the Pomio Kivung stands (or has stood) in relation to various external agencies: the missions, the colonial Administration, the independent state, the Tolai, the whiteman, and neighbouring communities.

External Relations

The Pomio Kivung emerged and spread among populations whose experience of Christianity derived largely from the efforts of the Catholic Mission of the Sacred Heart, which founded a base at Malmal in 1931. In spite of the fact that Kivung ideology borrows substantially from Christianity, followers of the movement are basically anti-missionary. Pomio Kivung supporters maintain that the reason for the many similarities between mission practices and those of their movement is that Catholicism deliberately and cynically combines true and false elements, in order to confuse the native and undermine his chances of meriting salvation. Since some mission teachings are true, they are also persuasive and an unenlightened person can readily be tricked into thinking that if part of a message is recognizably sound, then the whole thing is credible. I have also heard Pomio Kivung members declare that certain true elements of Catholicism have been revealed by missionaries out of a sense of cruel irony, and a desire to ridicule the ignorant layman. The underlying motive attributed to missionaries is the desire to make space for their own kinsmen in Paradise, at the expense of black New Guineans. But it is held that the missionaries will not succeed, for God will punish them for their violations of the Eighth Law.

In spite of its fundamentally hostile orientation to Catholicism (and other churches generally), the Pomio Kivung has long pursued an outwardly conciliatory policy towards the mission. Many Pomio Kivung members continue to baptize their children as Catholics, and to attend Sunday Mass. In spite of doubts or outright disbelief in the efficacy of confession, Pomio Kivung members even go through that weekly rigmarole. Such behaviour is seen as virtuous because it promotes harmony and goodwill in the external relations of the movement. If the Pomio Kivung deliberately contributes in any way to conflict and bad feeling then this is a violation of its own precepts. Nevertheless, members often believe that they are the victims of attack through no fault of their own, and in such cases they predict divine retribution for their persecutors but in the meantime leave them to get on with it. Thus, Pomio Kivung supporters generally treat missionaries with tolerance and goodwill, even to the extent of co-operating in and contributing to their missionary projects and rituals. But they do so in the knowledge that missionaries have little reciprocal goodwill, and are driven by fundamentally selfish and even vindictive motives. After the occurrence of the miracle, it will no longer be necessary to participate in the Catholic charade, and the missionaries will ultimately be subject to God's judgement.

Although the Pomio Kivung orientation to the Catholic mission which I have summarized goes back a long way, it is not clear that negative attitudes were present at the very outset. There is some indication that Koriam originally entertained sympathetic views on the motives of missionaries but that Bernard's more jaded outlook ultimately prevailed (see also Trompf 1990*a*: 67–8). It also seems likely that the negative reactions of some missionaries to the movement's activities has played a major role in reinforcing any anti-Catholic inclinations. At least, as far as the tone of outward relations between the two religions is concerned, it appears that the initiative has tended to lie with the missionaries. Pomio Kivung attitudes seem to have been generally conciliatory and instances of overt conflict involving the movement's leadership seem to have been instigated by the mission. Representatives of the Pomio Kivung have expressed the situation as follows (Koimanrea and Bailoenakia 1983: 185):

The Catholic Church has . . . opposed the Kivung on the grounds that it weakens the faith of people to receive Holy Communion because of the Kivung beliefs and the practice of offering food to the ancestors. Our response was: 'Go ahead and excommunicate us if you want to, but we still have our faith in God.

On the other hand, there are some aspects of the dynamics of political life at the community level of organization in the movement which occasionally produce unprovoked hostility towards the mission. When such conflict occurs, it is highly localized and tends to be disowned by the central authorities of the movement. I present a detailed description of these processes in Chapters 4 to 6.

Relations between the Pomio Kivung and the organs of constitutional government are similarly 'layered' and complex. It is clear that the Pomio Kivung makes use of Western models of government in various ways. At the community level, the roles of magistrate and lawyer are modelled on the colonial offices of *luluai* and *tultul*, which provided the Administration with local agents for the implementation of its policies in native villages. Meanwhile, the orators, in addition to resembling catechists, priests, and other sermonizers, assume roles which are comparable to those of modern councillors, magistrates, and other local officials established in the wake of national independence. Nevertheless, as with the Christian influence over Pomio Kivung institutions, the adoption of colonial and inherited models of political organization does not indicate an acceptance of Western-introduced structures and those of the independent state. On the contrary, Pomio Kivung members view their institutional arrangements as an alternative to, rather than as an extension of, the external Administration. Having said this, the orientation to outside authority is highly contextual. Attitudes to colonial authorities varied over time and space and with regard to specific institutional arrangements rather than to the 'colonial package' as a whole. Likewise, since independence in 1975, Pomio Kivung members have tended to take a more favourable view of national government than of provincial and community governments and, with regard to community government especially, attitudes within the movement have varied regionally in accordance with specific local experiences. Nevertheless, valid generalizations can be made once the basic orientations of Pomio Kivung members to the most influential foreign powers in their region have been broadly characterized.

It would not be too gross an over-simplification to say that Pomio Kivung attitudes towards the Tolai are essentially negative, and towards the whiteman (barring missionaries) are essentially positive. One of the most striking ways in which anti-Tolai feeling is expressed in the Pomio Kivung is through the refusal to chew betel-nut. The Tolai are renowned throughout Papua New Guinea as great chewers, and it is scarcely possible to enjoy the company of Tolai if you are disgusted by the habit. It is also possible that Kivung attitudes towards betel-nut are connected with separatist aspirations more widely construed. Eric Hirsch argues that betel-nut has come to be 'seen as an index of formative "national culture" developing throughout the country [i.e. Papua New Guinea]' (1990: 18). Abstention from betel-chewing may amount to a repudiation of this 'national culture', and certainly it has to do with the Kivung aspiration to be 'like the whiteman' in certain respects, rather than like other native New Guineans.

Hostility towards the Tolai is most commonly expressed verbally with reference to the uneven pattern of development in East New Britain. Colonization brought the Tolai considerable advantages and improvements in terms of wealth, infrastructure, public services, and political representation. The Tolai benefited most markedly in the post-war years, and in conspicuous contrast to the Pomio–Baining peoples who experienced comparatively little assistance. From the mid-1960s, Pomio Kivung leaders formulated and proposed solutions to these concerns. They envisaged their people as being held back by the Tolai, whose capacity to take full advantage of Western-introduced opportunities (and, above all, to exclude others from doing so) resulted from their proximity to the administrative and economic centres of Rabaul and Kokopo. The Pomio Kivung therefore identified the need for an urban centre of its own, which would attract and facilitate modern industry and public services. Until this occurred, it seemed that the Tolai would secure all the benefits of modernization for themselves. National independence was anticipated with some distress in the Pomio Kivung because members suspected that it would greatly consolidate Tolai control of economic and political power in the region. It was supposed that the worst iniquities had been avoided under the colonial system, that the Australians had at least shown some interest in protecting the less developed areas from Tolai domination. Pomio Kivung members frequently recall positive images of colonial officials pursuing justice in the face of Tolai self-interest. But there was a general feeling that the Tolai were the stronger force and, with the establishment of the Mataungan Association, were able to drive out the whiteman.

Since Papua New Guinea's independence, Pomio Kivung members have tended to regard all areas of state administration from the provincial level downwards with profound distrust and sometimes open hostility. This whole system of government is denigrated as 'belonging to the Tolai', and in spite of attempts to penetrate the system and change it from within, Pomio Kivung members have had little sympathy for its institutions and policies. The infiltration of community and provincial governments by the movement has for the most part been an attempt to weaken the negative influence of the state over the Pomio Kivung. But at a grass roots level, many followers have as little as possible to do with the state: they are reluctant to use its courts and schools, and often avoid paying its taxes even in the face of prosecution. Hopes for the future are pinned instead on the establishment of self-government. Although this is part of a millenarian vision, political leaders (especially Alois Koki) have long pursued the establishment of a separate Pomio-Baining province by parliamentary means. Their efforts were recently rewarded by the establishment of a 'Pomio-Baining Area Development Authority' with a promised grant of K5.37 million to be allocated over five years (1988–1993). But this assistance was obtained from central government with the approval of Prime Minister Wingti, serving to reinforce positive attitudes in the Pomio Kivung towards national government, and doing little to alleviate continuing hostility at a grass roots level towards the provincial government.

The remaining area of ongoing importance in the movement's external relations concerns the many indigenous non-Tolai communities of East New Britain who reject or oppose the Pomio Kivung. Some of these communities supported the movement at one time and have subsequently renounced it, while others have remained consistently indifferent or critical towards it. It is difficult to generalize about the movement's relations with such communities since the key factors involved are often regionally specific. In some cases, the Pomio Kivung is opposed on the grounds provided by Christian missionaries, or because it is seen as an obstacle to a group's development plans. In other communities, people abstain from Pomio Kivung practices but do little to oppose them. But more pervasively still, there is a sense of concern that non-members will be excluded from full participation in the Period of the Companies. Outsiders may express cynicism with regard to the efficacy of Pomio Kivung rituals but they are not entirely persuaded of the futility of such an enterprise.

The attitude of Pomio Kivung supporters to their detractors tends to be markedly tolerant, as it is towards the mission. Pomio Kivung communities behave cordially and co-operatively with neighbouring communities, to the extent that their efforts are cordially received. Relations of this kind are viewed in the movement as necessary in the short-term for the promotion of general harmony, but they are pursued in the idiom of material reciprocity (based around bonds of the flesh) rather than on 'deeper' solidarity (based around bonds of the spirit). Moreover, when the miracle occurs, it will no longer be necessary to maintain these onerous ties. For their part, outsiders who adopt a conciliatory policy likewise perceive their relations with Pomio Kivung communities as superficial, and they particularly deplore their renunciation of betel-nut. Abstinence stereotypically causes the mouths of members to 'stink' and prevents them from being 'genuinely' sociable.

Notes

1. Published sources on the Pomio Kivung are: Koimanrea and Bailoenakia 1983; Panoff 1969, 1988; Tovalele 1977; Trompf 1984, 1990*a*; Whitehouse 1989, 1990, 1992*b*, 1994, forthcoming *a*, *b*.
2. Trompf 1990*a*: 69.

3. The point should be stressed, to avoid confusion, that the term 'Village Government' is used in the Pomio Kivung to refer to all the ancestors who will return, and not to a particular category of them.

4. These are the Ten Laws of the Pomio Kivung and their standard exegeses:

1. *We must worship one God.* Worship is held to consist of a reciprocal relationship between humans and supernatural agencies, exemplified by pre-contact magico-medical practices. When Christian missionaries arrived, they tried to wipe out this form of worship. The Kivung has 'reawakened' everybody to the value of spiritual reciprocity, by providing a repertoire of suitable rituals for cultivating close reciprocal relations with God.

2. *We must not abuse the name of God.* It is blasphemous to use God's name as a swear word, to call any person by an offensive name or to ridicule a person's deformities or physical blemishes (because all persons are God's creations), or to invoke the name of God when tainted with sin (see n. 5, below).

3. *We must worship God on Sunday, and perform no labour.* Worship is enacted through the same Kivung rituals performed on other days of the week. Any sin committed on Sunday automatically constitutes a violation of the Third Law as well.

4. *We must respect everybody.* People must respect all the rights and duties which accrue to them in their cultural setting. It is sufficient to obey the most 'morally important' rules and to disregard trivial or 'less moral' rules when the latter conflict with the former. The main thing is that people are willing to obey rules and reluctant to disobey them. (Much is made of the importance of obedience, and less of the specific rules which must be obeyed.)

5. *We must not kill people.* This law not only forbids murder, but also any unreasonable verbal attack (including gossip or 'character assassination'), all forms of physical attack, self-mutilation, masturbation, contraception, and abortion (these last three because they 'kill' the potential for life).

6. *We must not have sexual relations outside of marriage.* This Law also forbids lustful thoughts about a person to whom one is not married.

7. *We must not steal.* As with the Sixth Law, thinking about the act is forbidden, as well as the act itself. 'Stealing' is broadly construed to encompass adultery (the stealing of sexual rights) and gossip (the stealing of a person's good reputation).

8. *We must not deceive.* Lying includes the withholding of information in order to mislead, the assumption of a disguise for nefarious purposes, and the breaking of agreements.

9. *We must not sexually desire another person's spouse.* Whereas the Sixth Law does not make adultery any more serious than experimentation among adolescents, the Ninth Law ensures that adultery is a particularly grave offence.

10. *We must not covet other people's property.* Once again, this makes stealing a more serious crime than it would otherwise be.

Of the Ten Laws, the Fifth occupies a special position because no matter which law a man breaks, he also automatically violates the Fifth inasmuch as, by sinning, he 'kills' (spiritually damages) himself. It is clear that many sinful acts constitute violations of several Laws. Murder and adultery are particularly grave offences, partly because they violate so many Laws at once.

5. The use of euphemisms, in addition to creating an atmosphere of secrecy when outsiders are around, is often explained by Kivung members as an attempt to avoid violations of the Second Law which proscribes the wrongful use of ancestors' names. According to Pomio Kivung members, to invoke the name of an ancestor or of God implies that one is speaking on behalf of the agency to whom it refers, and this is an intrinsically perilous business. Not only might the divine will be misrepresented, but the speaker may be personally tainted by sin for which absolution has not yet been sought. To speak piously when in fact one is sinful is the standard example given of how a person can break the Second Law. Consequently, Pomio Kivung members invariably refer to God indirectly as 'big man' rather than by name. The reluctance to utter sacred names probably has less in common with Christian or Hebraist conceptions of blasphemy than with the long-standing indigenous concern with guarding esoteric knowledge. In many parts of Papua New Guinea the avoidance of using names, especially of ancestors, has been shown to play a pivotal role in the reproduction and transformation of political systems (e.g. Harrison 1990). Moreover, since names are thought to embody supernatural power, to speak a name is often thought to invoke this power, to set it loose within the speaker. Visitors to Baining areas, prior to missionization, were struck by a reluctance to utter the names of gods (e.g. Klemensen 1965: 173). In Christian teaching the wrongful use of the Lord's name has the capacity to offend an external transcendent power, whereby a human agent acts upon a supernatural one. For Pomio Kivung members, by contrast, the invocation of God's name unleashes His power within the speaker, such that the two agents become fused, and whether this is for good or ill depends entirely on the moral condition of the speaker which is established through ritual, especially the rites of absolution.

3

Routinization

It's not good for us to think too much about what it will be like
when the ancestors come. We have to think about our many tasks
today, and obey the rules, otherwise the miracle will not occur. Or,
alternatively, if I don't put my head down and think of my work
today, another man will take my place at the time of the miracle.

(The Second Orator in the Kivung community of Dadul)

IN the last chapter I outlined the institutional system operating more or
less uniformly in all Pomio Kivung communities, including Dadul. Each
community in the movement performs a similar set of rituals, informed
by a common body of doctrines, disseminated from a central seat of
authority at Malmal in the Pomio region. A striking feature of these
community institutions is that they are highly routinized, being reproduced primarily in daily and twice-weekly repetitions. This emphasis on
repetitive or routinized activity is connected to the ways in which ideas
are codified and religious experience is cultivated. The style of codification and cultural transmission is related in turn to the scale and structure
of the mainstream Pomio Kivung movement.

My wider concern is to draw out certain contrasts between the mode
of religiosity predominating in the mainstream movement, and the more
ecstatic forms of religious experience cultivated in a localized splinter
group, described in Chapters 4 to 6. Splinter-group activities tend to
recur every few years, and I will show that this periodicity is associated
with distinctive patterns of cultural transmission and codification, and
political organization. The emphasis is on non-verbal 'analogic' codification, sensual stimulation, and emotionality, in contrast with mainstream
Kivung religion which is more extensively verbalized, logically integrated,
unemotional, and repetitive. Thus, in describing the routinized community system of Dadul (as an exemplification of all community systems in
the movement), I intend to set up a model of a particular politico-
religious regime, with which the materials of the following chapters will
be contrasted.

TABLE 3. *Routinized community institutions*

Frequency of observance	Type of observance
Daily	*Haus Matmat* ritual (whole community participates).
Twice-weekly	*Haus Bilong Bernard* ritual on Tuesdays and Saturdays (whole community participates). Meetings in *Haus Kivung* on Tuesdays and Saturdays (whole community participates. *Haus Famili* ritual (widow(er)s only).
Weekly	*Haus Famili* ritual (married persons only). Thursday and Sunday observances (whole community participates).
Fortnightly	Sacred gardens ritual (whole community participates).
Monthly	Collective absolution donation on last Thursday of month (whole community participates).

The frequency of religious observances in the mainstream or routinized community system are summarized in Table 3. The most complex and elaborate forms of ritual activity, concerned with temple rituals and the repetition of religious doctrine, are reproduced in very short cycles, ranging from daily performances to ones which recur on a weekly basis. Less complex rituals, connected with the sacred gardens and collective absolution donations, occur slightly less frequently, in fortnightly and monthly performances.

In the following sections, a detailed description is given of the actions which are repetitively performed at the temples, sacred gardens, and monthly absolution donations. I then describe the role of community meetings in disseminating exegetical commentaries on these performances, and reiterating the details of Pomio Kivung doctrine. An analysis is then provided of the nature of religious experience in mainstream communities like Dadul, and the implications of routinization for the nature and scale of political organization.

Temple Rituals

The *Haus Matmat* or 'Cemetery Temple'[1] is situated on the edge of Dadul's graveyard. Externally, this temple differs little from ordinary dwellings except that it is larger and has lower walls than most of the latter, and is decorated at the front entrance by cordyline, also used as markers for graves throughout the region and therefore associated with the dead. Otherwise, the Cemetery Temple, with its blade grass roof, bark walls, and earth floor, looks very much like a typical dwelling.

Every day food is placed in the Cemetery Temple as an offering to the ancestors.[2] The task of food preparation is performed by one of four groups of women each composed of two married or widowed women and one young single woman. Such a group will prepare food on two consecutive days out of every eight.

The three women of a work group whose day it is to prepare food generally start work at about 10 a.m., when they go off to their domestic gardens or (with permission from an appropriate official) to a sacred Kivung garden to collect firewood for cooking and to harvest taro, sweet potato, and other foods which will be presented to the ancestors in the afternoon. Such excursions may be combined with fetching water from the creek, otherwise an additional trip is necessary. When they return to the village, the women may either prepare the food in the communal Kivung kitchen built for that purpose, or in the cooking areas associated with their own dwellings.

The task of preparing offerings for the ancestors is supposed to be quite distinct from the task of secular food preparation. When handling the offerings to the ancestors, the women should observe specified internal states. For example, the women should never think about eating the food as they prepare it for (although they may eventually eat their fill of it) the food at this stage belongs to the ancestors and must be prepared with a view to (in the local idiom) 'giving with the palm of the hand' (i.e. freely, generously, and unreservedly). If the cooks think of eating the food in the course of its preparation then it will come from 'the back of their hands' and the ancestors will reject it. In actual fact, it is not the material substance of the food which the ancestors consume, but the respect, goodwill, generosity, deep faith, and devotion which the living supposedly put into its preparation and presentation. It follows that any breach of Kivung morality on the part of the cooks during food preparation renders the offering useless, because such breaches imply lack of devotion and respect (in so far as they 'injure' the ancestors in the sense of causing them offence) and lack of faith (in so far as a true believer would be too afraid to sin during the food preparation). A typical sin on the part of the cooks would be for two of them to gossip about the third's laziness, such gossip being seen (in the local idiom) as the 'theft' or 'killing' of the third person's good name. By cooking for the ancestors separately the women avoid squabbles or covert bad feeling about relative labour inputs. Under no circumstances should a menstruating woman work as a cook (if she comes into contact with the food it will be polluted and unacceptable to the ancestors). Sickness and menstruation may reduce the labour power of the cooking group and this usually just means that less food is prepared.

At 2.30 p.m. the village bell is struck with a stick three times by anybody who knows the time (in Dadul the 'bell' is a bomb shell found in the bush and now suspended from a tree in the middle of the village). Of the men who come to take the food from the cookhouse to the Cemetery Temple when the bell is struck, not all necessarily have set duties to perform, some act merely as assistants. The men do not communicate with one another except by mouthing, gesticulating, or whispering, and they are supposed to observe the same morally sound internal states as the cooks. They enter the Cemetery Temple one by one through the front door and place the food and drink (e.g. bottles of water) on a sideboard.

The temple is internally divided into two rooms. The first room, accessible through the front door, is dedicated to lower-ranking ancestors and contains two tables with benches (one for deceased men and boys and the other for deceased women, girls, and babies) and a sideboard for storing food. A team of designated (all-male) helpers lays the tables in this room with plates, cutlery, and decorative flowers or leaves in vases. Other tasks include the final cleaning of crockery and other equipment with tea towels and the display of elaborate concern with neatness and tidiness in the room. Checks are also made on the provision of additional comforts for the ancestors who will come to eat, for example a blanket and pillow in case one of them is cold or tired. Finally, food is dished into plates on the tables.

A screen dividing the temple in the middle contains an open doorway into a second room, called 'the boss's room'. The boss of the Cemetery Temple in Dadul is an ancestor who was in his lifetime a fairly prominent figure in the early days of the Kivung community and in Dadul's relations with external agencies in general.[3] Just as this ancestor was something of a leader and village representative when he was alive, he is designated an influential figure among the ancestors of Dadul village in the afterlife.

The preparation of the boss's room is performed exclusively by one of the three men especially chosen for this task. They do not take turns on a rota but simply work it out among themselves on a daily basis. In the boss's room there is only one table with benches and it is laid with three or four plates (one of the plates being for the boss of the temple and the

FIG. 7. The man responsible for the boss's room at the Cemetery Temple arranges the offerings with meticulous care.

others, like the plates in the lower room, being for any other ancestor who wishes to eat). There is also a sideboard where any additional food is placed. The man whose job it is to look after the boss's room performs the general tidying, cleaning, and flower arranging tasks that were mentioned in relation to the lower room and he dishes out food into some or all of the plates on the table. Then he cleans the rims of each plate containing food throughout the temple and memorizes the condition of the food (see Fig. 7). His next task is to attend to the monetary offerings.

The principal monetary offering in the Cemetery Temple is the catharsis money. At any time (e.g. after an absolution donation at another location) individuals may come to the Cemetery Temple to make a catharsis donation. The result is that money, donated in pursuit of catharsis, accumulates in the Cemetery Temple every day. The man responsible for the boss's room removes most of the money from the catharsis receptacle just inside the front door. He cannot remove all the money because he must leave a residue of a few coins so that power can still be obtained from the glass by placing one's palm over it. The money which he removes from the glass (e.g. 80t) is separated into two equal amounts (e.g. 40t). One of these amounts is divided among glasses on the two tables in the lower room (e.g. 20t per table). The man then enters the boss's room with the remainder of the catharsis money (e.g. 40t) still in his hand. Then he inclines his face to the rafters and delivers a fairly lengthy and obsequious speech addressed to the highest religious authorities in the 'other' ancestral world, such as God, Koriam, and local ancestors asking them for spiritual guidance and protection from evil and inviting them to eat the food which has been laid out and to receive the monetary offerings. Then he places his hands on the table and concludes with the Lord's Prayer. Finally, he places the remainder of the catharsis money (e.g. 40t) on a plate on the boss's table. This means that both categories of ancestor will have received equivalent monetary offerings, and neither group can feel overlooked or offended. After one last check over the house (especially on the state of food served on plates) he makes his exit and another male official, who meanwhile has been waiting outside, now enters the empty temple to take up his vigil.

The official who keeps a vigil in the Cemetery Temple (between approximately 2.50 p.m. and 3.45 p.m.) plays the part of a kind of observer. His Pidgin title of *kuskus* (literally 'clerk' or 'bookkeeper') associates him with Western government structure, particularly the officials who keep records on what is said at meetings. I will refer to the *kuskus* as a 'witness' (of which there are three in Dadul). After entering the temple the witness goes to sit in a small cubicle, built in the corner of an external wall and a wall dividing the two rooms of the house (see Fig. 8). According to Kivung ideology, he remains seated until 3.45 p.m. During the period that he sits there, the witness may hear a knocking at the door indicating the arrival of the ancestors, or he may hear a faint clattering of plates, cutlery, or bottles, or the creaking of a door. Such sounds are caused by the ancestors who have come to receive the offerings. Although they create noises, the ancestors are never visible. An analogy with the wind is often made, for just as the wind moves the branches of trees yet is itself invisible, so the spiritual substance of the ancestors moves objects in the Cemetery Temple thereby creating noise. These noises always cease before 3.45 p.m. and their cessation may be marked by another sound of knocking on the door. When the noises have stopped, it means that the ancestors have finished eating and have departed. Sometimes the witness hears nothing in the course of his vigil.

The task of the witness is to keep a mental note of any noises which occur during his vigil, representing evidence that the ancestors came to receive the offerings. All the men who act as witnesses are supposed to possess considerable courage and moral fibre since proximity to spirits, even the 'good' ancestors, is held to be dangerous to those who possess

FIG. 8. In the Cemetery Temple, a special cubicle and seat is provided for witnesses holding vigils.

inadequate conviction and faith and who therefore have reason to fear the wrath of God and the ancestors. The nature of such danger is twofold: in the face of presumptuous behaviour on the part of the morally weak, the ancestors may confer sickness upon them; and also the fear of the morally weak can itself cause sickness.

At 3.45 p.m. the village bell is struck three times once again, indicating that it is time for those villagers wishing to eat and to hear the news from the witness (this could be anybody in the community) to gather outside the front door of the Cemetery Temple. The man in charge of the boss's room is the first to arrive at the cemetery. He knocks on the door of the Cemetery Temple, announces his identity, then opens the door and enters. The witness remains seated in his cubicle while this man checks the plates containing food, first in the lower room and then in the boss's

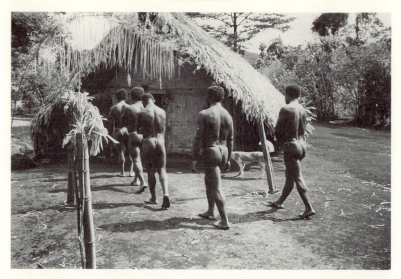

FIG. 9. Daily processions to remove offerings at the Cemetery Temple are gravely undertaken.

room. He may find that the food has not been disturbed, or he may notice that the rim of one or more of the plates has been splashed with food or that there are other signs of disturbance (e.g. a hole in a taro tuber where a morsel of food has been removed). If such signs are discovered he will show them to the witness who, until that moment, presumably does not know of their existence. Meanwhile, a team of helpers removes the food from the house (see Fig. 9) and places it on leaves and tables in the open air. Then the witness and man in charge of the boss's room emerge from the Cemetery Temple into the light to find another kind of official (an 'orator') standing there with his back to them, facing a gathering of some or all of the villagers (depending on who wanted to come). The man in charge of the boss's room goes to join the throng while the witness goes to stand a little to one side and behind the orator. The hushed chatter of those gathered sinks into silence while the witness whispers into the orator's ear, informing him either that the ancestors did not come or that he heard certain noises and the food was disturbed indicating that the ancestors did come. The orator in turn conveys this information to the gathering. If the ancestors did not come, it means that the living have committed some offence, thereby contaminating the offering and rendering it unacceptable to the ancestors. In such a case, the orator urges the people to consider how they have caused offence (it may be that all, some or just one of them is/are to blame). He tells them that a monetary collection must be performed soon to wipe the slate clean and restore moral purity in the village. He probably reiterates the impossibility of being reunited with the ancestors if evil continues to flourish among them, or he may focus on the horrors of damnation. If the ancestors have come, the orator relates the evidence to his audience and urges everyone to continue along the righteous path which they have evidently found and to strengthen themselves against corruption by Satan. This task of addressing the people could in principle be performed by the witnesses themselves but it is rare for them to do so. Thus, in practice, Dadul's three orators take it in turns on a rota (two days on and four days off) to address the gathering. After brief applause, the orator, the witness, and the whole gathering repeat together the Lord's Prayer and everybody shakes hands. The Lord's Prayer has a special significance for Kivung members in so far as it seems to focus on the themes of returning ancestors ('Thy kingdom come'), the harmony of the group ('as we forgive those who trespass against us'), and other central principles of Kivung doctrine.

After this, people talk to one another or help themselves and others to the food which has been removed from the Cemetery Temple. There are certain rules pertaining to the consumption of this food. The food from the boss's room should be eaten only by the adult men, the status of 'adult' accruing to those who possess an acknowledged role in the Kivung community (e.g. witness, orator, etc.) or those who are too sick or infirm to fulfill a role. In Dadul, there are no post-pubescent, healthy males who are without such a role or roles. Similarly, the food from the males' table in the lower room is supposed to be eaten by the boys (i.e. immature males) of the village and the food from the females' table there is consumed by the women, girls, and infants of both sexes. If, however, the mature men cannot consume all their food, the surplus can be eaten by anyone who so desires and the same applies to excess food from tables in the lower room although, in practice, sharing between females and boys seems often to occur before the existence of specific surpluses has strictly been established.

The atmosphere during the meal is light and relaxed, particularly if the offerings were received by the ancestors. Joking is now permitted (as long as it is in keeping with Kivung morality, including the normal conventions applying to behaviour between unrelated people, kinsmen, or affines). If a marsupial is sighted nearby, a team of boys might hunt it down and slaughter it. In other words, normal secular behaviour can recommence.

Even the food itself is no longer sacred and, if there are surpluses which nobody will eat, these can be disposed of in any way at all (e.g. fed to livestock).

The plates and other utensils with which the food was offered to the ancestors belong to the community as a whole and form part of the material ritual apparatus of the Kivung. These are washed on site with water collected in saucepans and bottles by the cooks during the morning. Men tend to take the lead with washing–up, assisted by anybody who spontaneously volunteers. The utensils are then returned to the side-boards within the Cemetery Temple. Meanwhile the gathering gradually disperses. During the meal, most people have eaten from their own plates which they have brought along for that purpose and they now take these utensils back home with them.

The ritual uses of the Cemetery Temple are not confined to the after-noons. At any time (except when there is food on the tables) any Kivung member may go the Cemetery Temple to put money in (or place a palm over) the catharsis glass just inside the door. It is a combination of individual circumstances (e.g. needs and faith) that determines if, when, or how frequently a person goes to the catharsis glass each day and nobody tells another person to do this. But every morning, at least some men go into the Cemetery Temple to make sure that it is tidy and clean and may wipe over the utensils which were washed the previous day, and on these visits the men always donate money in the catharsis glass or (if they have no money to spare) place their palms over it. The task of checking the Cemetery Temple is not allocated on a rota. All the men aim to perform this every morning and only fail to do so if they are sick, absent from the village, or waylaid by other pressing jobs. Therefore, in practice, some of them always turn up at the Cemetery Temple.

Just as there is only one Cemetery Temple in any Kivung community, so there is only one *Haus Bilong Bernard* ('Bernard's Temple'). In Dadul, Bernard's Temple is situated at the beginning of the path which leads from the conceptual centre of the village to the cemetery and its associ-ated temple. Bernard's Temple is very much like a smaller version of the Cemetery Temple, and thus resembles an ordinary dwelling except that it is decorated with the special leaves associated with graves (and there-fore the dead).

The ritual uses of Bernard's Temple are very much like those of the Cemetery Temple and it is internally divided along similar lines with a conceptually lower room and a boss's room, in which food and money are offered to the ancestors. The number and distribution of tables is the same as in the Cemetery Temple and the ceremonial sequence surrounding the presentation of offerings and removal of food follows the same structure and timetable (i.e. between bell rings at 2.30 p.m. and 3.45 p.m.). Moreover, it is performed by the same personnel as in the Cemetery Temple (i.e. the men responsible for the boss's room in the Cemetery Temple are also responsible for the boss's room in Bernard's Temple and the official helpers in the lower room of the Cemetery Temple perform the same duties in Bernard's Temple). Therefore, rather than allocate space to a description of all the rituals associated with Bernard's Temple, it is simpler to state that all the rituals described in relation to the Cemetery Temple apply to Bernard's temple with the following principal exceptions.

Food offerings are only presented at Bernard's Temple twice a week (on days which are fixed by convention in every Kivung community). The food and water prepared by the cooks on these two days are divided between the Cemetery Temple and Bernard's Temple. There are also some minor differences in the distribution of monetary offerings. Moreover, unlike the Cemetery Temple, Bernard's Temple is not attended by a witness when offerings are made, nor are the offerings there tampered with by the ancestors. It is assumed, however, that if a witness were stationed there, the noises made by the visiting ancestors would be heard. The boss of Bernard's Temple must be different from the boss of the Cemetery Temple. In the case of Dadul, he was (in his earthly existence) an early member of the Kivung and widely thought to possess knowledge about traditional customs. But unlike the boss of Dadul's Cemetery Temple, he was never a leader in the eyes of the colonial Administration and is not remembered as an orator or organizer. Finally, unlike the Cemetery Temple, Bernard's Temple is the venue for donations of money in an absolution receptacle.

The community as a whole has only one absolution receptacle, kept on a platform outside the front door of Bernard's Temple. Strictly speaking, this glass is not really connected with Bernard's Temple ritual but is kept at that location in Dadul because people wishing to put money into it have to concentrate very hard to assume the correct internal state and Bernard's Temple just happens to be located in a quiet spot conducive to that purpose (three absolution glasses were formerly kept at the respective houses of the three orators but this arrangement did not work out because the village children tended to play in these locations and thereby distract the persons coming to make donations).

The third kind of temple is the *Haus Famili* or 'Family Temple'. Every married couple and widower in a Kivung community has a special house or room called a 'Family Temple', which is set aside exclusively for the presentation of offerings to dead parents and other close relatives, and of monetary donations in personal absolution and catharsis receptacles.

Widows do not ordinarily have a Family Temple of their own but use one belonging to another married couple. This is because the work of building houses is performed by men, and houses built for the use of one domestic unit are very rarely built by men who are not members of that unit (unless they owe labour to a man who is head of the household in question, in which case the latter directs and participates in the building with the other men and boys acting as helpers). If a widow has a mature unmarried son he might agree to build a house for his mother but not necessarily. Thus, a widow is usually assimilated into the domestic unit of a kinsman or male in-law and is obliged to use the Family Temple of this unit or indeed of any unit which invites her to do so (collective pressure is exerted, if necessary, in Kivung gatherings led by the orators to ensure that at least one household head tenders such an invitation).

The rituals connected with the Family Temple occur in a single chamber, very much like the boss's room in the Cemetery Temple or in Bernard's Temple in so far as it contains one table and sideboard where offerings are laid out, a catharsis glass on the table for monetary offerings, and cordyline leaf decoration within and also at the entrance. In addition to the catharsis glass, there is an absolution glass too. The absolution glass is not directly connected with the ritual functions of the Family Temple and could, in principle, be kept in the domestic living quarters.

Every married person leaves offerings in his or her Family Temple once a week on a day which he or she has especially chosen for this purpose. Widows and widowers leave such offerings twice a week, once on their own behalf and once on behalf of their dead spouses. The food prepared as offerings may be taken from one or both of the sacred Kivung gardens with the permission of the men who oversee the care of these gardens, but it is generally taken from the donor's domestic gardens. The task of food preparation falls more heavily on women. Married women and widows generally prepare their own food offerings, perhaps obtaining some assistance from their unmarried daughters with the work of cooking and fetching water, crops, and firewood. A woman's husband or sons may agree to help her with these tasks to a lesser extent, especially if she is ill. A menstruating woman must delegate all such tasks entirely as well as the presentation and removal of offerings. Married men may prepare their own food offerings, but if their wives are not indisposed or menstruating, the latter usually undertake the bulk of the work. Widowers prepare their own offerings more frequently than married men unless they have one or more unmarried daughters to do most of the work for them. Ideologically, the main concern is not who prepares the food but that the job is performed with the correct moral attitude (as described for the communal cooks).

Food is presented in the Family Temple on the appropriate day at 2.30 p.m. and removed at 3.45 p.m. Usually, individuals perform the ritual by themselves on their own behalf, dedicating the offering to their own close relatives who have died. If individuals are obliged to delegate this task (e.g. due to sickness, menstruation, etc.) then they are violating the First Law (by failing to worship in the proper fashion), and should perform an absolution donation.

As with the offerings at the Cemetery Temple and Bernard's Temple, the food left at the Family Temple no longer belongs to the ancestors once it has been removed at 3.45 p.m. It may at that time be brought into the living quarters for immediate consumption by the family, any surpluses being distributed among other families with whom exchange relations are established. It may be put aside until later, while the family members assemble to eat the food which has been removed from the Cemetery Temple (and, on Tuesdays and Saturdays, Bernard's Temple). In short, the food removed from the Family Temple is disposed of in the same fashion as any other food belonging to a household.

The ancestors who receive temple offerings are all thought to be members of the so-called 'Village Government' over which God presides. The sharing of food and money with the Village Government (i.e. God and the perfect ancestors) is a way of bringing these parties closer together, a way of uniting them in a common goal. In the local idiom, commensality is a way of 'enticing' the ancestors. It is thought that the ancestors must love and care about the living, they must have strong affective ties with them, otherwise they will not be motivated to leave their perfect spiritual world and return to a corporeal existence.

The element of commensality and affective bonding is most pronounced in Family Temple ritual. This is not surprising since, when a person presents offerings in the Family Temple, he or she is expressing a relation to kinsmen who, when they were alive, shared food and bonds of affection and common interest with him or her. The ancestors who receive offerings in a Family Temple are, of course, also members of the

Village Government (and are therefore morally perfect and omniscient) but it is not in their capacity of members of the Village Government (which gathers in large meetings with the salvation of the whole population in mind) that the ancestors visit a Family Temple. Rather, it is in the capacity of a father or mother or uncle or other relation. As such, the manner in which catharsis donations and food offerings are made is not the same in the Family Temple as in the Cemetery Temple. In the Family Temple, donations and offerings are made with speeches which stress kinship relations and personal interests (e.g. requests are made for help with personal endeavours such as hunting). The language used is more direct and informal than would be considered appropriate in the Cemetery Temple. A different kind of affective bonding is sought in Cemetery Temple ritual. The Village Government which gathers there is so exalted, and therefore remote, that it is not closeness through kinship which is sought but a Christian-syncretic vision of atonement that the offering of food, containing the most moral aspects of the living, is intended to excite. In fact, in the Cemetery Temple, the ancestors most clearly represent God Himself and offerings to them are also offerings to God.

Thus, commensality is intended to cultivate bonds of two basic sorts between the living and the dead. Both are based on a kind of reciprocity, the one engendered in kinship and the other engendered in the 'Christian' notion of humans giving devotion, hard work, and moral commitment to God in exchange for mercy, forgiveness, and the promise of favour in His heart. This latter exchange is really a definition of Kivung 'worship'. In Bernard's Temple, elements of both kinds of bond are involved. On the one hand, since it is built and ministered by and on behalf of the community at large, it is more like the Cemetery Temple than a Family Temple and is therefore conceptually a 'big temple'. On the other hand, it is not the meeting place of the Village Government and so is not as 'big' or sacred as the Cemetery Temple. The awesomeness of the Cemetery Temple is enhanced by its physical proximity both to the cemetery (where the bodies of the ancestors reside) and the immense pole erected there on which the names of all known village ancestors are written, starting with the name of God (*Nutu* in the Maenge tongue spoken at Malmal) followed by the name of the boss of the Cemetery Temple (see Fig. 10).

Temple rituals are among the most elaborate and time-consuming activities within Kivung communities. Simpler and less frequent rituals concern the sacred gardens and the collective pursuit of absolution.

F IG. 10. The old Cemetery Temple in Dadul is dismantled. The cemetery post, listing the names of local ancestors, can be seen in the background.

Garden Rituals and Collective Donations

Each Kivung community maintains two sacred gardens adjacent to the cemetery and tended fortnightly by the whole community. Any productive individual who fails to turn up at these work sessions is fined K1, payable to the officials in charge of the gardens. One of the sacred gardens is called 'Paradise', and is described as the 'home' of the Village Government. The Paradise garden belongs to those ancestors who (like Adam and Eve) do not have to labour on the land for it to bear fruit. The fact that the living community does have to labour in the garden is seen as appropriate because in this way it enacts God's punishment for original sin. Because the garden is the Village Government's Paradise, it is a place in which no evil can occur and it is imperative that no sin is committed in this garden. Moreover, when taking on the role of 'man in charge' of Paradise, the official-to-be must undergo purification rites. The fruits of Paradise contain the most moral aspects of the living (like the offerings at the temples) and belong to the Village Government, not so much in their material form as in their moral essence. For this reason, the living must seek the permission of the man in charge of the garden before harvesting its fruits, lest they deceive or steal from the ancestors.

The second sacred garden is associated with the Maenge leader Bernard, and occupies a more hazy ideological position. It is said that when the ancestors come they must be presented with food from Bernard's garden. Beyond this, however, the purpose of the garden is not widely agreed upon and, like Bernard's Temple, it is somewhat extraneous to the overall ideological scheme.

Collective absolution donations are performed on the last Thursday of every calendar month. The aim of this ritual is to gain absolution for the souls of all (anonymous) people who have died but who have not entered the Village Government. In so far as these monthly collections cannot do anything for the donors (except that they constitute another form of worship, expressing the reciprocal relationship between humans and God) they are thought of as charitable. It is assumed that these monthly collections are responsible for the continuous release of souls from a kind of purgatory or limbo into the Village Government.

The ritual begins with the gathering of the whole community in the village clearing in a state of profound gravity and silence. An orator announces the reason for the collection and places the receptacles on any available platform. Then, one by one, the people come forward to put money in the receptacles, or place their palms over them. The children who are too young to perform this action on their own are manipulated through the motions by their parents. After the collection has been made, the amount of each donation is recorded by a bookkeeper especially chosen for the task. Then the crowd disperses quietly.

Collective absolution donations are also performed when ancestors reject offerings presented at the Cemetery Temple. The intention is to eliminate whatever moral impurity in the community has offended the Village Government. Moreover, public collections are sometimes mounted for charitable purposes (e.g. to excite pity in the Village Government for a local family whose members are outside the Kivung and therefore in constant danger of some Satanic affliction, such as an illness). The money collected at such times is always presented to the Village Government in the Cemetery Temple along with the day's individual catharsis donations. The times of such donations are announced by the orators at a convenient moment, such as a community meeting.

Community Meetings

All the members of Kivung communities (barring those with good excuses) are obliged to attend two public meetings every week, convened in a special building known as the 'Meeting House' (*Haus Kivung*). These meetings are scheduled to coincide with the performance of rituals in Bernard's Temple, taking place while offerings are left to stand in the temples. In Dadul, Tuesdays and Saturdays are the occasions for meetings and for rituals in Bernard's Temple. In other communities, different days may be selected, although Thursdays and Sundays may not be used, in view of their special sanctity.

People begin to gather in the Meeting House after the bell is rung at 2.30 p.m. When the male officials arrive back from their task of presenting offerings at the two big temples, the meeting begins. Women, girls, and very small children occupy positions on benches or the dirt floor at one end of the meeting house, while men and boys occupy the other end of the house. The only absentees are any menstruating women (who should confine themselves entirely to the domestic sphere and keep clear of all Kivung ritual), any sick people, and the witness at the Cemetery Temple.

Throughout the public meetings, the three orators take it in turns to address the community. The speeches may deal with any aspect of Kivung doctrine. The orators reiterate the basic moral propositions of the movement and elaborate upon themes in the group's cosmology. For this reason, the public meetings form part of the socialization process for children, drumming home morals and other ideas that inform the daily activities which they observe or in which they participate. Above all, however, the explicit intention behind the speeches is to persuade the community to become more virtuous. The orators may single out people at the meeting who should change their ways lest they let down the whole community. The orators stir up a deep horror of the Devil and his many wives (evil female spirits), by stressing how sinners are separated from their social universe and sucked into a wilderness of hunger, fear, and loneliness and by focusing on the horrors of eternal damnation. The orators speak in elaborate and grisly metaphors which capture the imagination and instil fear into would-be sinners. They employ rhetoric and raised voices, charged with emotion. In view of the frequency of these meetings, the key speakers have highly developed oratory skills and powers of persuasion.

Whether it is in the context of temple ritual or public meetings, the orators play a vital role in generating moral strength in the community. Their task is to cultivate within audiences ever greater support and commitment to the Pomio Kivung. The orators are attributed numbers (one to three) in Dadul (e.g. *namba wan komiti* is the formal title of the 'first orator') but this is not intended to imply some kind of ranking. In fact, the numbering refers to the order in which the three men acquired the role of orator. The orators are supposed to co-operate in the idiom of brotherhood (embracing a principle of 'equivalence') in their attempts to raise moral standards in Dadul.

The community meetings are occasionally used for the resolution of disputes. Most arguments, though, are settled in private when the disputants confidentially seek the assistance of the two special legal officials in the community. These officials suggest an amount of money which the disputants should exchange at some discreet location. This exchange of money is supposed to do three things: (i) it helps to remove some of the guilt and shame which is supposedly obsessing the disputants (who are, by definition, also sinners), although further absolution and catharsis donations are obligatory; (ii) it removes resentment and bitterness; (iii) it reinstates harmonious relations. The exchange of money is performed by means of two handshakes, the clasped hands transferring the currency, and this symbolizes the re-established good relations between the parties. Disputes of a very serious nature (i.e. ones which provoke arguments or fighting in full public view) have to be resolved at the public meetings. The same procedures as those used in private settlements are undertaken before the whole community, except that: (i) the amounts of money exchanged are increased (in proportion to the presumed increase in the shame of the disputants); (ii) the orators take a prominent role in exhorting the disputants to relinquish all bitterness or hidden malice, and the legal officials (if they speak at all) simply reiterate these instructions. Once a dispute escalates to the public level, its resolution is a foregone conclusion because it is perceived as a threat to the whole community (undermining the attempt to achieve the goal of collective moral strength), and any person who temporarily refuses to shake hands is subjected to extreme public pressure until he or she gives in, or is forcibly expelled from the community.

Whatever the content of a particular public meeting, the orators call a halt at 3.30 p.m. and one of them delivers a more or less fixed sermon on one of the Ten Laws for fifteen minutes. For this sacred period, smoking is forbidden and a respectful silence observed. Over the weeks, each Law is covered in sequence, the Tenth Law being followed by a fresh cycle beginning with the First Law. The orators take it in turns, only one of them speaking about one Law at each meeting. This has the effect of familiarizing every single person with all (known) methods of violating the Ten Laws. After a boy is sent to strike the bell at 3.45 p.m., the whole community shakes hands and leaves the Meeting House to gather at the cemetery for the removal of the temple offerings.

Routinization, Cognition, and Politics

Community meetings constitute the most important forum for the transmission of Pomio Kivung doctrine. It was primarily through these meetings that I came to learn the authoritative interpretations of the Ten Laws, and the array of ideas about the afterlife, the Village Government, and the eschatological themes concerning the Period of the Companies and of the Government. I was exposed also to Kivung ideas about the mission, the state, and surrounding villages. I simultaneously absorbed the meanings of ritual activities as the conditions for the occurrence of the miracle became clear and the exegeses of various taboos and positive ritual acts began to fall into place. Initially, I had to be guided through the metaphors and euphemisms of orations, but as my understanding improved, my need for guidance lessened. Nevertheless, as time passed and my learning curve levelled out, I found that the amount of new information which I could collect at meetings was diminishing, and that much of what was said merely repeated what I already knew. My attention began to shift onto the question of why such frequent repetition took place. Clearly, most attendants at meetings had long since acquired expertise in the religious ideology, and they obviously did not share the academic interest in orations which motivated my own intense concentration.

Whatever the historical explanation for frequent repetition of Pomio Kivung doctrine, it is not to be found in Dadul. The practices connected with meetings in the *Haus Kivung* were established in the Maenge-speaking centre of the movement at Malmal, several years before they spread to the Mali Baining. The latter were obliged to adopt the whole package as a prerequisite for inclusion in the Pomio Kivung. The emphasis on uniformity and routinization in the movement was probably part of a conscious policy on the part of leaders to sustain unity. According to one Maenge informant I met on a visit to Malmal, Koriam regarded meetings as a form of 'schooling' and the *komiti* as 'teachers' of his ideas.[4] He observed, however, that after graduating from school, children forgot or confused what they had learned very rapidly (*tingting i paol*—literally, 'thoughts are lost'). In order to prevent his own ideas from suffering a similar fate, Koriam insisted that meetings must be both regular and ongoing. This was intended to prevent variation in the way Koriam's ideas were represented in different communities, an aim which was reinforced by patrolling supervisors, dispatched from the movement's headquarters at regular intervals. This explanation for the routinized character of transmission in the Pomio Kivung concerns only Koriam's alleged intentions, rather than the actual effects of Pomio Kivung practices. A crucial question is whether these effects, many of which were presumably unforseen by Pomio Kivung leaders, have in fact coincided with the movement's aims of expansion and unification.

Pomio Kivung doctrine is elaborate and logically integrated, as the foregoing material illustrates. This body of doctrine is not enshrined in written texts, but sustained almost entirely through oral transmission, mainly in the context of community meetings. Such materials are encoded in cognitive memory (see Connerton 1989: 27–8), and it is obvious that unless they are reviewed on a regular basis they will be difficult and perhaps impossible to recollect with any degree of accuracy. Some of the ideas reiterated at Kivung meetings are repeated more frequently than is strictly necessary for any mnemonic purpose. For example, the Ten Laws are extensively interpreted in five-week cycles, whereas such materials could be effectively preserved in memory over longer periods than this. Yet exegetical commentary on rituals is not provided according to such a strictly predetermined cycle, and some important ideas may not receive thorough interpretation for months at a time. This is because much of the subject matter of orations is affected by unpredictable events: a detailed coverage of ideas about menstrual pollution is likely to be triggered by a breach (or alleged breach) of taboos; an extended interpretation of Catholicism is likely to follow from developments in the community's relations with the mission. Since orators take pride in their art, they generally seek to hold the attention of their audiences and therefore to avoid the kinds of repetition which will be received with a low level of interest. As far as possible, orators focus on themes which are due for re-examination, which tie in with contemporary events, or which lend themselves to colourful imagery and impassioned rhetoric. I have elsewhere (Whitehouse 1992b: 785) likened orators' speeches to sermons, with the caveat that:

whereas a church sermon is not supposed to repeat substantially another recent sermon but rather to illuminate in 'new' ways principles enshrined in text (and is not, in consequence, particularly memorable), Kivung speeches are the 'text', in the sense that they are constitutive of authoritative religious ideology and are required to sustain it accurately through regular repetition.

If Koriam's insistence on the frequent repetition of his teachings through deputized orators was originally intended to sustain doctrinal uniformity over time and space, then his strategy has been more or less effective. It is certain that if Koriam's ideas, which were codified in the form of elaborate, interconnected arguments, had been transmitted only very irregularly then they could not have been sustained intact. Moreover, during the long gaps between these periods of transmission, Kivung ideology would not have lived in people's minds, and therefore constitute the basis for a movement in any meaningful sense (see Whitehouse 1992*b*: 786). There is more to say, however, about the highly routinized character of non-verbal performances, especially the rituals connected with temples which are performed in daily, twice-weekly, and weekly cycles. Whether it was an intended or unintended consequence of Koriam's liturgical programme, repetitive ritual was substantially consistent with the movement's proto-nationalist aspirations.

The first thing to note about the sorts of rituals enacted in Pomio Kivung communities is that they are not (nor could they be) individually remembered. What is encoded is a script, specifying the culturally approved models for ritual performances. The cognitive mechanism which this entails is commonly referred to as 'semantic memory'. Over the past twenty years, theories of this type of memory have become increasingly sophisticated, due in particular to the innovative work of Shank (1982*a*, 1982*b*) on 'memory organization packets' and 'thematic organization points'. But what even the most up-to-date models have in common with early definitions of semantic memory (Tulving 1972), is the assumption that routine behavioural sequences, such as catching a bus every day, are not remembered as separate, unique experiences. A person can say that, two months ago, he walked to the bus stop at about 8.30 a.m., as usual, that he purchased a ticket from the bus conductor, that he alighted from the bus at a particular place, and then walked to his office. Unless this routine substantially differed from his model of a typical journey to work, he will almost certainly be unable to remember anything unique about the experience. This would apply to his memories of the people he saw on the bus. If, for example, he often sees five regular commuters, he could say that any of these people might have been on the bus two months ago, but would be unable to confirm this with certainty. If most of the passengers on a given day are unfamiliar, he may remember them as an amalgam of many impressions of strangers, anonymous faces that were not really there two months ago, who perhaps were never there at all, and distributed around the fixed interior of the bus in an entirely imaginary pattern. In the Pomio Kivung, routine ritual performances are remembered in much the same way, with certain consequences for how the movement is conceptualized by members and the emotions that it inspires.

In the case of the daily rituals performed in the Cemetery Temple,

there is a core of people in every community who almost always participate, but there are also usually a few visitors from other Pomio Kivung
villages who are obliged to join in, and even to assume the crucial roles of
witness or orator. Particular visitors come and go on a regular basis and,
over the long term, residents in a community are similarly mobile, so that
the participants in temple ritual at any location constitute an ever-shifting
category. This means that rituals at the Cemetery Temple are remembered in much the same way as a commuter remembers his daily journeys
to work. Fellow participants in the rituals may come and go, like passengers on a bus, and the routine is not inextricably bound up with a fixed
group of people. This is entirely consistent with the central assumption
of Pomio Kivung members that the Period of the Companies will result
from their collective efforts, as they all pull in the same direction. Members see themselves as part of a brotherhood within which there is freedom of movement. Some travel extensively (especially 'supervisors' based
at the headquarters), but it is recognized that nobody has seen all the
other members, and they constitute a kind of imagined community (cf.
Anderson 1983). Routinized ritual, uniformly performed within the movement by groups of ever-changing composition, is highly consistent with
the formation of this sprawling, imagined community (see Whitehouse
1993). In semantic memory, the details of actual events and people are
discarded in favour of conventional scripts for ritual performances, which
are envisaged as extending across time and space. In the following chapters, I describe the attempt in Dadul to create a very different kind of
community, much smaller-scale, intimate, and bounded, based around
contrasting types of transmission, codification, and memory.

In closing, it is necessary to acknowledge a few of the drawbacks of
highly routinized rituals in the Pomio Kivung. The first and most obvious is that these rituals are time-consuming (Table 4). People not surprisingly maintain that Pomio Kivung ritual is hard work, and the fact that
these unremitting demands continue year in and year out, without having
yet resulted in the anticipated supernatural transformation, has often led
to frustration. Such feeling formed an important part of the background
to the developments which I describe in the next chapter.

It is also plain that the characteristic activities of Pomio Kivung members are not intrinsically very exciting. A glance around audiences in the
Haus Kivung usually reveals a good deal of fidgeting among children and
many glazed eyes among the adults. Temple rituals are performed somewhat mechanically, like other uninspiring chores, and seem to be neither
intellectually challenging nor emotionally arousing. This is not to say that

TABLE 4. *Average weekly time inputs into the Kivung (Dadul)*

Title	Av. no. of hrs. per person per week	No. of persons with this title	Total 'man hrs.' per week (av.)
Adult males:			
Orator	2.75	3	8.25
Witness	0.50	3	1.50
Boss's room man	1.50	3	4.50
Temple helper	1.25	11	13.75
Bookkeeper	1.00	1	1.00
Garden keeper	1.00	2	2.00
Garden labourer	0.50	14	7.00
Lay observer	2.75	11	24.75
Inspector	1.75	14	24.50
Adult females:			
Cook	7.00	12	84.00
Labourer	0.50	12	6.00
Lay observer	2.75	12	33.00

participation in such activities is not rewarding for many people (see Chapter 7), but it is not productive of the kind of high excitement that is stereotypically associated with Melanesian 'cargo cults'. The splinter group, which I am now going to describe, provided an altogether more intense and arousing experience.

Notes

1. The Pidgin term *Haus Matmat* means literally 'Cemetery House', for there is no special word for a house which is dedicated to the presentation of offerings. In the Mali language, there is likewise no equivalent for the word 'temple' and so the *Haus Matmat* is described as a 'house' (*abuga*), typically the 'big' house (*abuga amorka*), a phrase also sometimes rendered in Pidgin (*bikpela haus*). These terms all designate a special type of building by attaching an adjective, as in the compound *hauskuk* (literally 'cookhouse') which translates readily as 'kitchen'.

2. When this practice was first explained to me, the offerings were described in Pidgin as *kaikai bilong tumbuna* ('food for the ancestors'). But the word *tumbuna* (ancestor) is rarely used in everyday discourse, in case it might one day be overheard by outsiders. Most visitors to Dadul who are not members of the Pomio Kivung are well aware of the significance of temple ritual, and often refer to it pejoratively as 'feeding the dead' (carrying the connotation of 'feeding livestock'). It is believed, however, that ridicule is less likely to occur

openly if visitors do not hear overt references to ancestors, and this is the reason typically given for avoiding the word. The term 'big man' is often used as a euphemism for ancestor, but since God is also referred to as 'big man', there is always an element of ambiguity here.

3. I never heard his name uttered in everyday discourse, however, for he was always referred to as the relative of a living person, using the appropriate kinship term.

4. The analogy between the Pomio Kivung and 'schooling' is still prevalent among members in other contexts (see Chapter 4).

4

Transformation and the
Remembrance of Things Past

Some men may feel sure that they are innocent, that they have done
nothing wrong. But in the eyes of the ancestors at the Cemetery
Temple, there is another kind of knowledge—these eyes see all our
thoughts and deeds, and the things we say. The ancestors can sometimes discern observances and violations of the law, even though we
are not aware of what we are doing. Later, if we have been doing all
the right things, a report may occur reassuring us that we are on the
right path, and entreating us not to change our thoughts and deeds,
for they are now beyond reproach. Now, today, I want to advise
Kivung supporters in Dadul as follows: when the reports tell us that
something is wrong, then there is no point in all the men arguing
about it. We must ask the ancestors to show us what is wrong and
help us mend our ways. We must get the ancestors to show us
exactly how we have violated the laws. We must ask the ancestors
to inspect our souls for the marks of sin and to give us more
reports. . . . When it comes to the kind of report in which we are
told that we are doing something wrong, I can sometimes see what
it is that's wrong. . . . If what I say is correct, then soon enough the
witness receives a report from the ancestors supporting what I have
said.

(Tanotka, leader of the splinter group in Dadul and Maranagi)

KIVUNG practices in any given village were resistant to change in certain respects. In Dadul I was told stories about local individuals who,
having advocated radical modifications to mainstream institutions, had
been expelled from the movement altogether. Thus, deliberate contradic-
tion of the authoritative rules and ideas of the movement, as dictated by
the supreme authorities in Malmal, constituted grounds for expulsion.
Minor innovations had sometimes been tolerated. Examples from Dadul
included the lowering of the fine for failure to turn up at a work session
in a sacred garden, and the 'discovery' of a new kind of sin (which,

through ignorance, had not until then been recognized as a violation of one or more of the Ten Laws). The proposal and acceptance of such modifications were dominated by the orators, who were ordinarily the key figures in any debate. The orators, however, could not have imposed an unpopular innovation of the other men and, on the contrary, tended to propose changes which originated in (or had been established as being consistent with) the consensus of the whole community. Thus, individuals could only influence the practices of their Kivung community in a way which was compliant with the consensus and existing ideology.

Reformist ambitions in the Kivung community had to be pursued within tight constraints. A balance had to be struck between the desire for innovation and the need for consistency, and between the aspirations of reformers and the mood of the community. In the middle of 1987 two classificatory brothers of outstanding political ability began an impressive campaign. Both men were young. The eldest, Baninge, was in his late twenties (married with two children under the age of five years) and a permanent resident in Dadul where he kept the Kivung financial records but held no other official position. The other man, Tanotka, was scarcely out of his teens (also married with a small baby) and a permanent resident in Maranagi where he was just one of many young lay members of the Kivung. Unlike his fellows, Tanotka had received a few years of high school education (an extreme rarity in the region).

Possession, Myth, and Reincarnation

The campaign began in August 1987, when Tanotka had an unusual experience. The account of what happened to Tanotka became standardized within a few weeks. In a sense, it was mythologized almost as soon as the events occurred. I arrived in the field more than a month too late to witness Tanotka's unusual experience and so I cannot attest to the historical accuracy of the accounts I collected. But like everyone else, I soon learned the basic story by heart. It ran as follows.

Sometime in August 1987 Tanotka fell ill while participating in a small drinking party. He complained of chest pains and giddiness. Shortly after sunset he made his way, unsteadily, to the house of his classificatory brother, Baninge, to lie down and recuperate. Between about 7 p.m. and midnight Tanotka lay on a bed in Baninge's house, speaking as if in a delirium. At first, Baninge attempted to treat him with traditional medicines on the assumption that he had a straightforward illness. Then

Baninge surmised that his brother was not ill, but had been possessed by an ancestor. Tanotka's hands were cold and this suggested the presence of an ancestor (i.e. because coldness was associated with inaction, corpses, the damp earth in graves, as well as being an inversion of ordinary sickness which produces fever). From time to time Tanotka would say 'I am Wutka'. In addition, he repeated three cryptic statements: (i) 'I am a post'; (ii) 'I will stand in two villages'; (iii) 'recall [imperative] the story of Aringawuk'.

In the course of the evening Baninge invited a number of important male officials (such as the orators) to witness Tanotka's behaviour and these men later claimed that they had heard the intelligible (if peculiar) statements mentioned above. By inviting the orators to witness the event, Baninge implied that the occurrence was significant in the context of the Kivung. But Baninge did not immediately proclaim his view that Tanotka was being possessed. For their parts, none of the male officials claimed retrospectively that they had recognized Tanotka's state as one of possession. The fact that Tanotka recovered totally and suddenly at midnight did, however, suggest to all the villagers that his 'sickness' had been very unusual.

In the following weeks Tanotka spent a good deal of time in Dadul, but it was Baninge, a permanent resident there, who (by all accounts, including his own) took the key role in promoting interest in the statements made by Tanotka during his sickness/possession. In particular, Baninge appears to have concentrated his efforts on convincing the first orator that a genuine possession had occurred. The first orator was a very persuasive and intelligent man, and was looked upon by external agencies as the representative of Dadul. Together with the first orator, Baninge organized a series of discussions among the male officials in the community, held in the Meeting House. At these meetings Baninge suggested (what might have been obvious) that Tanotka had been possessed by a specific ancestor called Wutka, who wanted to use the youth's body to tell the living how to bring about the miracle (the Period of the Companies). Baninge argued that the essence of Wutka's plan was encoded in the three cryptic statements made during the possession.

Wutka had tried to say then that he represented the post on which the Ten Laws were inscribed. The law post was planted in the ground (at the entrance to Dadul) so that only part of it was visible. This signified that although ordinary mortals knew most of the ways of violating the laws, some sins were hidden from them (i.e. hidden underground). Wutka therefore wanted to say that he would clarify all the hidden aspects of morality through Tanotka, by 'being the post'. The people of Dadul had to be enlightened in this way, prior to the miracle.

In addition, the idea of the 'post' was associated in people's minds with the central pole in a traditional Mali round-house, on which the whole construction was conceptually supported. The revelation conveyed by this metaphor was that Wutka would 'carry' the whole community in the sense of bearing and overcoming the sins of the people. Evil was always described as 'weight' or 'heaviness' and the idea was that the post (i.e. Wutka) had the moral strength to withstand this burden and to carry the community to salvation. The roof of a round-house is composed of rafters which converge on a central post, uniting there. This in turn conveyed a notion of moral unity, and multiple posts (persons) uniting at one post (uniting as one person), conjoining in moral perfection. This reading of the metaphor connoted obedience to the Laws (i.e. convergence on the post representing the Ten Laws). So the reference to the post made by Wutka (speaking through Tanotka) had a number of meanings which Baninge was able to cultivate through suggestive remarks.[1] The interpretations I have mentioned were supplied by a variety of male officials as speculative or personal understandings and were not attributed directly to Baninge. Nevertheless, Baninge's objective was achieved in the course of this process in so far as the idea of the post, whatever the specific nature of the metaphor, demonstrated the need for *obedience* to Wutka's statements.

The implications of this innovation were far-reaching. Whereas the existing community system enabled the consensus to assert itself through the orators, the embodiment of an ancestral voice in one man created the potential for a new political order. It was plain that Tanotka had to tread carefully. If he claimed superiority over the orators then he ran the risk of being denounced by them as a man possessed by Satan, masquerading as an ancestor. By that time, such a procedure for dealing with upstarts in the Kivung had been well established.

Wutka's statement about 'standing in two villages' was meanwhile interpreted by Baninge to mean that the Village Government had decided that only two Kivung villages in the province were capable of bringing about the miracle, and it seemed obvious that the two villages in question were Dadul and Maranagi, the residents of which were descended from Wutka. Not only were the people of these two villages closely related genealogically, but they could also be distinguished from other Mali groups by subtle dialectal and cultural differences. Most importantly, the people in Dadul and Maranagi were all Kivung members (with only a few exceptions). It was a combination of these three factors which made the pairing of Dadul and Maranagi natural. Thus, although the Dadul-Maranagi genealogical chart could have been extended to include all the people of Sunam, the latter had lost their cultural purity and were said to have become like the Tolai (even foregoing their birthright to Mali land). And, of course, the people of Sunam rejected the Pomio Kivung.

Finally, Wutka's directive to recall the story of Aringawuk generated a complex string of ideas. When Tanotka first mentioned Aringawuk during his possession, few people recognized the name or had heard the stories about him. But in the ensuing weeks Tanotka (with Baninge's assistance) developed the story as follows.

A long time ago, before the arrival of the whiteman in East New Britain, a young man (from Aringi, near the current site of Maranagi) was possessed by one of his ancestors and guided to a hole in the ground, which was the 'eye' of the Village Government. He passed down into this hole and entered the world of God and the ancestors. The name of this young man was Aringawuk. By a different means, Koriam also entered the Village Government at this time (implying, of course, that Koriam was born centuries ago, an idea which had been widely disseminated in the Pomio Kivung from its early days). Both Aringawuk and Koriam learned from the Village Government all the basic tenets of Kivung ideology and in particular the importance of the Ten Laws for the pursuit of salvation. After five years Koriam returned to his native village of Ablingi in Kandrian Sub-district (West New Britain), and Aringawuk in turn went back to his Mali kinsmen. Aringawuk tried to teach his fellows about the Ten Laws and he shook hands with them all. When he had finished, Aringawuk started to pull away the black skin on his head, revealing white skin underneath. In this way, Aringawuk intended to release his spirit back into the Village Government (i.e. by 'peeling off and discarding his earthly self, as if it were nothing more than a shirt'). But Aringawuk's brothers stopped him, saying that he must not go back alone but should wait until the whole community had achieved the same moral state as he, and could go with him. Aringawuk's elder brother, Gwasinga, came forward to replace Aringawuk's black skin and seal it once more on his head. And so, Aringawuk remained with his kinsmen for a period, but was disappointed to see that not all of them had believed him and many continued to break the Ten Laws. Aringawuk decided that the community was wasting his time and would not return with him to the Village Government. Tired of waiting, Aringawuk went into the forest and hanged himself, thereby delivering his soul into the Village

Government. Just as ancestors in the Village Government could not be persuaded to leave their perfect world when their living descendants remained sinful, so Aringawuk could not be persuaded to remain in 'this world' as long as it was contaminated by sin and faithlessness.

Suicide by hanging was an established method of shaming kinsmen who had unjustifiably caused injury or offence. Aringawuk, however, killed himself because of the sins of the community in general and not because of sins against him personally. In this regard, his death connoted the crucifixion of Jesus, as that sacrifice was understood in Dadul. When Aringawuk's body was recovered, it was found to be peppered with bullet holes suggestive of the mutilation of Christ's body on the cross. In addition, these bullet holes constituted a prophesy that Western technology and military power would soon come to East New Britain.

This story constituted a re-working of the traditional myth of Aringawuk, known to just a handful of old men. The authenticity of Tanotka's version was never publicly questioned, but it certainly introduced a number of new and important ideas. To begin with, the story showed that the Kivung did not originate in the Pomio region, as had previously been assumed. Rather, the 'roots of the Ten Laws post' (in the prevalent metaphor) 'grew' among the Mali in the first instance (and perhaps simultaneously in Koriam's natal village, the members of which had since lost sight completely of Kivung ideology). Aringawuk became impatient of his fellows and took his life so that Koriam was the only prophet left in 'this world'. Therefore, it fell to Koriam to enlighten the living people and he happened to begin his work in the Pomio region. Like Aringawuk, however, Koriam finally chose to die (for such figures are never the victims of an untimely death, but always leave this world of their own volition) and passed his work on to Kolman. Of course, there was never anything natural or inevitable about the designation of a Maenge leader and now, perhaps, the time had come for Kolman to pass on his work (i.e. of 'holding the key to the fence') to Wutka, speaking through Tanotka. In this way, history would complete a neat circle with the 'roots of the Kivung growing back towards their original source'. Wutka's claim that he would stand in two villages seemed less revolutionary and more appropriate (or legitimate) with the 'rediscovery' of the story of Aringawuk.

The story also provided a kind of blueprint for the emergence of new inspirational leaders. In the story, Gwasinga attempted to utilize the power of Aringawuk by keeping him in 'this world' so that the whole community might be delivered into the Village Government along with him. In the same way, Baninge would utilize the power within Tanotka on behalf of the community. But this time the story would end differently. The two communities (Dadul and Maranagi) would this time faithfully obey the edicts of their inspired leader and would reverse the scenario in which the community or just the leader leaves 'this world', so that instead the Village Government would leave the transcendental world to be reunited with the living on earth.

The story of Aringawuk came to be used in the legitimation of further ideological (as well as other types of) change. But in the weeks after Tanotka's delirium, these were the basic strings of ideas which emerged in the informal meetings. There is little doubt that Baninge generated a large proportion of these emergent ideas, often inspired by Tanotka's more general visions. For Tanotka soon developed a habit of speaking in riddles, making statements of such obscurity that it fell to all the men to suggest clarifications. If Baninge took a leading role in this process, it is probable that Dadul's first orator and several important officials from Maranagi (who were hurriedly summoned) also participated in various ways.

The status of these new ideas was, for a long time, unclear. Some children may have taken all (or most of) the emergent ideas to be as true or authoritative as the older ideology associated with the mainstream movement. But, for the most part, people regarded the new ideas as exciting but unproven and possibly dangerous. They were exciting because people felt that they had all been waiting too long for Kolman to announce that the miracle was about to occur. The collectivity was undoubtedly sympathetic to the principle of the Dadul-Maranagi group breaking away and proceeding alone. On the other hand, however, people feared that the new ideas may create conflict with various groups (particularly with the Pomio Kivung leadership). Therefore, discussion of these ideas in the all-male gatherings was shrouded in secrecy and only Baninge and Tanotka had the courage to make reference to them in the twice-weekly community meetings. Nobody claimed to know for sure that these new ideas were authoritative. Even Tanotka would only go so far as to claim that he believed he must have been the bearer of statements from Wutka during his possession because that was how other people had interpreted the events. But Tanotka would not say that he knew this to have been the case. Tanotka suggested that since the possession he felt that Wutka still resided within his body and spoke to him (Tanotka) as if over his shoulder. This enabled Tanotka to offer (coded) insights into the meanings of signs but Tanotka could never be sure that a particular insight came from Wutka; he only ever thought it might or should be so.

Then, on 8 October 1987, in the midst of these developments, two white-skinned ancestors left the Village Government and turned up in Dadul asking if they might live there for a couple of years.

The two white people arrived in Dadul on foot, from the direction of the Uramot Baining village of Riet. By the time they were in the village proper, it seemed as if it had been deserted. Some of the inhabitants were away in their gardens. Others were hiding, some watching through cracks in the walls of their houses. The Uramot guides led the white couple out of Dadul to the nearby hamlet of Stanis Naden Joanis, the Provincial Member for the Sinivit region.

My wife and I felt that it was a necessary courtesy, as well as potentially useful, to meet Stanis before deciding on a location for our respective fieldwork projects. It turned out that Stanis had a house in Dadul which he and his family did not intend to occupy because of strained relations between the villagers and Stanis' domestic group. Moreover, there was no effective institutional mechanism for resolving this disharmony because, although Stanis had been urged by the highest political authority in the Pomio Kivung to join the movement, he had refused. Stanis installed us in his empty house. It was made from bush materials, except for the roof which was formed from sheets of corrugated iron weighted down with large stones.

Just before sunset on our first day in Dadul, Tanotka demonstrated his leadership qualities by being one of the first men in the community to talk to us outside our house. What is more, he spoke to us as 'brothers' or equals rather than in a mode which would have been more typical between a villager and whites (e.g. priests, government officials). That evening, the whole community (including the visitors from Maranagi who had come in the wake of Tanotka's possession) gathered in the Meeting House and we were invited to sit, facing the audience. Stanis explained that we had come to ask questions about the local customs and it became clear to us that we were expected to ask them all right away. That evening, and every evening for a period of time, we asked questions in the Meeting House (using broken Pidgin), and the orators and other men answered them eagerly. After we left these meetings and at other convenient moments, people evidently pondered the significance of our arrival. No anthropologist had visited the region before, and it was not easy for people to accept the stated reasons for ethnographic research. As the days passed, our interviews were conducted in less formal situations and we developed a reputation for following people around and observing them when they were engaged in all sorts of trivial pursuits. This behaviour was consistent with the idea that the Village Government keeps the whole community under continuous surveillance. It was suggested that the word 'anthropology' was a blanket to cover up the real purposes of our research projects. Perhaps we had come from the Village Government as a sign that the miracle was at hand, and to find out which people would answer questions truthfully and which would tell lies. The orators would occasionally refer to us with the terms used euphemistically to refer to ancestors, rather than as *masta* or *misis* ('whiteman' or 'whitewoman'), and warn people never to try to deceive us. But nobody appears to have asserted that we were reincarnated ancestors. It was a matter for individual belief. It would have been inappropriate for an orator, for example, to say that my wife and I were ancestors. He could hint that, in his view, this was the case but like all living people any orator is 'blind' or 'unenlightened' (*aipas*) so that he cannot know for sure what the meaning of any sign or portent really is. The significance of our arrival was like the significance of a dream: everybody recognized the imagery involved but nobody could swear to the validity of their interpretations. This was both an expression of respect or deference to the omniscience of the Village Government as well as an avoidance of violations of the Eighth Law.

A very similar response was simultaneously evident in relation to the alleged possession of Tanotka. People were familiar with the suggestions concerning the significance of Wutka's cryptic statements but nobody (not even Tanotka) was prepared to swear to the validity of any interpretations, except to say that they thought most of them might or should be true. The fact was that it would have been immoral (i.e. deceitful) for people to claim that they knew for certain (i.e. possessed authoritative views on) who my wife and I really were. But the idea that such things were a matter for personal belief also suggested that people were required to strengthen their own convictions. On these grounds, some men (e.g. Baninge) told me that ideas which 'come from within the person' are more 'powerful' (i.e. stable, unshakeable) than ideas which are imposed on the person by figures of authority. For those who wanted the belief in Tanotka's possession or our hidden identities to spread, it was also strategically efficacious to keep quiet in case these beliefs were subsequently undermined and the exponents of them publicly humiliated. It gradually became obvious that the creation of divine authorities required a departure from such tactics, a departure which was facilitated initially by the advent of *ripot* ('reports' from the ancestors).

The Legitimation of Emergent Ideas: (1) The Reports

The aim of this section is to describe the development of an institutional mechanism for the legitimation of emergent ideas. This mechanism, incorporated into big temple ritual, provided a method of receiving statements or reports from the ancestors. These reports imparted authority to emergent ideas which formerly only mainstream ones had enjoyed. It also provided a basis for the legitimation of splinter-group institutions yet to be devised. At the same time, it served to disguise Baninge's influence over the religious ideology. With the advent of reports, it seemed that emergent ideas came from the ancestors, who conveyed them to the witnesses, who conveyed them to the orators, who conveyed them to the people. Less obvious was the fact that Baninge actually loaded this ideological conveyor belt.

In the previous chapter, I described how the task of the witness, in the mainstream community, was to testify whether, on a given afternoon, a meeting had occurred (and the offerings had been accepted). In February 1988 the role of the witness was expanded. From that time forward, he would not only be a witness to the fact that a meeting had occurred, he would actually be addressed (in the Mali language) by one or a few of the ancestors attending the meeting. Sometimes, the ancestors speaking would identify themselves (e.g. as Wutka or as the boss of the Cemetery Temple), but often the ancestors would speak anonymously to the witness. Moreover, on Tuesdays and Saturdays a few ancestors would always gather in Bernard's Temple as well to make statements, so it was necessary to install a witness in Bernard's Temple on these two days each week. In the beginning, the witness would actually hear the ancestor(s) speaking in the same way that a person hears the voice of a living person. Partly because one of the witnesses could not honestly claim to have heard voices in this way during his vigil, the idea was soon changed so that the witness only needed to hear the voices 'in his head' rather than 'through his ears'. The length of time between bell rings every day was increased (from 2.30 p.m.–3.45 p.m. to 2.30 p.m.–4.45 p.m.). In a couple of hours it was inevitable that anybody would have at least a few thoughts and it became the task of the witness to recognize which of his thoughts were trivial and personal (i.e. internally generated) and which were morally important (i.e. implanted by the ancestors). Statements received from the ancestors in this way were called 'reports'. As soon as not only Baninge, Tanotka, and the witnesses, but also the orators were prepared to assert that these reports came directly from the Village Government, the community was morally obliged to accept this view as well.

The very first reports were received in the temples at Maranagi (December 1987). This would seem to suggest that the idea did not originate in Dadul. But there are some indications that Baninge had a hand in the emergence of the earliest reports, not least because the first man (in both Maranagi's and Dadul's temples) to receive a report from the ancestors was Baninge's father (who, in other respects, did not have a history of innovative behaviour). It is necessary to reiterate that those who performed Kivung rituals in Dadul (as in other villages) frequently included visitors from neighbouring Kivung communities. Once Baninge's father (who normally lived in Maranagi) had shown the way, Dadul's resident witnesses could follow suit in the receiving of reports. The fact that Baninge's father was elderly (i.e. an object of respect) meant that it would have been very awkward for anybody (except perhaps another old man) to denounce his claims. Even if somebody of equal seniority had challenged Baninge's father, this would have been construed as a bad thing, an attempt to generate disharmony. In principle, the male officials as a group could have prevented the concept of reports from becoming established (e.g. by means of a collective assertion that the statements received by Baninge's father came from Satan). But this did not occur. Indeed, from the very start, it was regularly reiterated by all my informants (men and women) that the reports should be celebrated as 'proof' that the community had found favour with the ancestors and the miracle was now close at hand.

Over a four-month period, after the first report was heard, more than eighty separate statements from the ancestors were received by the witnesses and recorded on paper by a special official. A large proportion of these reports (43%) demanded improvements in the behaviour of the community (or of certain persons within it). By contrast, a few reports (12%) congratulated the community and promised that the miracle would soon occur. A handful of reports (4%) warned that Satan was close at hand, waiting for opportunities to tempt weak souls into evil and damnation. But a great many reports (41%) asserted the authority of all emergent ideas transmitted by Tanotka and Baninge, and urged the community to unite behind these two leaders.

In a less overt way, almost all the reports were an expression of the increasing influence of Baninge and Tanotka. This is because Baninge was allocated the task of asking questions of the Village Government when offerings were presented in the big temples. Now, as far as most people in the community were aware, Baninge used to ask his questions before the witness had come into earshot. But, in reality, if the witness did not overhear the questions, Baninge would tell him about them briefly before the witness took up his vigil. Since most reports were therefore formulated in response to Baninge's questions, Baninge clearly enjoyed considerable influence over the answers (i.e. over the content of reports from the ancestors). Since Baninge and Tanotka held many private conversations, it is likely that Tanotka also influenced some of Baninge's questions to the Village Government. Nevertheless, if only because Tanotka still spent a good deal of time in Maranagi, Baninge was the more influential of the two in relation to the reports in Dadul.

The reports introduced a very subtle mechanism. Although Baninge's questions normally implied the kind of answers he wished to receive, ultimate control over the content of reports lay with the witnesses. Nevertheless, a witness would never hear a report which he knew would run counter to the consensus, because such a report would not be accepted (e.g. it would be attributed to Satan who had come to the temple disguised as an ancestor). Moreover, if a witness regularly heard incongruous reports whilst those of the other witnesses were reliable, it might appear that the former was lying about the messages from the Village Government. All the same, a witness could run the risk of these sanctions if he chose and especially if he thought that popular opinion would be sympathetic. For example, he could in principle hear a report denouncing Baninge. The fact that this never occurred meant that Baninge and Tanotka were able to take the reports as an indication of support at a grass roots level (and particularly among the witnesses) and as a vindication of the ideas implied by Baninge's questions to the Village Government. Moreover, Baninge and Tanotka could now claim that they themselves had not come forward as leaders but that the ancestors (via the witnesses) had forced them into these roles.

An obvious advantage of the new institutional role of the witness was that it served to widen the base of 'this wordly' support for change. This was vital, because Baninge and Tanotka knew that they could not succeed in mobilizing the community behind their cause, if they were the only two people campaigning for such changes. But, in addition to the witnesses, Baninge and Tanotka needed to be seen to have the substantial backing of the orators as well (since they were the long-established purveyors of morality). In the context of community meetings this was not immediately forthcoming. Therefore, Baninge used his influence over the content of reports to place pressure on the orators to rally behind him. Reports like these were regularly received by the witnesses: 'Tuesday, 1 March 1988: reports continue to occur but the leaders do not habitually pay attention to them.' Or again, 'Wednesday, 2 March 1988: I [Wutka] am pleased with Baninge; when will the orators stand by the side of Baninge? It is true that the orators tell everybody to obey the Ten Laws but who will stand by the side of Baninge?' The problem was that the orators were initially still using the public meetings to say the same old things (e.g. about the Ten Laws) and were still assuming that the community's moral obligation was to plead ignorance on the matter of the validity of Tanotka's possession. In fact, after the first few weeks of reports, the orators were persuaded to amend this view.

Prior to the advent of reports, not only had there been a moral pressure to keep an open mind about Tanotka's possession, there had also been no ideological basis for Baninge's assumption of authority. Unlike Tanotka, of course, Baninge had not been possessed and there was nothing on the face of it to distinguish him from his fellows who described themselves as 'blind' or 'unenlightened'. What the reports revealed was that Tanotka and Baninge. were the only two people in Dadul and Maranagi whose spirits had already entered the Village Government. Therefore, like Kolman, Baninge and Tanotka were thought of as being physically in 'this world' but spiritually with God. This also meant that some of the reports from the big temples actually came from the spiritual manifestations of Baninge or Tanotka, who announced their identity before making statements. For example: 'Saturday, 20 February 1988: the witness received this report from Tanotka. I always enlighten you on [the subject of] various things but you do not believe [what I say].' With the advent of such reports, as well as those from other ancestors asserting the authority of Baninge and Tanotka, came a moral pressure to cast off the veil of humility and ignorance and to accept the truths ensuing from Tanotka's possession by Wutka.

The Legitimation of Emergent Ideas: (2) Collective Ritual

Until the end of 1987 the emergent ideas generated by Tanotka and Baninge had enjoyed only a tentative reception, even if many people had wanted to regard them as true. But the reports made them true. In reports, the ancestors themselves were saying that everybody must believe the emergent ideas and unite behind Tanotka and Baninge who knew the way. In this sense, emergent ideas managed to acquire the same legitimacy as older ones. Nevertheless, the legitimation of these ideas was not complete. There had been at least two dimensions to the legitimacy of mainstream ideas. Of course, one was that these old doctrines had come from God and the ancestors (via Koriam, Bernard, and Kolman). But, in addition, the people of Dadul used to demonstrate their collective commitment to the doctrines by gathering as a single large unit at public donations, meetings, and other rituals, and by observing the various rules enforced at these gatherings. Kivung ideology had always maintained that the community of Dadul, as a whole, must demonstrate to the ancestors its willingness to satisfy the preconditions of the miracle. But collective gatherings had another significance, one which was not explicitly recognized by participants. That is, they demonstrated to the living community that the Kivung had the backing and support of the population. Reports could not imbue emergent ideas with this kind of legitimacy. The method of receiving and disseminating reports engaged a fairly large personnel (i.e. witnesses, orators, etc.) but it did not encompass the community as a whole. In short, there was no social context in which each person in Dadul could see that everybody else had thrown in his or her lot with the new leaders.

By March 1988 the idea of unity was being constantly reiterated in reports and at the public meetings. The prevalent metaphors were: 'we must stand as one man [i.e. stand united]' and 'all the people must become one person'. This dictum was associated with the idea of rafters in a round-house converging on a single post, a metaphor which had arisen from Tanotka's original possession. It was not just that the people should obey the Ten Laws and other long-standing Kivung rules, but that they should be unified in their commitment to emergent ideas as well. The first ritualized expressions of this new unity took the form of large dances and feasts.

It just so happened that reports in March 1988 were complaining about the poor condition of Dadul's Cemetery Temple, which was several years old and had developed an irreparably leaking roof. In consequence, a new temple had to be constructed (see Figs. 10 and 11). It was usual to celebrate the completion of such large projects. Baninge and the first orator, however, argued that the opening of the new Cemetery Temple should be celebrated by a particularly large daytime dance, known as the *awan* (see Chapter 1).

A performance of the *awan* had not been contemplated in Dadul for a very long time. Much discussion ensued, concerning the reasons why the *awan* had been abolished. It was decided that the clubs traditionally wielded by the *awanga* should be replaced by stems of wild ginger (see Fig. 12), and that the crucial aspect of the *awan*, which merited restoration, was its celebratory character. It will be recalled that this had also become the *raison d'être* of the Uramot night dance, as a result of missionary criticism. Tanotka played a major role in creatively developing a fixed itinerary for the *awan*. In practice it involved not only a feast and the dances of *awanga* but also singing and dancing throughout the night. Moreover, the *awanga* were accompanied by another costumed figure, traditionally absent from the *awan*, known as the *ilotka* (see Fig. 17). The *ilotka* had, in the past, figured prominently in the *mendas* (see Chapter 1). Their conical bark head-dresses were a brilliant red but, in keeping with Kivung prohibitions on self-mutilation, this colouration was produced with paint rather than blood collected from the tongue.[2] The round the clock celebration provided a blueprint for future collective rituals, explicitly mounted to demonstrate the unity of the people behind emergent ideas.

It seems probable that Baninge was keen on the idea of a big celebration for the new temple in order to test out the ability of the community to mount such activities at short notice and on the say-so of a few male officials. The celebration for the opening of the new Cemetery Temple did not have anything very much to do with emergent ideas. But it was evidently clear to Baninge that such rituals could be used to great advantage. On the very night that everybody else was dancing and singing in celebration, Baninge crept home and had a dream.

The following day Baninge described his dream to me as follows: 'I fell asleep and the ancestor [Wutka] came to me. He followed me and asked me this question: "Do you know this man from the past [Aringawuk]? Now a young man [Tanotka] has arrived and he is here. Watch this man well, this young man, he will start working." That is all. That is my dream.' The circumstances in which Baninge had this dream were familiar from oral myths or histories in which (time and time again) heroic figures slipped away from their fellows at a celebration to encounter some transcendental being. When Baninge's dream became public knowledge, nobody was in any doubt as to the persons, named in brackets, who figured in the dream. Both the circumstances and content of the dream embodied familiar themes, euphemisms, and metaphors. When Wutka said that Tanotka would 'start working' (i.e. in the very near future) this was recognized as the phrase applied to Kolman's 'work' of holding the key to the gate in the fence. There could be no doubt that Baninge's

FIG. 11. The new Cemetery Temple in Dadul is constructed in the shadow of the old.

FIG. 12. Most *awanga* carry stems of wild ginger instead of the traditional clubs, but women and children run for cover nevertheless.

dream signified that Tanotka would soon take over Kolman's role. Just as Aringawuk had been the first to assume this role, Tanotka would be the last. It is not simply that Baninge's dream could be taken to mean these things, it was in fact patently obvious.

Baninge's dream did not introduce any radically new ideas. Since Tanotka's original possession, the distinction between Tanotka's and Wutka's voices had become increasingly blurred. Although at first it had been assumed that Tanotka was just a medium for the ancestor Wutka, Tanotka had since become a member of the Village Government and a sort of ancestor in his own right. As early as March 1988 reports were declaring that Tanotka himself was the 'post' referred to in the original possession. Kolman was meanwhile being described as a 'post which is loose' and Tanotka was said to be the new post which would replace the old or loose one. By contrast, the Tanotka post would stand firm. Kolman himself had at one time replaced an 'old post' (Koriam) when it was 'loose' (when Koriam died). Just as Koriam had been assisted by a right-hand man (Bernard) and Aringawuk before him (i.e. by his brother Gwasinga), so Tanotka was blessed with such a figure (Baninge). Thus, a report in mid-March 1988 declared: 'Baninge has emerged as a leader for this post.' The idea that Tanotka would replace Kolman as the 'post' or 'holder of the key to the gate' was not new. But Baninge's dream suggested that Tanotka's ascendance was now very imminent. As such, Baninge believed that his dream should be celebrated.

Having just witnessed the celebration of the opening of the Cemetery Temple, Baninge realized that a technique at last existed for imbuing emergent ideas with an authority which reports, dreams, and possession could not provide. It was clear that in the form of dances and feasts, the community as a whole could, in principle, actively and publicly demonstrate its support for Tanotka as a potential replacement for Kolman. But Baninge could not simply stand up at a meeting and say that another feast and/or dance must be mounted in support of Tanotka. As a matter of etiquette and tradition, these things had to be organized by the men as a group under the leadership of a man (or men) much older than Baninge. Mythological characters (usually young men) had organized dances, but Baninge would have run the risk of causing offence and, in any case (as with the reports), he wanted to disguise his influence as far as possible so that the decisions taken in the course of changing the community system in various ways appeared to originate in the community as a whole (or, at least, among a broad base of its officials).

What Baninge actually did was to approach various influential officials in private with the account of his dream, hinting that this vital portent be celebrated on an appropriate scale. In his private conversations with certain officials, Baninge did more than hint, indeed he was quite explicit about the 'need' to mount a collective display of support for Tanotka. Publicly, Baninge disguised his influence very carefully. He described his actions after receiving the dream as follows: 'Firstly I told X [one of the men responsible for the boss's room], then my in-law [a key figure in the organization of dances] along with my brother [Tanotka]. Then all the leaders discussed my dream. They discussed it but I didn't know [i.e. I wasn't there when they discussed it]. Later, they came and told me that we were to make a feast . . . The leaders had to be told first. It is up to them to tell everybody of my dream. The dream does not belong to me. It is up to the leaders to tell the dream.' Ideally, as in the case of reports, Baninge wanted his influence over dreams and festivities to be almost invisible.

The celebration of Baninge's dream took place on 11 April 1988 (five days after the celebration of the opening of the new Cemetery Temple). In the large-scale rituals mounted on this day, the whole community (for the first time) actively demonstrated support for the ideas which had started to emerge with the possession of Tanotka. In celebrating Baninge's dream, the whole community was agreeing to follow Tanotka in the place of Kolman. That very day, when the community gathered for the feast, a report was announced: 'I [Wutka] have come to speak in support of my post [Tanotka] who now stands up and to whom they [the Village Government] have already given the work [i.e. the work of 'holding the key']. You must all be obedient and harmonious. This man [Tanotka] is the origin place [spiritual origin or destiny or, in other words, 'Paradise']. What is happening is enormously important.' The report reiterated the ideas in Baninge's dream, although an over-enthusiastic witness made Tanotka's assumption of Kolman's work a *fait accompli* rather than something which would soon occur. But the point is that the whole community, by participating in the feast, was actively expressing support for the emergent ideas. Nowhere was this more striking than after dark in the Meeting House when the men started the proceedings with a song about Aringawuk. Having gathered in private to learn and practise a version of this song (which in some form was said to have been in existence for generations) several days in advance, the men were able to synchronize and project their voices with great confidence. Meanwhile, all the women danced around a central post in the house (see Fig. 13), specially installed there (signifying the new leader and their allegiance to him). Emergent

FIG. 13. Women in the splinter group dance around a post, especially installed in the Meeting House.

ideas now resounded and danced in the night air, endorsed by the ancestors and celebrated by the living.

The role of dreams as a cue for collective action was established in a different way just a few days later (on 15 April) when, in response to a dream which Tanotka had, a donation was organized (i.e. similar in appearance to the kind which regularly occurred on the last Thursday of every month). This public donation ritual once again constituted a collective, positive affirmation of support for the emergent ideas.

It should be clear by now that the establishment of Baninge's and Tanotka's roles in the newly emerging community system was not a simple concomitant of reports. Certainly, the reports endorsed these roles, even pre-empted dreams and other portents in the production of certain central ideas. But reports in themselves could not demonstrate collective support among the living for the ideas which they contained. This support was displayed and thereby (in a real sense) established through dances, feasts, and donations. Although dreams, rather than reports, explicitly justified the first manifestations of these collective acts, reports soon came to be the reasons for later collective rituals in the same way that Baninge's dreams continued to be. The fact that all such influential reports and dreams started (in an empirical as opposed to an ideological sense) with Baninge, was cleverly disguised by the mechanics of the new institutional role of the witness and the seeming alienation of Baninge from the production, interpretation, and social consequences of his dreams.[3]

Assuaging Fear: Kolman and the Competition Metaphor

By mid-April 1988 there was clear collective support in Dadul for Tanotka as Kolman's replacement and for Baninge as Tantoka's right-hand man. But there was also an undercurrent of fear. For many years the communities of Dadul and Maranagi had looked to Kolman as their religious leader and had participated in the Pomio Kivung as part of a broader organization (encompassing the Pomio-Baining region as a whole). The highest political authority in this organization was a formidable character (Alois Koki) whose infamous temper literally terrified the stereotypically passive and shy Baining peoples. If Tanotka were to usurp Kolman's position without permission then the Kivung officials in Dadul and Maranagi feared that they may come under attack from the Pomio leadership. Such an attack, they believed, might be mounted in the name of public relations, and in defence of the credibility of the Pomio Kivung as a unified political and religious movement. In order to consolidate further the support which they had obtained, Baninge and Tanotka needed to demonstrate that the mainstream authorities did not pose a threat to their emergent institutions.

On 19 April 1988 Baninge, Tanotka, one more of their brothers from Maranagi, and Dadul's first orator set off to see Kolman. They promised that they would obtain Kolman's support for the emergent institutions and that Kolman would willingly hand over the 'key' to Tanotka. On 6 May 1988 they returned bearing good news. According to Baninge, Kolman had told him that there was now a competition within the various villages who regarded themselves as Pomio Kivung members. Some of these groups were led by false prophets but whichever group had the right leader, a leader who could illuminate the correct way forward (i.e. ritual observations—particularly those based upon traditional culture) would 'pass the examination' and 'be granted entry into high school'. Kolman's (alleged) metaphor was an appropriate way of talking about the pursuit of the Period of the Companies because, not only were places in high school a notoriously scarce resource for which there had to be stiff competition, but the metaphor suggested a competition specifically for Western technological knowledge.

The competition metaphor was later steeped in controversy. Baninge was the only man who claimed to have heard Kolman use this metaphor during the group's visit. But it would have been a strategically intelligent move on Kolman's part to have used such a metaphor. Since Koriam's death, Kolman had presided over the establishment of numerous factions. Experience would have taught him that many splinter groups can be reclaimed by the mainstream movement if allowed to discover for themselves that their leaders are false ones. This was also a policy often favoured by colonial and provincial governments in relation to other cult movements. Moreover, there were no compelling grounds upon which Kolman could have persuaded Baninge and Tanotka to surrender their factional aspirations. From Kolman's viewpoint, a hostile response might have run the risk of alienating the villages of Dadul and Maranagi in the long term, possibly forever (thereby undermining the electoral base in two constituencies). Moreover, a hostile reaction would also have been ideologically ungrounded because Tanotka's ascendancy in Dadul and Maranagi rested upon the same presuppositions as Kolman's authority. Finally, Kolman could afford to be indulgent, in so far as his authority was only being questioned in the context of two distant villages (and there, he assumed, only temporarily). Although, in the egocentric thinking of the Dadul-Maranagi group, the ascension of Tanotka meant the abolition of Kolman's leadership in a universal sense, such ideas would not (indeed could not ever) have touched those villages all over the province who still claimed allegiance to Kolman.

In any case, the four men returned with an effective vindication of Tanotka's authority and widespread fears about the prudence of forming a Dadul-Maranagi splinter group were successfully allayed. Reports reconfirmed that Tanotka now 'held the key' in place of Kolman. Such gratifying reports henceforth required collective donations of money for report glasses kept in the temples. In this way the community expressed thanks to the Village Government.

During the following fortnight, Baninge's and Tanotka's roles, now quite clearly formulated, were consolidated by more dreams and reports

over which Baninge exerted a less carefully disguised influence. For example, on 19 May 1988 Baninge dreamed that Tanotka (his transcendental
self) came to him and shook his hand, saying: 'I am pleased with you.
You help me well. We are good friends and companions in the work of
the Kivung.' But Baninge did not inform the other men of his dream
(Tanotka himself had by then returned to Maranagi). Instead, Baninge
went to the Cemetery Temple at 2.30 p.m. the following day to ask the
ancestors to comment on his dream. The report which followed was
'heavy' in the sense that it warned the community to observe the First
and Fourth Laws more faithfully. Baninge took a leading role in the
speeches at the Saturday public meeting, when he interpreted both his
dream and the report which occurred in response to it.

Baninge's dream meant that he was being a faithful and obedient
servant (or right-hand man) to Tanotka, but the report stated that the
rest of the community was faithless (a breach of the First Law) and
disobedient (a breach of the Fourth Law) in this regard. This enabled
Baninge, with the backing of the orators, to launch a diatribe against the
'doubting Thomases' in Dadul who were offending the ancestors by their
failure to rally behind Tanotka, and thereby delaying the miracle. In fact,
at this time, the community could scarcely have been more firmly behind
Baninge and Tanotka, but such urgent sermons were a valuable means of
sustaining public enthusiasm and excitement. Baninge later conceded
that the faith of the community was almost perfect but he stressed over
and over the importance of obedience (an element of Kivung ideology
which was now more frequently reiterated in reports than any other
single idea). At last, Baninge was beginning to come out of the shadows
and assume a more visible role of leader, firmly backed by the consensus
and by the moral requirement of obedience to him on the part of the
community. It was on the night following this meeting that Baninge first
dreamed of a ring.

Further Institutional Innovation: The Ring

Baninge dreamed that there was a huge ring with a fence stretching across
its diameter, thereby creating two semicircles. In one semicircle stood the
Village Government and in the other stood Tanotka and Baninge himself.
Among the ancestors in the Village Government was the boss of the
Cemetery Temple (Dainge). Tanotka called out to him across the fence:
'Dainge, what do you think about your people? Do you want to bring
them into the ring or not?' But Dainge was angry and did not reply to

Tanotka. Presently, Tanotka asked him again: 'Dainge, what do you think about your people?' But again Dainge did not reply because he was angry. Baninge stood by the side of Tanotka and was silent. Only Tanotka, because he was the 'post', had the authority to speak across the fence. Finally, Tanotka cried out for a third time: 'Dainge, your people are obedient and pious, and yet they cannot enter this ring.' Still, Dainge did not reply for he remained angry.

This dream introduced a modification to mainstream ideology concerning the miracle and salvation. The ring represented God's chosen few, and anyone who entered the ring was guaranteed salvation. But whereas formerly there had only ever been a simple dichotomy between the chosen (perfect, omniscient spirits) and the well-intentioned Kivung members (the living), now the picture had become more sophisticated. The semi-circle in which Baninge and Tanotka stood was to contain the living people who were not omniscient (i.e. because they were still 'earthly') but who were nevertheless 'chosen by God' and guaranteed a privileged place beside Him on Judgement Day. Baninge and Tanotka appeared in the dream as their earthly selves who had now entered the ring (it was assumed that their spirit selves had some time ago already entered the other semicircle, that is, the Village Government). The spirit selves of Baninge and Tanotka could not transmit continuous omniscience to their earthly selves but at least there was now moral unity between their earthly and spirit selves, represented by the ring. The goal was not to transport the rest of the living (i.e. in Dadul and Maranagi) into the Village Government in a spiritual form, but to make the living people morally fortified (like Baninge and Tanotka) so that they could all enter the ring in the 'earthly semicircle'. When that finally occurred, the fence would soon after be broken and all the people within the ring would be united on earth (i.e. in the Period of the Companies).

Whereas ordinary people might be satisfied with a guarantee of personal salvation, Baninge and Tanotka were deeply concerned about the eternal destinies of 'their people' and were therefore clearly cast in the roles of heroic figures. To put this another way, the task of the post and of his right-hand man was altruistic and charitable (reflecting both the perceived essence of Christianity and of indigenous mythological representations of heroism). The reason for Dainge's anger in the dream was that the community had not yet achieved moral purity in the fashion of Baninge and Tanotka. Therefore, the obedience and piety of the living was not in itself sufficient. The community had to remove every stain of sin before it would be admitted to the ring. The immediate goal before

Baninge's and Tanotka's earthly selves was therefore to help the living to achieve moral purity.

On Sunday, 22 May Baninge explained his dream to the orators and also to the witness who would be in the Cemetery Temple that afternoon. The witness later received the following report from Dainge (boss of the Cemetery Temple) confirming Baninge's dream: 'within this ring only two [men] now stand inside. When will you all come inside?' As a result of Baninge's dream, and the report which reiterated it, a public donation was held immediately after the offerings had been consumed at the cemetery. This was a collective effort to eliminate the sin of the community and assuage the anger of the Village Government which was impatient for the collectivity to enter the ring. As such, the donations went into the absolution glass. Yet, in contrast to private absolution donations where the donor sought personal absolution, or the monthly public donations where the donor sought absolution for anonymous ancestors, the public donations on this occasion were directed at the purification of the living community as a single unit. There was not any question now of individuals joining Baninge and Tanotka in the ring in dribs and drabs. Henceforth, the whole community (except for Baninge and Tanotka) would be either chosen or damned as a single unit. Therefore, private donations were now (even more clearly than before) about collective salvation, since personal absolution from sin could only be understood as being in the interests of the community at large. As a result, all donations were increasingly public and collective from that point on (although, in principle, private donations were expected to continue) and they took on a more elaborate ritual form, based on the metaphor of the ring.

Donations, however, were not the only method of purifying the collectivity. Moral strength was also sought through the rapid transformation of time allocation in the community. In general, the goal was to increase collective, unified, community-level activity and to reduce solitary domestic activity. Therefore, on the one hand, public gatherings in the Meeting House were rescheduled on a daily timetable (in place of the 'old' system of twice-weekly meetings) and, on the other, people were urged by the speakers at these meetings to remain as far as possible in the village clearing. People were told not to linger at their gardens or in the bush: time devoted to gardening, washing, and hunting and gathering should be curtailed so that the collectivity would be physically together for most of the time. Moreover, the people should avoid journeys to non-Kivung settlements (e.g. to visit relatives or sell cash crops). In such places there was a danger of contamination or corruption by evil.

Henceforth, any person wishing to undertake an excursion beyond Dadul was obliged to inform Baninge, or one of the orators, in advance.

By 28 May 1988 it was assumed that these various innovations had supplied the community with sufficient moral strength and unity to enter the ring together. A physical ring was marked out with beer bottles (embedded upside-down in the ground to form a circle) in the centre of Dadul. At dawn, all the villagers gathered in this ring, forming a human circle. Baninge maintained that dawn divided the state of darkness (i.e. night-time) in which the living were situated, from the state of enlightenment (daytime) enjoyed by the ancestors. Daybreak signified the breaking of the fence which the community hoped, at some time in the near future, to achieve. Tanotka stood alone in the middle of the ring and, one by one, the people came forward solemnly to shake his hand and give him money before rejoining the circle of people. Then everybody shook hands with everybody else, the ring of people snaking back on itself until the circle diminished and vanished (see Fig. 14).

The ritual of the ring was one which, henceforth, would be repeated many times, although some elements came to be modified. The significance of this first performance of the ring ceremony was clear: the community had now become God's chosen people and had entered into a contract with Tanotka wherein they presented him with an offering (of money) and their allegiance (expressed through handshakes) in return for guidance along the path to certain salvation. Henceforth, Tanotka was officially or ritually encumbered with the tasks which had formerly accrued to Kolman.

There was an additional feature of the imagery of the ring ceremony which, for the participants, may have been the most striking. That is, the collectivity performed the ritual wearing only genital coverings. As a sensory experience, this made the ritual quite different from any which had been performed before in the name of Kivung ideas. First, the participants were exposed to the cold mists of dawn in their naked state. Secondly, their nakedness had a startling visual effect. Ideologically, the purpose was to demonstrate solidarity with the ancestors (who were stereotypically naked) and a renunciation of the shame which missionaries had imposed upon them. People should no longer be ashamed of their ancestral customs and particularly of the nakedness of Adam and Eve in paradise. Moreover, the rejection of foreign clothing demonstrated profound confidence in the moral fortitude of the community and its achievement of sexual asceticism: it was at last safe to expose erotic features of the body, since violations of the laws were now unthinkable. In practice,

FIG. 14. At the end of ring ceremonies, the circle of people snakes back on itself so that everybody can shake hands with everybody else.

universal nakedness probably did excite erotic thoughts in the participants (especially men) and certainly produced intense shame in the women. Yet, after this first ring ceremony, the people performed all Kivung rituals in a state of virtual nakedness (i.e. wearing only the genital coverings of the forefathers) and even avoided wearing clothes during secular activity, except when outsiders visited Dadul. Consequently, the initial visual and psychological effects of this practice rapidly decayed, and nakedness was increasingly taken for granted.

The Pressure for Progress

There is a problem which all millenarian movements must come up against at some point. That is the point at which the conditions of the millennium appear to have been satisfied and nobody can think what to do next. Taking stock of the position which had now been achieved in Dadul (as well as in Maranagi where the same or similar rituals were more or less simultaneously underway) it will be noted that the community had now been chosen (or had entered the ring) and therefore presumably the Village Government no longer had any excuse to delay its re-entry into 'this world'. By the end of May 1988 Tanotka had been given the key to the fence (several times in fact) and should have been ready to announce a date for the start of the Period of the Companies. The obvious next step was to generate new rituals connected with awaiting or welcoming the ancestors. But on this score, there was a shortage of imaginative ideas. Baninge became so desperate in fact that he even asked me if it was true, as he had heard, that in some countries religious groups held something called a 'Last Day' and if so, how they went about it. With characteristic unhelpfulness, of course, I said that I had no idea.

Following the first ring ceremony, there was a period (lasting about three months) in which the same emergent ideas already described were reiterated over and over, and the emergent rituals were repeated again and again. Occasionally, the community was side-tracked by entertaining or even apparently progressive events but, by and large, progress towards the miracle during this period entailed the pretence of having taken a step back so that it appeared that everybody had entered the ring for the first time (again) or Tanotka had obtained the key from Kolman (again). In order to sustain popular enthusiasm in such confusing circumstances, the confusion itself had to be cast as mystery or inscrutability. During this period, the quintessential purveyor of inscrutable ideas, Tanotka, remained almost continuously in Maranagi. Two reasons for this were widely disseminated in Dadul: (i) Tanotka was becoming increasingly weak and less mobile as his life force diminished and his spirit longed for release, or as he became less 'native' and more 'white' or less 'worldly' and more 'ascetic' or 'cold' etc. (the metaphors varied); (ii) Tanotka, like everybody else, wanted to remain increasingly within his own community and not to venture out into the places (e.g. Arabum on the way to Dadul) where evil supposedly lurked. All this meant that it fell increasingly to Baninge to find acceptable justifications for the confusing lack of progress. Baninge regularly used two justifications: (i) the community itself was slowing down progress through sinfulness, especially inadequate faith; (ii) the intentions of the Village Government were mysterious and people should strive towards enlightenment on their own account and not expect him (Baninge) to explain everything to them.

The period from the end of May to the end of August 1988 was one of stagnation in which the innovations established before June 1988 (and mostly after January 1988) were continually in evidence, whereas almost no new ones were created. I have pointed out that Baninge justified the absence of progress in terms of the failure on the part of the community to maintain a secure position within the ring. This, of course, was also the justification for repetitions of the ring ceremony. But this state of affairs was potentially confusing and demoralizing and, to counter this, there needed to be a sense that progress was imminent and under control within Dadul. Although Baninge could not commit himself to a specific timetable for progress or even the general ceremonial form which it would take, he needed to convince the community that he had worked all this out. In other words, Baninge had to claim to know what would happen even if the rest of the population did not. In order to make this claim credible, Baninge needed to establish a really powerful aura of authority and mystery. Increasingly, therefore, Baninge started to contradict the orators at meetings, thereby demonstrating his superior knowledge of the true cosmology. He began to make cryptic statements which it would be the duty of the people to try to understand or interpret. On one occasion, Baninge even set himself up as a confessor or priest when he ordered everybody to gather outside his house at dawn and enter one by one to list which (out of four of the ten) Laws they had violated in their lifetimes. At the time, this whole business seemed to be an attempt to instill fear and shame into one of the witnesses whom Baninge believed was having adulterous relations with his wife. But it added to Baninge's impressive and exalted image. Shortly after this (in July 1988), a report announced that Baninge had a 'number' which was taken to mean that he was a mouthpiece of God (e.g. as a 'number two' man or minister is sometimes a mouthpiece of the 'number one' man or the prime minister). Following a later report at the beginning of August, the first orator told a public meeting that Baninge was now a 'staff' (or 'walking stick') in the same way that Tanotka was a 'post'. At the same time that Baninge's divine powers were being crystallized, the idea arrived from Maranagi that Tanotka was Jesus Christ.

Of course, the problem with claims of divinity and omniscience was that they would ordinarily be disproved. The fact that Tanotka no longer visited Dadul meant that the people there had no evidence on which to base any doubts concerning his spiritual condition. In Maranagi itself Tanotka was becoming increasingly a recluse who did not answer questions and who only appeared publicly to make cryptic statements. Clearly, though, Baninge had to veil himself in mystery for the same reasons. He too refused to answer questions, although continuing to make statements of his own choosing. Like Tanotka, he insisted that people should themselves strive for enlightenment. He claimed, for example, that if people truly desired the miracle then they would be enlightened (as he himself had been). But this could only work as a short-term tactic.

During the first week of August, there were signs at last of demoralization among the men. In several private conversations (including a conversation with me) one of the orators subtly expressed resentment with regard to Baninge's continual overruling of the orators in meetings and his assumption of personal superiority in all areas of cultural life. If an orator said one thing about a Kivung law and Baninge said another, then everybody was obliged to accept that Baninge's statement was the correct one. Even in matters of tradition, in which the authority of the old men had once been unquestioned, only Baninge (scarcely, or not even, out of his twenties) was now supposed to know the definitive facts. The orator asked: 'How can this be? Does not Baninge come from the same village as all of us?' But the orator stopped short of denying Baninge's authority. Similarly, another orator complained that, because he was old-fashioned in his orations (i.e. stressing ideology associated with the mainstream movement rather than with the 'new' developments), he was being pushed out of his role and dominated by Baninge and the other two orators. Although these views were disguised as neutral observations which were not motivated by bad feeling, they constituted complaints nevertheless. Only the first orator showed no signs of resentment. But there were indications of demoralization within the male population as a whole, particularly some cases of rule breaking (which would probably not have occurred when morale ran high).

On Tuesday, 9 August Baninge attempted to counter this trend by announcing that a new and exciting ritual would occur within a few weeks. In a nocturnal meeting Baninge described a traditional round-house which had recently been built in Maranagi (and which he himself had recently gone to see). Baninge said that the people of Maranagi would congregate in the house after dark and remain there until dawn. Women would occupy one half of the house and men the other. During the night, people would hear a terrible noise outside the house created by the cries of dogs and wild pigs (manifestations of Satan and his wives). People would see the animals through cracks in the bark walls but, because the posts had been firmly planted, the animals would not be able to force their way into the house. During the night, Tanotka would touch everybody in turn to see if their skin was soft and cold (like a white person's) or firm and hot (like a native's). Tanotka would shake anybody whose skin was 'black', to remove the evil. But if a person still remained hot, he would cast him or her out of the door to be consumed by the wild pigs. By dawn, only 'good' people whose skin had become 'white' would remain in the house. By this, Baninge meant that everybody remaining would have entered the Village Government at a spiritual level although they would still appear physically as themselves. They would now have white skins underneath (and hidden by) their external black skins. As such, all the people would be like Baninge and Tanotka, their eyes would be opened and they would not need to be contradicted nor would they need to ask questions. Baninge said that the people of Maranagi were fortunate because they had already constructed their round-house and could hold the all-night vigil and enter the Village Government as soon as they pleased. After that, they would all know what preparations to make for the Period of the Companies. By contrast, the people of Dadul had not yet built a round-house in which their own leader (i.e. Baninge) could perform the role for his people that Tanotka would perform in Maranagi.

By Wednesday, 22 August the men had not yet got very far with the building of a round-house, a fact which suggested continued general demoralization. Baninge, who had recently paid a further visit to Maranagi, now held another meeting in Tanotka's office with the mature men. He spoke fiercely, accusing the men of being lazy and went on: 'my brother [Tanotka] has told me not to bother giving orders to you any more, to do this or that work, or to build a traditional round-house like the one in Maranagi. If you all have sufficient faith then you will do it without my urgings. Moreover, I am tired of being the only one among you who is enlightened with regard to the old [i.e. moral and ancestral] path. . . . if you want to obtain this vision you must do as they [are doing] in Maranagi.' The first orator supported Baninge in castigating the other men, who in turn quietly accepted the criticisms.

Later that day, after the performance of a traditional marriage which (for reasons connected with practicalities and rules of kinship) took place in Baninge's house, Baninge spent several hours addressing the community in a special meeting (also at his house). He warned the gathering that the people of Maranagi would soon leave them all behind and that if, eventually, a round-house was built in Dadul and an all-night vigil performed, then in all likelihood many people would be thrown to Satan and consumed by the wild animals. Baninge also stressed that people were wasting years of commitment to the Kivung for want of the faith

and enthusiasm to unite behind him now. Baninge's oration was so persuasive (as indeed were those of his staunchest supporters, such as the
first orator) that by midnight, when the meeting broke up, the whole
village seemed to be buzzing with excitement. The first orator led a group
of men on a moonlit search for flowers which they weaved into necklaces.
The younger children, who knew that the adults were high spirited,
charged around shouting and chasing one another. At sunrise, the men
adorned Baninge with the flower necklaces they had made and plastered
lime powder on their faces and arms as an expression of joy. The whole
community once again formed a ring (wearing traditional costume as had
become compulsory in all Kivung ritual since the first ring ceremony)
while Baninge stood alone in the middle of the ring. As it had done some
months before for Tanotka, the community came forward (one by one) to
shake Baninge by the hand and to give him money. Henceforth, it was
Baninge's task to lead the community of Dadul on Tanotka's behalf,
whilst Tanotka restricted himself to the work in Maranagi.

With the community firmly behind Baninge (once again), progress
could no longer be postponed. Little more than a week later, a new twist
was set to occur. Baninge announced that he would not lead the people of
Dadul to the miracle after all, for the necessary preparations would waste
too much time. Instead, they would all evacuate the village of Dadul and
unite in one large community with the people of Maranagi, at whose
round-house their spirits would be delivered altogether into the Village
Government and their earthly selves would be launched into the Period
of the Companies.

The Transformation of Mainstream Institutions

The rituals and ideas of the splinter group differed from those of the
mainstream movement in a number of ways. The most striking difference
was that the splinter group formed an ideologically self-contained unit,
whereas the old community had been part of a much larger organization,
centred in Malmal. Correspondingly, the structure and nature of personnel had changed.

Whereas the highest living moral and cultural authorities in the
routinized community had been the orators and the old men respectively,
Baninge was now the supreme authority in both of these provinces. This
had the effect of placing the orators and the elders on a par with the blind
and morally deficient general population, although an orator (or an old
man) was still regarded as a sort of first among equals by virtue of his

oratory skills and long-standing respectability. But whereas the influence of the orators over community ideology (e.g. idea production and selection) had been highly constrained because their views had always been fallible, Baninge's influence could not (as a matter of moral principle) be subject to constraint or obstruction by the other members of the community. In practice, there *were* constraints on Baninge, ranging from the limitations of his imagination to the morale of the population (which would have been adversely affected by many of the possible moves available to Baninge, including those which contradicted the logic of existing cosmology). Yet the nature of Baninge's influence was different from that of the orators because he was expected to assume a dynamic role in radical institutional change whereas the orators were not (and never had been). It should be reiterated that the actual mechanics of Baninge's influence were somewhat disguised from the community at large (less so, perhaps, by August) but the orators and witnesses were daily subject to the effects of his influence.

In addition, the volume of collective activity was increased in the course of the emergence of the splinter group. Formerly, community rituals had demanded, on average, six hours of input from men each week, and about ten hours from women (due to the heavy demands of cooking). Yet the demands of the splinter group were far greater. Meetings alone demanded as many as 12 hours input from community members each week and, taking into consideration the dances, feasts, and ring ceremonies, it is clear that the allocation of time to Kivung rituals was greatly increased. The distinctive *quality* of collective activity in the splinter group is harder to summarize. Ring ceremonies and the various kinds of celebrations all constituted collective displays of commitment to radical and exciting ideology. Attendance at community meetings did not (unequivocally) express support for emergent ideas since most attendants sat in silence and much of what they heard was a reiteration of the ideology associated with the mainstream movement. But participation in ring ceremonies and celebrations explicitly demonstrated support for emergent institutions, and cultivated a more intense experience of religious life, as I explain in the next section. An obvious factor is that these institutions ostensibly implied the imminence of the miracle (in contrast to the old institutions which de-emphasized the miracle because it was, at that time, immoral to think about it at length) and were, for this reason alone, extremely exciting and revolutionary.

Having said this, the community meetings of this period were not the same as the old ones. Although the old familiar morals and sermons on the Ten Laws figured highly in all such meetings, these were now integrated into orations as responses to reports and were presented alongside repeated assertions of Baninge's authority and visionary knowledge. Among the commonest new themes were: the imminence of the miracle, the need for collective unity and obedience, the importance of staying in the village clearing as much as possible, and the danger of damnation if donations were not continually made. On average, Baninge and the first orator each spoke for about 40 per cent of the time in community meetings, with the remaining two orators claiming about 10 per cent of the available speech time each (excluding the fifteen-minute sessions at the end of the meetings). The content of the speeches by Baninge and the first orator were very similar except that Baninge occasionally produced cryptic statements and the first orator made frequent reference to Baninge's superior authority.

The rituals of the splinter group were inherently less stable than those of the mainstream community system. In the case of the latter, most of the rituals were reproduced in cycles, with reference to an established calendar whereas, in the splinter group, many of the institutions were not reproduced according to a fixed agenda. Ring ceremonies (associated with donations and repetitive assertions of the community's guarantee of salvation or of Baninge's and Tanotka's assumption of divine authority) were always mounted in response to authoritative portents acquired through reports, dreams, or statements from the two leaders. Such portents did not occur according to any recognizable, pre-set schedule but relied upon the continued imagination and enthusiasm of various key parties (the leaders, the witnesses and, to some extent, the orators). Whereas diminished enthusiasm and imagination were unlikely to affect the performance of a mass donation scheduled for the last Thursday of any given month (i.e. because the failure to mount such a performance would have constituted an active challenge to, or violation of, morality), the failure to generate grounds for collective festivities or ring ceremonies remained perfectly feasible throughout the period.

Another important difference between the mainstream community system and splinter-group organization was that the institutions of the latter modified domestic life in a number of ways. Firstly, the splinter-group ideology discouraged and penalized regular excursions to markets and other selling points for cash crops, thereby reducing a major source of domestic incomes. Against this it might be argued that most of the money obtained from cash cropping in the past represented the surpluses of a stable agricultural production level, which were ordinarily channelled into the Kivung. But the loss of revenue did affect domestic life during this period because a proportion of surplus income was ordinarily retained within households as an insurance against future misfortune as well as a source of necessary funding for manufactured foods and basic household items (e.g. nails, tools, etc.). As I shall show in the next chapter, Baninge and Tanotka would need to take large sums of money from the Kivung funds and this meant that many of the reports during the May–September period demanded increasing donations from each domestic unit. Such demands were justified because moral improvement and protection from Satan were much more vital at this stage than they had formerly been. Even livestock (i.e. pigs and chickens) were demanded by the reports as sacrifices to the ancestors and so many of these domestic investments were publicly consumed. With the reductions in monetary incomes, domestic savings were being depleted rapidly. Plantation work was forbidden because it removed people (usually boys) from the village. Therefore, the only realistic source of income was the sale of cocoa to Tolai fermentary owners who sent a car to Dadul each week.

The second source of interference in domestic life was the discouragement of crop production. On the one hand, the splinter group demanded a large amount of time input (e.g. in house building, feasts, and dances) and participation in exhausting rituals (e.g. nocturnal dances) which necessitated sleeping in the daytime, and on the other, it stressed the importance of gathering together in the village clearing as much as possible so that excursions to gardens and cocoa blocks were reduced to a minimum. Most families in Dadul were not yet experiencing any hardship (except for lack of ready cash) and no household's subsistence was immediately threatened. But with the emphasis on harvesting rather than clearing, planting, and weeding, it was clear that the agricultural production level had dropped dramatically in all households even if domestic life was otherwise proceeding more or less as usual. Problems would obviously arise when previously established gardens were exhausted, unless (as was generally asserted) the miracle occurred first.

The Remembrance of Things Past

Many of the institutional innovations described in this chapter were explicitly regarded in the splinter group as an attempt to restore obsolete traditions or *kastam*. Much of the oratory in meetings at this time concerned the importance of remembering cultural materials which had been renounced in the past, largely in the face of missionary pressure. The influence of Christianity in this respect was criticized with increasing intensity and bitterness. The church was frequently likened to an electric wire from which the metal interior had been removed. This conveyed the idea that Christianity had only the semblance of an efficacious ideology, signified by the defective item of foreign technology. Indigenous forms of worship, based around the cultivation of relations of reciprocity with the transcendental world, were said to have been virtually destroyed by missionization. If a missionary saw a man performing rituals to cure a sick friend, he would kick the sacrificer and say he was doing the Devil's work. Traditional worship was often likened to a fire, which the mission-aries had attempted to scatter in the dust. The splinter group, meanwhile, was described as a 'wind' which sought to 'rekindle the flames' which the missionaries had almost extinguished.

The recollection of traditional religious principles in the splinter group had diverse manifestations: the attempt to salvage the myth of Aringawuk, to restore the near-naked attire of the forefathers, and to reinstate the *awan*, the performance of feasts, and the old songs. The process was not simply one of remembering, of course, but in some cases of creatively reconstructing traditional practices. Tanotka's version of the myth of Aringawuk was substantially different from the version which I collected from the elders at Maranagi. Accordingly, the song relating Aringawuk's adventures was far from being a faithful rendition of an earlier version. Yet many of the other songs performed at night had been subject to more frequent transmission over the years, having escaped the censure of missionaries and, in many cases, having been performed at Christian celebrations.

Of all splinter-group activities, the construction of Mali *awanga* and *ilotka* costumes at secret locations in the bush presented perhaps the most significant demands on memory. In this context, considerable emphasis was placed on accurate recall and the faithful reproduction in minute detail of ancestral techniques of costume production and performance. It was hoped that the ancestors would be moved by the care and attention with which the living sought to restore the Mali *awan*, and expert advice was continually sought from authoritative sources (not just the enlight-ened leaders, but the Mali elders). I was accordingly obliged to collect extensive data on the specific materials and techniques used in the pro-duction of a variety of costumes. It was clear that the men expected me to take a keen interest in these activities and to be gratified by them, not as an ethnographer but as one who had participated in these activities during a former existence. Initiations into the mysteries of the *awan* were performed by elders but it was never proposed or even hinted that I should undergo these rites, in spite of the fact that the secrets were paraded before me, and I dressed and danced with the other men.

Whether or not the details of myths, songs, feasts, and even the *awan* were faithful reproductions of past performances, they were explicitly described as such by participants. Gaps or discrepancies in the memories of elders were not regarded as insuperable because an even more authoritative source of information was at hand, in the form of Baninge and Tanotka. In this context, the body of Mali *kastam* was likened to the trunk of a tree, and its many branches represented the obfuscations of foreign influence. Tanotka, as an enlightened leader, was often attributed the ability to cut away the branches and reveal the valued trunk (a variant on the metaphor of the post).

The institutional framework within which the elders and enlightened leaders pieced together fragmented memories and insights reverberated in various ways with the obsolete system of initiation. In the pre-contact era Mali Baining initiations were performed roughly every seven to ten years (oral testimony, Maranagi). Prior to each performance, the men responsible for directing these activities (stereotypically the mother's brothers of novices) had to meet secretly to share their memories of past initiations and thereby to plan the sequence of ritual actions by means of which novices would be exposed to the revelations of the male cult. In these secret meetings, out of the earshot of women and children, the men would practise songs and prepare their ritual paraphernalia. The all-male meetings, now convened at the *Haus Kivung* or in the bush, were modelled on these former gatherings of initiators. The resonance of one with the other was cultivated in the splinter group by the conspiratorial character of the meetings ensuing from Tanotka's possession, the masculinity of participants, and subsequently the content of discussions which revolved around the technicalities of choreography and costume production.

The restoration of tradition involved a shift of emphasis away from the codification of materials in *language*, and towards the cultivation of concrete metaphors through *collective ritual performance*. The basic form of collective celebrations was established at the time of the opening of the new Cemetery Temple. The women were summoned to cook in the night by the secret male bullroarer (*angarega*). At dawn, the *awanga* and *ilotka* converged on the village clearing from the men's sacred site in the bush and from the Paradise garden (see Fig. 15). When they had gone, the female dancers performed in the clearing. Then the women were chased

FIG. 15. A mixture of *awanga* and *ilotka* converge on the village clearing and begin to charge energetically in a circle.

away by the returning *awanga* and *ilotka*. The symbolism of this perform-ance inhered in two phases: (i) the *awanga* and *ilotka* (representing the ancestors emerging from Paradise) converged on the centre of the com-munity (thereby enacting the miracle of re-entry into 'this world'); (ii) the female dancers (representing 'this worldly' forces such as menstruation, sexuality, childbirth etc.) were driven out of the community by the male dancers or ancestors (the second phase therefore enacting the ultimate supremacy of asceticism or, in other words, the achievement of the 'Period of the Government'). The significance of the performance was never explicitly expressed in words by participants. Nevertheless, my crude interpretations of the drama were widely recognized, judging by the knowing smiles and nods which greeted my speculative exegesis. The *awan* was followed in the afternoon by the presentation of a feast to the ancestors at the big temple(s) and, two hours later, the consumption of the food in public by the whole community. Then, throughout the night, there was male singing and female dancing (profane partying in contrast to the sacred dances of the *awanga* and *ilotka*).

Numerous meanings were also transmitted non-verbally in the context of dancing, and the installation of a post in the *Haus Kivung*, around which the women danced, seemed not to require any kind of exegetical commentary. It went without saying that the women's dancing celebrated the emergence of Tanotka as a post in place of Kolman.

In the case of some of the emergent collective rituals, exegesis was made available to some but not all participants. The first performance of the ring ceremony was scheduled to coincide with the break of day, signifying the breaking of the fence separating the living and the dead. This understanding was expressed in words by Baninge at an all-male meeting, but not all participants in the ceremony (and very few of the women) had had the idea explained to them. Nevertheless, the link between sunrise and spiritual enlightenment was accessible to all participants, by virtue of the use of light and darkness as metaphors for knowledge and ignorance in a variety of contexts.

Through the extensive use of 'concrete metaphors' or 'analogic codification' (see Barth 1975: 207–14, 1987: 32–7) in splinter-group activities, a different kind of religious experience was being creatively developed—different, that is, from the routinized model of the mainstream movement. The latter regime incorporated collective rituals, but the meanings of these rituals could not (on the whole) be inferred on the basis of a concrete relationship between the actions and their metaphoric referents. For example, collective donations entailed the depositing of money in receptacles, the significance of which could only be expressed in *words*, conveying principles of catharsis, absolution, and charity. By contrast, the actions of the *awanga* and *ilotka* spoke for themselves and exegetical commentary could add little or nothing to the understandings conveyed through non-verbal performance. In the case of mainstream rituals, religious knowledge was acquired mainly through an appreciation of verbalized cosmology, whereas the concrete metaphors codified in splinter-group rituals cultivated revelations through a more implicit, inferential process. A striking thing about concrete metaphors which are sustained in collective physical activity is that the activity itself can be productive of emotions and sensations which language alone cannot hope to cultivate.

The image of dancing around a post, by means of which the women expressed allegiance to Tanotka, was a *collective* act of communication, unlike a verbal statement which could be made by any *individual*. The act of communication itself was therefore simultaneously productive of feelings of solidarity. It provided not only a statement, but also an expression, and an experience of solidarity. The output of the dancers and singers was meanwhile sensually stimulating in a variety of ways. The haunting melodies and stirring rhythms, the dust kicked up and the perspiration, the flickering of the fire, the nakedness of the performers, the interlocking of female arms, and the reverberation of male percussion—all these stimuli bombarded the senses and, at the same time, emerged out of a single communicative act for which words could never have substituted.

The same rich mixture of transmission, revelation, emotion, sensation, and expression characterized ring ceremonies. It is one thing for a leader to tell his people that they are the spiritual elect, but it is quite another to experience the promise of salvation through the formation of a human ring, visibly and physically joined to enclose the leader and to present an impenetrable barrier to the evil forces lurking outside. The transition from cold air on naked skin to the warming rays of daylight not only communicated ideas about salvation, but provided an experiential taste of deliverance from a world of suffering to a Paradise of well-being. Likewise, the transition from darkness to clear visibility produced an experience of revelation incomparable to the effect of light/darkness metaphors in language.

Institutional innovation undertaken by the splinter group was not exclusively based around non-verbal codification. The radical ideas of the new leaders were transmitted in language to a considerable extent, and relied heavily on cryptic statements, mythology, reports, dreams, and orations, as I have described. The point is that there was a gradual shift of emphasis. Initially, Baninge and Tanotka needed to demonstrate logical consistency between their ideas and prevailing (mainstream) doctrine. Thus, they were obliged at the outset to operate in the medium provided by the routinized movement, in which the privileged vehicle of cultural transmission was language. Words, however, were not sufficient to stimulate and demonstrate collective support. Thus, in due course, there was a proliferation of collective rituals which provided a different kind of legitimacy for emergent ideas, and a different experience of revelation. The emphasis was no longer on an abstract unity with the mainstream movement, based around a presumed uniformity of ritual practices, but on a concrete experience of local unity and allegiance, the expression of which was intrinsically moving, stimulating, and pregnant with meaning. The *awan* had a climactic character, being concerned with the production of highly memorable performances—imparting meaning in a graphic and simple manner, and charging the experience of revelation with emotive and sensually provocative stimuli. The considerable power of this model for millenarian activity is demonstrated even more dramatically in the next chapter.

Notes

1. The image of a post is a recurrent feature of New Guinea religions (e.g. Wagner 1986, Weiner 1991, Barth 1975, O'Hanlon 1992, etc.), and has been siezed upon in other 'cargo cult' rituals (e.g. Inselmann 1944, Berndt 1952/3, etc.).

2. Self-mutilation is construed throughout the Pomio Kivung as a violation of the Fifth Law, based on the Commandment prohibiting murder (see Chapter 2: end note 4). This was the most compelling argument also for arming the *awanga* with mock weapons, instead of the real thing.

3. The split between the role of prophet (in this instance Tanotka) and that of an organizer, perhaps operating behind the scenes (here, Baninge), has been widely reported in studies of Melanesian 'cargo cults' (e.g. Worsley 1957: 271, Steinbauer 1979: 120–1, Thrupp 1962, Talmon 1966, May 1982, etc.). I am grateful to Raymond Firth for drawing to my attention the relation between Sabbatai Zui and Nathan of Gaza (Scholem 1946), which strikingly parallels the early phases of Baninge's and Tanotka's roles in the splinter group. Further details of this phase in Dadul's recent history are provided in a collection of essays to be published in honour of Sir Raymond Firth (Whitehouse forthcoming *a*).

5

Climactic Ritual

Tanotka and I are the last remaining men whom God has enlightened and we will wake up this country. Nobody will come after the
two of us; we are the last. The whitemen did what we are doing, but
they never finished the work. Now we will put an end to illness,
sadness, hunger, and toil. There will be no night-time, no pain, no
tropical ulcers, and no sickness.

(Baninge, leader of the splinter group in Dadul and Maranagi)

A T the end of August 1988 Baninge told me that demoralization could
destroy the splinter group unless a credible programme to prepare for the
returning ancestors was set in motion. On a visit to Maranagi (29–30
August) Baninge explained the situation to Tanotka and presented him
with a provisional plan for climactic rituals, entailing the fusion of Dadul
and Maranagi. Baninge set out his plan roughly as follows, in the form of
a detailed programme.

On Wednesday, 31 August Baninge would announce a general prohibition on participation in the Catholic confessional. On Friday, 2 September he and Tanotka would go to Rabaul to book themselves on a flight
to Malmal. On Saturday, 3 September, or thereabouts, Baninge would
launch a campaign to expand his following by drawing various outsiders
into the Kivung. Between Sunday, 4 September and Wednesday, 7 September he and Tanotka would aim to visit Kolman in Malmal to inform
him that the miracle was about to occur in Maranagi. Also on Wednesday
the elderly and sick persons in Dadul would embark upon the walk to
Maranagi. On Thursday, 8 September every remaining person in Dadul
would walk to Maranagi carrying their livestock and, that evening, they
would slaughter and cook every remaining pig from Dadul and Maranagi.
Then, on Friday, 9 September, a great feast would be presented to the
ancestors to pay a backlog of debts which had accumulated in the wake of
reports demanding offerings of meat and money. When these offerings
were removed, the living would satisfy their craving for sensual pleasure
through over-indulgence in a massive feast and drinking spree. After this,

they would renounce all hedonistic delights forever and enter the round-house to hold an all-night vigil (referred to as a 'preparation ceremony') during which Baninge and Tanotka would separate sinners from those who were guaranteed salvation. Any sinners who were identified would have a brief period (i.e. until 15 September) in which to obtain absolution. Then, on Thursday, 15 September, another all-night vigil would be held in which all the people would be united in moral purity and would start to develop white skins under their black skins. In the course of this vigil there would be a great sign (such as thunder or a supernatural portent). Thereafter, everybody would be enlightened as to the method of producing the miracle. They would all become increasingly weak as their black skins began to loosen and sag and their white skins to grow. Tanotka would no longer appear as a mere boy but as the manifestation of God which he really was. Moreover, Tanotka would no longer hide his knowledge behind cryptic statements but would announce the date when the ancestors would return and would be recognized far and wide as the one true leader of Mankind. But most people outside the Dadul-Maranagi group would now be too late to obtain absolution for their sins and would be destined to suffer eternal punishment following the Day of Judgement. That is, after 15 September, God's pity would be exhausted and only the few chosen before this date could now merit salvation.

Baninge apparently formulated the above plan more or less independently. The only date in his programme which he claimed to have obtained from the ancestors (in the form of a report received in Maranagi) was 15 September. But Baninge claimed (in a private interview with me) to be the author of all the other elements in the plan, for which he had obtained Tanotka's approval.

The idea that the people of Dadul should migrate to Maranagi was tactically appropriate for a number of reasons. In the first place, Baninge realized that such a migration was capable of boosting morale. The ring ceremonies, and other collective rituals already established, had a considerable psychological impact on the participants, partly because they demonstrated the group's numerical strength, solidarity, and unity, and Baninge realized that this collective conscience would be greatly enhanced by the fusion of Dadul and Maranagi. By combining these two populations, collective rituals would take on an even more dramatic and awesome character. Moreover, the evacuation of Dadul would promote excitement in so far as it would temporarily relax the constraints on people's movements which had more or less bound everybody to the village clearing for several months. Baninge also hoped that it would demonstrate his conviction that the miracle was imminent. Unlike the splinter-group activities already in place, which were more or less furtively undertaken (e.g. were postponed when outsiders visited the village), the evacuation of Dadul could not fail to catch the attention of villages and other agencies external to the Dadul–Maranagi group. The fact that Baninge and Tanotka were now ready to run the risk of exposure to external criticism through public acts (like the evacuation of Dadul), demonstrated their certainty that the Village Government would arrive very soon and provide adequate protection from critics and opponents. Finally, the fusion of Dadul and Maranagi may have seemed ideologically necessary because the two villages had been linked from the time of Tanotka's original possession, when it had also been established that the 'eye' of the Village Government was at Maranagi rather than Dadul.

Baninge's new plan was an improvement upon the one put forward a week earlier involving wild pigs and dogs which was supposed to be implemented twice (first in Maranagi, then in Dadul). This was because unspecified portents (particularly the sort which naturally occur quite frequently, such as thunder storms and earthquakes) could be better relied upon to occur than an invasion of wild animals, and even if nothing happened on 15 September (e.g. because of intervention by Satan) persistent repetitions of the vigil were likely to produce a good portent in the end.

Another advantage of the new programme was that it contained additional drama and ritual (e.g. the visit to Malmal, the preparation ceremony and so on) which would elongate and intensify the new phase of millenarian activity. In practice, Baninge's plan became even more complicated (and, in some respects, more effective) before and even after it was underway. To allow for this flexibility, Baninge was careful not to announce his whole plan publicly but to put it into practice (more or less) day by day and to improvise along the way (indeed, it seems that Tanotka and I were the only persons to whom Baninge confided his whole plan in advance).

Transforming External Relations

Many of the elements in Baninge's plan were concerned with the defiance of various agencies external to the Dadul–Maranagi group. The prohibition on the confessional was a means of alienating the Catholic Church; the visit to Kolman was seen as a challenge to the religious wing of the

Pomio Kivung; the drive to expand Baninge's and Tanotka's following contravened the orders of a Pomio Kivung political leader; the migration to Maranagi expressed a rejection of secular government; a number of the elements in Baninge's plan were also calculated to alienate surrounding villages. For some time, Dadul's external relations had ranged from being harmonious to being implicitly hostile. Baninge's plan now demanded that all external relations should be characterized by open and explicit conflict. Baninge confided to me in a private interview that his intention, in alienating all these external groups, was to demonstrate beyond doubt the depth of his conviction that the Period of the Companies was at hand, and the diplomacy and compromise demanded by life in 'this world' could at last be abandoned. By 'proving' that the miracle was imminent (i.e. by burning all the established bridges required for existence in the 'old world'), Baninge planned to stimulate such intense and enthusiastic support for himself and Tanotka that the two of them could (if only temporarily) assume an openly dictatorial role in the creation of climactic rituals. Although such a plan could easily have failed, its implementation turned out to be a resounding success.

On 31 August 1988 Baninge declared (at a mass gathering for a public donation ritual) that the people of Dadul should no longer confess to the Catholic priest on his fortnightly visits. Baninge's argument was that, since the priest only pretended to be able to grant absolution for sins, confession entailed participation in deceit (a breach of the Eighth Law), which could not be tolerated now that the demands for moral purity in the community had intensified.

On 2 September 1988 Baninge publicly announced a few details of his plan (although he made no mention of the special significance of 15 September). This announcement, like the prohibition on the confessional, excited Baninge's followers because of its revolutionary character. The following day Tanotka declared that he had sent 'provocative' letters to the Principal of the Community School at Arabum and one of the Kivung orators at another Mali village, near to Maranagi, known as Reigel. Moreover, he said that he intended to broadcast a message of defiance to the world in general, on Radio Rabaul. I was unable to discover for certain whether the provocative letters had been Baninge's or Tanotka's idea, but the announcement that they had been sent greatly intensified group morale. Perhaps Dadul's first orator was more intoxicated by these developments than other people, but in any case he was inspired to write letters of his own to Sunam village and to the Minister for Lands in the Provincial Government, letters which later caused many more problems for the people of Dadul than those sent by Tanotka (see Chapter 6).

On the same day that Tanotka described his offensive letters to an electrified public meeting, Baninge began his drive to expand the splinter group by persuading persons outside the Kivung to join his following. On 3 September 1988 Baninge laid on a meal for the respected elder Sawai, who was linked by kinship to the people of Maranagi and Dadul but who lived at Arabum (i.e. outside the Kivung). At Baninge's house Sawai and his adult children were entertained and, by ingenious forms of persuasion, induced to join the Dadul–Maranagi splinter group. Baninge maintained that Sawai was a particularly important recruit because of his reputation as a sorcerer, a man who could cast out devils. Since the battle between the splinter group and Satan had now become more intense than ever, it was clear that any reinforcement to the group's armoury against evil would be welcome. Yet the primary justification for recruiting outsiders was pity (*marimari*). That is, the attempt to bring more souls into the ring was supposedly motivated by charitable sentiments. Individuals targeted for recruitment were genealogically connected to the Dadul–Maranagi group and, therefore, descendants of the Village Government. At one level, the drawing of such persons into the fold was therefore an act of charity on behalf of the ancestors, who reserved special affection for their descendants. Such justifications for the new evangelism resulted in the recruitment of several adults from Dadul and Maranagi who had, until now, refused to participate in the Kivung. All but one of the new recruits from Dadul were members of Bapka's domestic group. Bapka was an infamous cynic who utterly repudiated the Kivung. Even now, Bapka himself could not be induced to join Baninge's following. He alone remained outside the community. Bapka explained his position to me as follows:

I don't like the cult. It forces people to work too hard, especially old people. They meet, sing, do all their ritual work and when are they permitted to sleep? The village is their prison and they cannot come and go as they please to visit friends in other villages or even to tend their gardens.

Bapka later became a vehement critic of events which occurred in the splinter group after the migration to Maranagi.

Like the prohibition on the confessional and the sending of provocative letters, the expansion of Baninge's following had negative implications for the external relations of the splinter group. It is useful to summarize the main areas of controversy which this element in Baninge's plan was intended to excite.

First, the recruitment of persons living outside of Dadul and Maranagi was in direct violation of the orders of a Pomio Kivung supervisor (Francis Koimanrea). On a visit to Dadul after Tanotka's original possession in 1987, Francis had forbidden Tanotka to seek followers in Reigel. According to the men of Dadul, he had also warned the people of Reigel that Tanotka was a false prophet.

Secondly, the manner in which Baninge brought outsiders into the Kivung was in violation of Pomio Kivung membership rules. Normally, membership fees were prohibitively high, and this was a method of deterring people from leaving the Kivung once they had invested so substantially in it. Yet Baninge declared that his new recruits would be able to undergo a membership ritual (based on the ring ceremony) at Maranagi and would be allowed to pay a joining fee of their own choosing. Moreover, the newcomers were not obliged to give up the chewing of betelnut. In defiance of Pomio Kivung rules, Baninge declared: 'We are following our own customs now, not those of the Pomio leadership.'

Thirdly, the recruitment of persons in Dadul, formerly outside the Kivung, was certain to provoke anger in other villages. That is because, unlike Kivung members, the new recruits (e.g. Bapka's wife and children as well as the wife of Dadul's first orator) had enjoyed close relations with their kinsmen in Sunam and other villages; the recruitment of the former into the Kivung entailed a renunciation of these close relations and considerable resentment (particularly in Sunam) was widely anticipated.

Fourthly, the expansion of Baninge's following involved the removal of certain children from school and adults from employment, and so here was a basis for confrontation with the education establishment (and therefore the government) as well as with private companies. Baninge's willingness to alienate so many external agencies without compunction or fear was still further evidence of his conviction that the miracle was imminent.

It could be argued that, in challenging external groups, Baninge not only persuaded people to strengthen their faith in the cause, but he also gave them a sense of protection from the dangerous concomitants of his actions. The two leaders made no attempt to argue that any living persons, other than themselves, had decided to challenge external agencies. Baninge and Tanotka acted unilaterally in their defiance of the outside world, and the rest of the population did not expect to be held accountable for following the dictates of their leaders. Baninge and Tanotka effectively assumed responsibility for the actions of the group and, in this regard, their new and exalted roles were not enviable. Such factors must surely help to explain the willingness of splinter group members to do extraordinary things at this time. Indeed, profound allegiance to the two leaders was a precondition for the implementation of the next two elements in Baninge's plan: (i) the visit to Kolman; (ii) the pig slaughter and the migration to Maranagi.

Baninge and Tanotka argued that it was their duty to inform Kolman that the miracle would soon occur. But they pointed out that the performance of this duty should not waste valuable time, and so it was evident that they would have to undertake the journey to Malmal by aeroplane. The K270 air fares (vastly more expensive than the cost of passage by sea) were paid for with money from the bank account to finance the communal car (serving the whole region's transportation needs). The account was held in the names of two men (both members of the Dadul–Maranagi group) who had always borne the responsibility of protecting the fund against misuse. Baninge now ordered these men to withdraw money for a purpose unconnected with the upkeep of the car. The fact that the order was obeyed without question demonstrates the strength of the leadership at this time and certainly suggests that Baninge's and Tanotka's followers considered that accountability for all developments now lay with the two leaders.

Baninge and Tanotka flew to Malmal on 5 September 1988, and returned two days later with the news that Kolman had bowed to their authority and had parted with K30 as a sign of his allegiance to Tanotka (the new 'post' or 'holder of the key'). It was on the day of their return to Dadul (7 September) that a male task force, on Baninge's orders, captured and slaughtered all the pigs in the village. These pigs represented years of domestic labour and were each worth a considerable amount of money. Baninge's authority at this time was particularly evident in the destruction of one very large pig, worth several hundred kina. This prize pig was looked after by an old man in Dadul, but rights in the animal were also held by persons in Sunam. The old man did not argue with Baninge's order to have the pig destroyed, even though it was widely recognized that this action would cause conflict between the people of Sunam and Dadul. I will return to this topic in the next chapter. The point here is that the old man, normally responsible for the pig, passed his responsibility on to Baninge without question. Regarding the fate of the pig, as regarding all things, accountability now lay exclusively with Baninge and Tanotka.

Fɪɢ. 16. A ring begins to form within the greatly expanded community at Maranagi.

The migration from Dadul to Maranagi was accomplished in two waves (i.e. on 7 and 8 September 1988). On the way up the mountain it was necessary for the cultists to walk through Arabum, bent double under the weight of pork and personal possessions. The migration of splinter-group members, marching in procession through Arabum, inevitably produced cries of derision from local residents.

Once in Maranagi the newcomers to the Dadul–Maranagi splinter group were instructed in the basic rules of the Kivung, and urged to put aside their clothes just as everybody else had done. At dusk a special ring ceremony was held to bring the newcomers into the fold. The most striking feature of the ceremony was the size of the population (see Fig. 16). The fusion of the two villages gave all collective ritual thereafter a greater sense of power. Older people, in particular, could not attend these gatherings without shedding tears of joy, for they remembered how their numbers had been depleted after the Second World War. It was assumed that a similar reaction to the rituals would prevail among the ever–vigilant ancestors.

Thus, the build–up to the migration to Maranagi (as well as the migration itself) involved the transformation of the group's external relations. This transformation occurred in ways which were ideologically indicated. In general terms, there had always been hidden tensions between Dadul's

Kivung on the one hand, and the church, all levels of government, and many surrounding villages on the other. But now that the miracle was imminent, and moral purity (e.g. honesty) more important than diplomacy, open conflict with the outside world was ideologically justified. Yet the transformation of external relations cannot be explained in these terms. One could equally argue (as occurred much later) that any kind of disharmony could never be consistent with Kivung doctrine. Instead, I would suggest that the defiance of external agencies occurred as a result of Baninge's conscious effort to furnish himself with dictatorial powers. On the one hand, revolutionary changes were exciting (e.g. providing evidence of the imminence of the miracle) and, for this reason, helped to consolidate support for the leaders. On the other hand, such changes made it desirable for most people to assume the role of sheep rather than shepherds (i.e. because the shepherd, and not his flock, would be held accountable for all developments). These two factors seem best to explain Baninge's success in seizing the role of dictatorial leader at this time. Once in Maranagi, however, Baninge and Tanotka were confronted with another task, namely the organization of a new programme of rituals, premissed upon the rapid production of the miracle.

The Preparation Ceremony

On 9 September 1988 two separate pork feasts were held on Baninge's orders. The first occurred at dawn to celebrate the official opening of Maranagi's ancestral round-house in readiness for the 'preparation ceremony' to be held that night. In addition to a feast, the morning celebrations included dances of *awanga* and *ilotka* (see Fig. 17), and a ring ceremony at which Baninge opened the door of the round-house. These rituals were slightly different from earlier versions, in accordance with new instructions from Baninge. The second pork feast, presented in Maranagi's big temples during the afternoon, was consumed at dusk. The purpose of the second feast was to pay off a backlog of debts to the ancestors, which had accumulated in the wake of earlier reports demanding meat.

One of the reports which followed the removal of the second feast seemed to predict a miraculous sign during that night's preparation vigil. In actual fact, the syntax of part of the report was conditional and the vigil to which it referred was inconclusive: 'If the children see a sign in the ancestral house, they must not be frightened or blaspheme. The

F IG. 17. *Ilotka* dance in a circle in front of the round-house at Maranagi, accompanied by a male choir beating lengths of bamboo on planks of wild palm.

orators must warn people to have courage. During the night, all the people will see proof of their work in the Kivung.' This particular report was received by one of the youngest witnesses who appeared to have become over-excited by the mood in Maranagi, for Baninge had not encouraged him to hear this report and it was most unusual for a witness to receive a statement suggesting some new development which had not been anticipated by one or both of the two leaders. As a result of this report, however, the mood in Maranagi almost reached fever pitch as people brought their gardening implements to the house of one of the orators to be locked away. People declared that they would not be needing these 'foreign' tools again.

After dark, the whole community gathered in a ring outside the round-house and shook hands in the established fashion. On Tanotka's order, the women entered the house first (just as whitemen were believed to make way for their women folk) and then the men followed until everybody was inside. Although the round-house was just large enough to accommodate everybody, it was severely overcrowded and people's legs were trapped in the crush and soon began to ache. Children had to sit in their parents' laps and they cried or moaned continually because of their confinement. Moreover, it soon became oppressively hot. For the first half-hour nobody spoke, although parents who were unable to stifle their children's whining were subjected to a barrage of tuts from the disapproving male elders.

Finally, Tanotka delivered a speech about the significance of the roundhouse, particularly the central post which marked the 'centre of Paradise' or the 'eye of the Village Government' as well as the 'work' with which he (Tanotka) had been encumbered. But Tanotka's speech was highly coded so that it could not be understood by newcomers to the Kivung, from whom many themes of splinter-group ideology were still being hidden. When Tanotka had finished, the other established orators in the community took turns to speak as if at an ordinary community meeting (although they also disguised their references to splinter-group ideas). This continued for $2\frac{1}{2}$ hours, during which time no great portent occurred. Since hearing that day's report from Bernard's Temple, most people had expected a violent storm or an earthquake. But the night was calm and the vigil was abandoned at 11 p.m. as if it had been little more than a regular public meeting.

Unlike Dadul, Maranagi had a 'men's house' in which men (especially single men and male visitors) habitually slept and to which all the men tended to repair at various times for the purpose of socializing in an environment where they could discuss 'male things' (e.g. secret male ritual) and generally escape their domestic responsibilities. The men's house was also a good place to keep in touch with the mood of the male consensus. On the day after the anti-climactic preparation vigil, the discussion inside the men's house was particularly interesting. The young witness who had received the report about the portent was insisting that there had been a sign after they had left the round-house but that only he had noticed it because everyone else had fallen asleep. The men wanted to know what this sign had been and the witness said that a 'great wind' had awoken him. So why had it not awoken everybody else? To this, the witness conceded that it had been more of a stiff breeze. The other men were not impressed. Their conclusion was that none of them should have expected a portent in the first place because the report must have been referring to another (later) vigil in the round-house. Then they made light of the matter by joking about their foolishness in giving up their gardening tools. The self-mockery was also an expression of humility before God, whose plan they had (slightly) misunderstood. Presently they would surrender their tools again and that time around there would be a real portent.

The Mass Marriage and other Tactical Innovations

Although the failure of the preparation vigil had been explained away, it remained a failure at some (psychological) level for the members of the community. Retrospectively, it seemed that Baninge should have followed the broadcast of the report from Bernard's Temple with an announcement to the effect that this report referred to a later vigil. This would have been consistent with his original plan. Perhaps he did not because he was prepared to believe that this really was an authoritative report which did relate to the first vigil, or because the short-term boost to morale was too gratifying to undermine. But the result was that the vigil lost direction somewhat. It began as a silent wait for the portent. Then, as the men lost confidence in the likelihood of a sign occurring, the whole vigil degenerated into yet another meeting. With hindsight, it would have been better if Tanotka had followed Baninge's original plan, and had used the vigil to separate the pure souls from those tainted by sin so that the latter might prepare themselves (through absolution donations) for the final vigil at a later date. At least the preparation vigil would not then have run the risk of failure.

All the developments described so far in this chapter had been intended (by Baninge at least) to generate in the community a state of maximum psychological commitment to emergent institutions, in readiness for the inevitable climax which would be a vigil marked by a supernatural portent. The mishandling of the preparation vigil meant that some rebuilding of this commitment was called for. In this context, Baninge came up (apparently on the spur of the moment) with an inspired stratagem, which was to organize a huge marriage ceremony to pair off the single Kivung members. This move was indicated ideologically because the Period of the Companies was also a period of temptation and it was appropriate for the younger girls in particular (whose morals were notoriously lax) to be constrained, or sexually placated, by marriage and therefore relatively safe from the temptation to have sexual relations with the reincarnated ancestors. In this respect, Baninge's plan to marry off the young people was further proof of his conviction that the miracle was imminent, so his stratagem had this clear psychological recommendation. It also paralleled Baninge's prohibition of the confessional or the sending of provocative letters in the respect that it constituted a challenge to external agencies. This was partly because Baninge urged the coupling of certain adolescents who were (in the context of normal morality and law) under-age.

The normal criterion for female marriageability was that the girl's breasts had begun to sag. But one bride in particular had not even begun to develop breasts, while many of the others still had firm breasts. Many of the boys were also too young since they did not yet have a strong growth of facial hair (the normal criterion for male marriageability). Moreover, Baninge insisted upon the formation of these marriages in the model of sister-exchange, thereby imposing severe constraints on the range of possible pairings. In consequence, betrothals which contradicted other more practical considerations (such as the wishes of the youths and their parents) were inevitable. No immediate obstacle was presented by these factors, and certainly no objections were (or were likely to be) raised by members of the Dadul–Maranagi group. But these members had relatives outside the Kivung who would normally have reserved the right to influence marriage arrangements. In particular, one of the girls on Baninge's list was the only daughter of Bapka (the one person in Dadul who had refused to join Baninge's following). Since Bapka valued his daughter's labour (especially so, because his wife was an invalid) it was obvious that he would object to her marriage to a grossly under-age youth without his opinion having been sought (let alone respected). From various points of view, it was clear to all and sundry that Baninge's plan for a mass marriage would strain external relations to breaking point, and possibly give rise to legal action. As such, Baninge was demonstrating his belief in the imminence of the miracle beyond question.

In order to mount a ceremony on a scale appropriate to a mass marriage, Baninge required money to buy desirable foods (e.g. rice, tinned fish) and drink (e.g. cordial, beers, and spirits). But a quantity of pork remained uneaten in the wake of the slaughter of all the domestic pigs in Dadul and Maranagi and so this resource, at least, was readily available for Kivung ritual. It will be noted that Baninge's original plan had involved a sort of 'feast to end all feasts' on the day of the preparation vigil, after which the population would renounce all hedonistic desires. Yet Baninge did not in practice attribute this significance to the feast on the day of the first vigil. Perhaps this was because Baninge realized that there was more pork available than could be consumed on that one day. Perhaps he also had the forethought to realize that the more he could elongate his original itinerary by supplying additional extravagent rituals, the more intense would be his support. However that may be, Baninge decided that an unparalleled feast for the mass marriage was now essential and that this would also be dubbed the feast to end all feasts, marking the renunciation of hedonism. The question, then, was how to obtain enough money for food and drink.

The financial problem was easily resolved in practice. Baninge simply ordered the orators to take money from the communal absolution funds and from the collections made in response to the demands of reports. The former method was not particularly controversial since the absolution fund had, for some time, been used to sponsor projects mounted for the sake of the community. The use of report money was more unusual. But the men argued that a recent stock-take of the financial records revealed that some of the demands made by the ancestors had been overpaid and they were therefore entitled to remove the excess money. For complex reasons, this argument was not mere fabrication although the figure taken to represent an excess in the report fund was probably inaccurate.

On Monday, 12 September a group of men went to town in the communal car to buy supplies for the great feast which (along with the mass marriage) was scheduled for the following day. Thus, only three days separated the less-than-successful preparation vigil and the mass marriage which would 'make up for it' as far as group morale was concerned. Baninge also used the Tuesday ceremonies as a way of dealing with another problem, which was the sudden influx of uninvited newcomers.

Over the weekend (10–11 September) a number of people had come to Maranagi from Reigel because they wanted to share in the fruits of the miracle. This was a problem because these people from Reigel did not share the same ancestors as the Dadul–Maranagi group and, therefore, had no right to join it. Reports occurred in the big temples, ordering the unwanted newcomers to leave, but they refused. Baninge's response was to hold a ritual on the morning of Tuesday, 13 September to finalize the membership ceremony of legitimate newcomers and to receive their confessions as he had done for the people in Dadul. After this, he declared that God's pity was finally exhausted and any living person now tainted by sin was henceforth destined for eternal damnation. This meant that all the members of the Dadul–Maranagi group (including the legitimate newcomers who had undergone this final purification rite) were spiritually secure, but the unwanted newcomers (excluded from the rite) could expect to gain nothing from remaining in Maranagi. In practice, this tactic seemed to fail in so far as the Reigel group did not leave. But their continued presence turned out to be useful to Baninge because they became the natural scapegoats to blame for the failure of a subsequent all-night vigil to produce a portent.

Another important tactical innovation was Baninge's decision to unify the big temples of Dadul and Maranagi. He argued that since the two villages shared one group of ancestors, and now even shared one village, so they ought to share one set of big temples. Therefore, when the men returned to Maranagi with supplies on Monday, 12 September, they brought with them from Dadul the ritual paraphernalia and monetary offerings kept in the big temples there. It is yet further evidence of Baninge's supreme authority at this point that he sent the news of this development to Dadul on the Monday itself so that it was conveyed by messenger to the men returning with supplies from town. The men proceeded to strip the temples and carry the contents to Maranagi, an act which would ordinarily have been unthinkable, but was now performed simply because Baninge had ordered it and before the men had heard his justifications for doing so.

The mass marriage and the immense feast to mark the end of hedonism occurred as scheduled on 13 September, and had a suitable impact on morale in Maranagi. There was singing and dancing throughout the night and nobody seemed to be troubled any more about the apparent failure of the first vigil. By then, the whole idea of a preparation vigil (i.e. to identify sinners who must obtain absolution) had become redundant in any case, because God could no longer forgive sinners. The next vigil would be of a different kind and it would certainly yield a great portent from God to mark the onset of an era in which the people enjoyed enlightenment and awaited the arrival of the ancestors in a state of serenity and relative inaction.

The Period of the Vigils

On the morning of Wednesday, 14 September a ring ceremony was held (on Baninge's orders) at which each person in the community was obliged to give 30t to Baninge in order to gratify God (of whom Baninge was a manifestation) and thereby encourage Him to produce a portent during the vigil which would be held that night. In private interviews with me, Baninge insisted that a sign would occur during that night's vigil which would herald a new period of mass enlightenment, thereby rendering his leadership unnecessary. That is to say, each person in Maranagi would be henceforth like an ancestor or like God and would know how and when the Village Government would return. According to Baninge, the material world would be unchanged following the vigil. Every person would still be black-skinned in physical appearance (though they would be spiritually white) and the village and forest would remain as before. This scenario, however, contrasted with the views of the population as a whole.

Most people recognized the above scenario but said that they believed it was now redundant. Instead, the portent would be followed the next morning by the actual return of the ancestors and the transformation of their forest into a modern city. Moreover, they would all peel away their black skin and appear as white people. Most informants said that the sources of their information on this matter were the senior officials (e.g. orators), although some said that Baninge himself had led them to imagine that the miracle would immediately follow the portent. In fact, Baninge's public statements had (to my own knowledge) been ambiguous (e.g. 'after the vigil, the companies will come', although this did not specify how soon after). It is possible that Baninge made a public statement predicting the miracle immediately after the portent and that I happened to miss it, but this seems unlikely since Baninge was adamant (in private interviews) that he had made no such statement.

This discrepancy constituted an interesting development, in so far as it was one of the first indications of Baninge's withdrawal from the limelight as a purveyor of authoritative statements. In the preceding weeks Baninge had made numerous public pronouncements which were clear and explicit as part of a dictatorial strategy. But after 14 September his strategy changed, and he later explained to me that he had decided to withhold his knowledge (*save*) or insights (*lukluk*) from followers, since it was now 'up to them' to obtain enlightenment for themselves. In practice, he did attempt to maintain some influence over ideology but he appeared to do this half-heartedly and inconsistently. In any case, on 14 September the people locked away their gardening tools and entered the round-house with the explicit expectation that the following day they would be reunited with their ancestors.

Things did not go as hoped. The uninvited newcomers from Reigel entered the round-house along with the legitimate community, in spite of numerous attempts to dissuade them. During the vigil, Tanotka and various orators complained at great length about the presence of the Reigel people. Finally, Tanotka said that they must abandon the vigil and hold it the following night instead. On Thursday, 15 September most people (including Tanotka) attributed the failure of the vigil to the interference of the uninvited Reigel people. There seemed to be no detectable demoralization in the wake of this failed vigil because the explanation was convincing. Under intensified pressure from the legitimate group, the unwanted Reigel people left Maranagi in the morning. Moreover, the information that 15 September had been the established date for the 'real' vigil was leaked to most of the community by the witness who had received the report in Maranagi at the end of August. In consequence, many people ate the pork fat which was left over from the recent feasts. It was widely believed that although pork fat tasted good, it produced nausea. For this reason, it had been collected in bamboo casks for use as an additive in cooking rather than as a food in its own right. But the unconcerned consumption of this fat on the 15th indicated that people believed the miracle was just a few hours away and the physical changes which they would undergo would prevent them from suffering any ill-effects from the pork fat.

The vigil on the 15th continued until 3 a.m. the following morning. In the hot, overcrowded round-house people groaned with nausea and there was incessant vomiting of pork fat and rushing off to the latrines or bushes. Meanwhile, the children screamed to be let out. Once again, the miracle failed to occur.

Some people suggested that the miracle had started to occur but had been aborted. This view was put forward by one of Dadul's orators who, returning from a latrine, had seen a light on the roof of the round-house. Another official from Dadul had seen a light from within the house, shining through cracks in the walls. All the same, the miracle did not actually occur as anticipated and the uninvited Reigel people, who had now left, could no longer be held responsible. On Friday, 16 September some of the legitimate newcomers also left Maranagi. In particular, Sawai's grown-up children from Arabum declared that they were Christians and did not believe in the Kivung and so departed. Baninge merely shrugged his shoulders and told them they would go to hell. These events were followed in the afternoon by a statement from the ancestors (received by Dadul's first orator in a dream) revealing that these legitimate newcomers had prevented the miracle from occurring because they had not belonged to the Kivung over a long enough period of time and lacked faith. At the afternoon meeting various other orators, with Tanotka's backing, added that the coming and going of people afflicted with nausea during the vigil had offended God and prevented Him from unleashing the miracle. A third explanation for the failure of the vigil was put forward by Baninge, who declared that God had been disappointed by the 30t-per-head donation and wanted the community to donate more. The total collection had amounted to K52.50 and this was not enough.

The meeting was shorter than usual and the offerings removed from the big temples an hour early. Strictly speaking, the offerings were ideo-logically redundant because the community had supposedly already sat-isfied the preconditions for the occurrence of the miracle. But since Baninge (in his new, quieter role) had not ordered the abolition of temple rituals and similar activities, they were maintained in a truncated form. Moreover, as long as Baninge and Tanotka were not willing to share all their knowledge with the population, reports remained an important means of obtaining information. That day's reports reiterated that the people had behaved badly during the vigil but also demanded that another vigil be held tonight because the portent would occur at midnight.

That evening, at dusk, a ring ceremony was held. The ceremony was mounted to collect more money to gratify God and to provide another opportunity for the orators and elders to castigate the people for their bad behaviour during the previous night's vigil. Baninge's 'brothers' (except for Tanotka) took a leading role in the ceremony and repeated that the portent would occur at midnight. Baninge himself was silent (this was the first ever ring ceremony attended by him which he did not use to address his followers).

If Baninge had been worried, then it soon became clear that he need not have been. The vigil on 16 September produced a good portent on the stroke of midnight: a girl from Dadul (approximately 18 years of age), called Lagawop, was possessed. Lagawop's possession lasted until dawn when she told everybody to gather for another vigil the following night. Lagawop's speech during the possession had consisted of the extensive repetition of Kivung doctrine, which she had encoded in memory as a result of long-term attendance at Kivung meetings (Whitehouse 1992: 785). Yet, from the viewpoint of Lagawop's audience, these were not the words of an adolescent girl but the inspired oratory of an ancestor. For Baninge, Lagawop's possession was a godsend in other ways. It meant, for example, that one (and probably many) more vigils would now be held before the population grew impatient and demanded a more substantial miracle.

On Saturday, 17 and Sunday, 18 September the vigils were repeated and Lagawop was possessed on each night. She did not speak continuously, however, and when she paused to recover her strength the whole community sang the song about Aringawuk. By the morning of Monday, 19 September, the participants were exhausted since nobody was obtaining adequate sleep during the daytime. Lagawop rested in the communal cookhouse, and as she lay there she was visited by her dead grandfather (the boss of Bernard's Temple in Dadul) and her dead grandmother. When the offerings were removed from the big temples in the afternoon, Lagawop sat on a stone and delivered a long speech about her encounter with these two ancestors. Gradually, a large congregation gathered to listen to Lagawop. This was probably the point at which Baninge, Tanotka, and certain key male officials decided to intervene.

At dusk, a secret meeting occurred in Baninge's father's house. Baninge's brothers (including Tanotka) certainly attended and it is likely that a handful of orators and elders was also there. I did not attend this meeting and cannot be sure what was said. But I heard second-hand that suspicions had been expressed at this meeting with regard to Lagawop's possession. There was a general feeling that she may be suffering from Satanic delusions. If she was being possessed by Satan rather than by good ancestors, then she would have to be denounced as a false prophet and the evil forces exorcized. These conclusions were reached in an environment of intense secrecy. No reference was made to them when the community gathered to enter the round-house later in the evening. Lagawop was possessed as usual and during the gaps in her discourse, the people sang as before.

In the small hours of the morning, however, one of Baninge's brothers (not Tanotka) asked Lagawop to name herself. She gave the name of her grandfather. He asked her over and over, and she gave the same reply. If the young man had cross-questioned a good ancestor in this fashion, then it would have shown profound disrespect, for which he should have been criticized. But nobody objected to the young man's behaviour. This gave Tanotka the confidence to speak out as well: he denounced Lagawop as a liar and said that Satan was wearing the face of her grandfather. Baninge's maternal uncle then seized Lagawop and shook her vigorously, shouting that she was possessed by Satan. He shook her and threw her against the walls and onto the floor. When Lagawop was sufficiently terrified, she cried out: 'I am possessed by Satan! Leave my body Satan! Go to your village, Satan! Go to Arabum!' Of course Arabum, being outside the Kivung, was a more appropriate stamping-ground for Satan than Maranagi. Lagawop then wept until an elder came to shake her once again. The vigil was abandoned. At dusk the following day, the ring ceremony was used to finalize the exorcism of Lagawop. The key roles were taken not by Baninge or Tanotka but by their brothers who told Satan to leave Lagawop's body and who shook her hand to signify her return into the fold as an ordinary teenage girl.

On the face of it, Lagawop's possession had been an asset to the male leaders in so far as it helped to sustain people's psychological commitment to the vigils. But she became a threat when she showed signs of aspiring to the role of a divine authority in her own right. Prior to her downfall, I heard murmurings in the community (from a few elders but mostly from the younger male officials) that Lagawop was becoming a leader like Tanotka. It would be facile, and at best a half-truth, to suggest that the conspiracy to denounce Lagawop constituted an attempt by Baninge and

Tanotka to maintain their exclusive position in the community. The main problem with Lagawop's ascendance was that her actions and statements were not subject to influence and constraint by the will of the male officials as a group. Being female, and little more than a child, it would have been extremely difficult to let her into the male meetings and sustain the exclusion of all other females. Moreover, even if she could have been made an honorary man, she lacked the maturity, sensitivity, and kinship connections to manipulate (and more importantly, to be manipulated by) the male consensus. In short, Lagawop was a classic upstart and would have been denounced even sooner during any other epoch in the Kivung's development. It is also possible that the male conspirators knew that the effect of Lagawop's possession on group morale could not be sustained because the community would soon become impatient with her moral discourse and expect the real miracle to occur. As long as Lagawop's possession was regarded as genuine, there was no method of explaining the failure of the miracle to occur. But by denouncing Lagawop, the leaders established that Satan was concentrating his energies on the obstruction of the miracle. This provided a necessary side-track or delay tactic. The male leaders announced that the community must overcome Satan before it could expect God to produce a genuine portent and unleash the Period of the Companies.

For a few days (20–22 September) no more vigils were held although there were several ring ceremonies to drive Satan out of Maranagi. There was an immediate subsistence problem too because the population in Maranagi was twice its normal size and local gardens had been virtually depleted. The leaders organized various fishing and gathering expeditions involving large male task forces (who collectively dammed rivers and netted fish in the traditional fashion). But many people complained of an insatiable hunger. Meanwhile, Baninge and Tanotka refused to announce any concrete plan for the immediate future. On Friday, 23 September one of the witnesses, apparently impatient of this hiatus, received a report in the Cemetery Temple ordering that a vigil be held that night. The vigil occurred but there was no portent. Another report the following day ordered another vigil with the same result. For five consecutive nights (23–27 September) the vigils were held and each time they failed. It was generally accepted that the reports from the big temples were really coming from Satan. By Wednesday, 28 September the population was exhausted and extremely hungry. Baninge led most of the productive members of Dadul back to their village where they hoped to gather food from their gardens. They were bitterly angry to discover that most of their crops had been stolen by enemies of the Kivung from neighbouring villages. The people of Dadul had a great many such enemies, particularly following the dissemination of provocative letters. Only Baninge reacted stoically. He said that he was too virtuous to feel anger and believed that the thieves would receive their punishment soon, on the Day of Judgement.

The population in Dadul shared what food it could find. On Saturday, 11 October Tanotka sent a note to Baninge in Dadul, quoting a fresh report saying that Satan had been defeated and the miracle could at last occur. Baninge persuaded the people in Dadul that they could not give up now, having come this far. My interviews with almost every adult in Dadul that day revealed that the people were frightened to risk exclusion from the miracle now that they had invested so many resources in the pursuit of it. Nobody expressed any reluctance to return to Maranagi and for several consecutive nights the whole community gathered for more vigils in the round-house. Less than a week later, officials in the Provincial Government were informed of the migration to Maranagi and sent a Health Inspector to Dadul. He found that the deserted village was in a state of serious neglect. The houses were dilapidated, and the bush was advancing into the clearing. He marched to Maranagi and told the people of Dadul to return home and clear up their village. He also ordered the demolition of the round-house on the grounds that the vigils held there were a danger to public health (i.e. because by now people were being prevented from leaving the house to go to the latrines, from sleeping during the vigils and so on). The people of Dadul left Maranagi saying that if they did not obey the Health Inspector then they would be prosecuted. But many of them were sick and all were exhausted and hungry so that these were even more compelling reasons to return to Dadul. One little girl, already weakened by long-term illness and malnutrition ensuing from it, was now close to death. Clearly, the physical survival of the whole population depended on the restoration of production.

Climactic Ritual, Leadership, and Political Scale

The vigils held in the round-house at Maranagi (mid-September to mid-October 1988) were unsuccessful in the obvious respect that they did not herald a miraculous transformation, ushering in the Period of the Companies. On the face of it, this would seem to be one of the greatest political weaknesses of millenarism—that its prophesies are never fulfilled. The mass gatherings and rituals which are mounted in the expectation of a miracle predictably break up, and the ideas surrounding them are liable to come under attack. Yet there are some important respects in which the vigils at Maranagi, and perhaps many similar activities in Melanesia, may be regarded as resoundingly successful in both political and religious terms.

The large splinter-group community, based upon the fusion of Dadul and Maranagi, was only temporarily sustained as a viable ritual unit. Yet the deeply impressive and memorable nature of splinter-group rituals meant that the solidarity created by these activities was enduring—certainly, it was bound to outlast the physical congregations themselves, in which these memories were cultivated and shared. Likewise, the religious experiences of participants in the vigils were so intense, moving, and conceptually powerful that they provided compelling and enduring revelations, capable of being sustained in people's thoughts and feelings long after the rituals themselves had ceased.

The vigils held in the round-house at Maranagi were symbolically similar to the ring ceremonies which preceded and accompanied them: the short posts from which the circular wall was constructed corresponded to a ring of bodies (splinter-group members); the tall, central post supporting the rafters corresponded to the leader (Tanotka or Baninge), who stood at the centre of the ring of people. The iconicity of the house and of the ring ceremonies derived from the seminal utterance attributed to Wutka: 'I am a post' (see Chapter 4). The metaphor was thus more or less fixed from the outset and conveyed a simple idea, that the members of Dadul and Maranagi formed a spiritual elect (a ring) which should be directed in its quest for salvation by a divine leader (a post). The metaphor was initially communicated in language but, as it came to be codified in collective ritual performances, its impression on people's minds was subtly transformed and greatly intensified.

This has been shown with reference to the initial performances of the ring ceremony which served not only to communicate the root metaphor but to provide an experience of its efficacy, partly through emotional and sensory stimulation. The promise of salvation was not merely being asserted but physically experienced, and solidarity was not merely demanded but realized through the act of collective participation (see Chapter 4). These features are even more strikingly apparent in the vigils at Maranagi. In part, this has to do with the fact that the first ring ceremonies in Dadul, along with the dances and feasts which were performed, were seen as preparatory to truly climactic rituals, heralding the Period of the Companies. Correspondingly, these rituals were somewhat constrained in the ways that they sought to cultivate novel experiences among participants. The taste of salvation offered by the first ring ceremony utilized the experience of a transition from slight discomfort (coldness) to mild pleasure (warmth), yet this process was no more impressive as a sensory experience than the satisfaction of day-to-day desires. It may be that the shame or sexual excitement induced by nakedness at the first ring ceremony was exceptionally stimulating, but the routine observance of nakedness at subsequent rituals undermined its initial impact (see Chapter 4). Likewise, the *awan*, feasts and nocturnal dances, whilst they undoubtedly cultivated unusual and impressive experiences, did not fully exploit the opportunities for extreme emotional and sensory excitation which were, in principle, available. For example, the fact that the *awanga* were equipped with stems of wild ginger instead of clubs, greatly reduced the sense of terror and drama which the *awan* must have induced in pre-contact times.

In contrast, the vigils at Maranagi were far more traumatic, involving severe deprivations, miseries, and even physical assault and, as such, they were conducive to a particularly intense experience of physical and emotional suffering, greatly intensifying the desire for supernatural deliverance and thereby providing some of the most memorable religious revelations of all splinter-group activity. The vigils were bound to make an enduring impression on people's minds, not only because they constituted the climax of millenarian activity, nor even because they were the most traumatic and large-scale rituals yet undertaken by the splinter group, but also because they transferred the burden of revelation onto the individual participant as an interpreter of the divine will and not merely as a recipient of authoritative pronouncements, issuing from the mouths of leaders.

The worst forms of suffering inflicted on participants in the vigils ensued from overcrowding, confinement, and lack of sleep. People were obliged to sit with their legs tightly crossed, and their bodies pressed together throughout the night. Due to lack of ventilation, it was oppressively hot and stifling in the round-house. At many vigils, people were prohibited from leaving the house during the night and were occasionally forced to urinate where they sat. The atmosphere was particularly unpleasant during one vigil, following the widespread consumption of pork fat, at which many participants vomited. Young children suffered acutely but were restrained by the adults from crying or complaining. Senior officials meanwhile prevented any of the participants from obtaining some temporary relief from their miseries, by falling asleep.

The role of senior officials (e.g. orators) in the Mali round-house was not unlike that of sadistic initiators in other parts of Papua New Guinea, for example among the Baktaman, where novices are incarcerated for four days in a house, where they are prevented from sleeping and forced to undergo severe overheating and dehydration (Barth 1975: 66). The kind of physical violence which is typical in New Guinea initiations was not apparent in the splinter group, although the aggressive exorcism of Lagawop tended in that direction. The overall experience for all participants, however, was one of intense discomfort and suffering.

There were probably several reasons for the infliction of suffering on participants at vigils. In part, their confinement had to do with the maintenance of unity. If people had been permitted to leave the house during the night, their absence might have prevented the miracle from occurring. In part, the endurance of suffering demonstrated the great value and importance which the community attributed to the metaphor of the post. In other words, the revelation of the round-house was not one which could be imparted lightly. This aspect of the rituals was particularly apparent during the early vigils, attended by new recruits to the splinter group. The newcomers were obliged to infer the meanings of ring ceremonies and vigils without exegetical commentary, and indeed the leaders explicitly forbade the provision of verbal explications of the metaphor of the post. The newcomers were thus treated as novices *par excellence*, and the long-standing members in their turn enjoyed a sense of superiority over them. Some of the latter probably felt that there was a certain justice in the fact that newcomers should suffer to obtain religious knowledge, otherwise acquired through long-term participation in the cult. Nevertheless, for those who already possessed a sophisticated understanding of Kivung eschatology, the suffering entailed in vigils served to deepen that understanding.

Ideas of salvation in the splinter group were never elaborated extensively in words. Even the mainstream movement had failed to provide a comprehensive vision of the Period of the Companies or of the Government—indeed, dwelling on these issues was held to be equivalent to thinking about eating temple offerings in the course of their preparation (see Chapter 3). Salvation was construed as deliverance from suffering, yet beyond the routine endurance of God's punishment for original sin, the suffering of Kivung members was hardly a pressing concern. By instituting prolonged and intense suffering in the vigils, splinter-group activities produced a more urgent and widespread longing for deliverance, and meanwhile brought into focus the otherwise vague notion of salvation as the converse of present miseries. The speeches delivered during vigils (by Tanotka and Lagawop especially) focused heavily on the theme of deliverance from suffering, and although the tears of their audiences seemed to be inspired by these words, they were no doubt triggered more directly by the desperate conditions in which they were received.

The nature of religious experience during the period of the vigils was conducive to a change in Baninge's style of leadership. During the fortnight preceding the vigils, it had been necessary for Baninge to assume a dictatorial role in order to mobilize the material and human resources required for the performance of climactic rituals. On the one hand, he had to command obedience in order to seize funds and foodstuffs and, on the other hand, he had to relieve his followers of responsibility for their actions. This was achieved through Baninge's campaign of defiance towards external agencies. But once the climactic rituals were underway, there was no further need for dynamic leadership. The people knew what to do and how to do it, and Baninge drifted out of the limelight as a director of social action. The vigils themselves took over (as it were) from Baninge as the source of religious transmission. Baninge made fewer statements and the rituals were left to speak for themselves. Certainly, the image of the round-house, like that of the ring ceremony, communicated the centrality of the leader, but this was a process over which Baninge himself no longer exerted any special influence. The situation was characteristic of a religious system which relies heavily on iconic codification because the idea, the conception, inhered in the collective act rather than in the words of the leader, who in turn became more of a figurehead than a dynamic social strategist.

A critical factor in the success of climactic rituals was the scale on which they were performed. I have observed that the fusion of Dadul and Maranagi contributed greatly to the excitement and intensity with which support for the millenarian programme was expressed. On the face of it, the greater the scale of collective rituals, the more impressive they would be, and this assumption clearly informed Baninge's drive to expand his following. But the splinter group was not as expansionary as all that. The leaders never sought a following among groups that were not descended from Aringawuk. But, even if they had not been constrained by this genealogical criterion of recruitment, there were limits on the capacity of Maranagi to play host to a large population. Even the influx of people from Dadul, bearing as much food as they could carry, rapidly depleted Maranagi's gardens and reduced the population to hunting and foraging for subsistence. In other words, the scale and longevity of collective ritual was determined by insuperable material conditions; the rituals of the splinter group had to be a temporary and politically localized phenomenon. The cult could not have spread more widely, nor been reproduced more permanently, without exchanging its collective and traumatic activities for a more routinized set of institutions, which could be reproduced independently at scattered locations, and unified by a body of doctrine spread by patrolling leaders. As such, it would have been a different kind of religion altogether, and much more akin to the mainstream Pomio Kivung movement.

Despite the predictable demise of the splinter-group rituals, and the inevitably modest range of their influence, they were successful in so far as they engraved upon the minds of participants a set of moving and compelling memories which, in the ensuing years, were certain to imbue more routinized activities with meanings that they would otherwise have lacked. The desire for salvation, for example, was cultivated in the splinter group in such a way that could never entirely be forgotten and yet could not have been generated within the mainstream Pomio Kivung. Thus, the millenarian outburst is rarely a failure in political and religious terms, but provides an enduring regime of cultural transmission rather like initiation—infrequently enacted, and yet sufficiently intense to exert an ongoing influence over group identity and religious experience.

6

The Aftermath

I've heard what has been said at this meeting in pursuit of a reconciliation between Dadul and Sunam. I myself received a letter . . . I
thought it meant that the time had come for their Kivung government to carry them to power. The letter that went to you in Sunam
was similar . . . I have long known that Kivung members believe
that those of us who mix with the Tolai and are outside the Kivung
will be separated from Kivung members when their government
comes to power. So I have waited and watched, but in fact their
government has not arrived. So my complaint is this: why did you
not wait before sending your letters? . . . You could have put them
on one side until your government arrived, and then you could have
sent them or spoken out . . . Nevertheless, you acted prematurely,
before you knew when your goal would be achieved. In fact, only
God knows when.

(Stanis Naden Joanis, Minister for Lands, ENBP Government)

A T the end of October 1988 the people of Dadul (having returned to
their village) were confronted with a series of problems. Perhaps the
primary problem was the inadequacy of the food supply but, in addition,
there appeared to be a serious danger of legal prosecutions over the mass
marriage, the removal of children from school, and the offensive letters.
There was also the threat of violence, humiliation, and ridicule at the hands
of disgruntled communities external to the Dadul–Maranagi splinter group.

The resentment towards the Dadul–Maranagi group which was har-
boured by various external groups tended to be focused on four major
criticisms. The first was that the mass marriage had entailed the coupling
of many under-age partners and that the arrangement of specific betrothals had not been undertaken with the knowledge or consent of appropriate parties.

A useful illustration of this point is provided by the events which
ensued from the marriage of Bapka's daughter to an under-age youth. It
will be recalled that Bapka was the only person in Dadul who refused to
join the Kivung and follow Baninge to Maranagi. Prior to Baninge's

emergence as a divine leader, Bapka had managed to prevent his own brother, wife, and two adolescent children from joining the Kivung. But as the splinter group emerged, Bapka's family increasingly feared exclusion from the fruits of the apparently imminent miracle. Pressure from Dadul's first orator, and from other members of the community, was placed upon Bapka's family to join the Kivung, until they finally agreed (although Bapka himself was still determined to abstain). When the vigils at Maranagi were abandoned and the people of Dadul returned, Bapka learned of his daughter's marriage and was duly enraged. His immediate reaction was to blame the first orator and to threaten him with legal action since this orator had played a prominent role in the persuasion of Bapka's family to join the splinter group.

Bapka chose a public location for his heated verbal attack on the first orator: the centre of the village clearing. The orator in turn defended himself by claiming that he had played no part in the organization of the mass marriage and that Bapka should address his complaints to the leaders (i.e. Baninge and Tanotka). Thus, the orator publicly disassociated himself from events at Maranagi and suggested that he had abandoned his conviction in the righteousness of the leaders' decisions. The first orator was under particular pressure to do this because, if he had been summoned to the community court in Sunam (as Bapka threatened) then he would have been confronted by many enraged relatives living there. Indeed, as a result of his (offensive) letters to Sunam village, he would probably have been in danger of physical assault.

From Bapka's viewpoint, the situation was also rather delicate. On the one hand, the loss of his only daughter in marriage presented him with particular difficulties. Bapka's wife was an invalid and virtually unproductive so that he relied heavily on his daughter's labour. If legal action was the only available method of retaining his daughter, then it would have been a feasible option because the court would probably have upheld his objections to the marriage (explicitly because it occurred in violation of ordinary local custom). On the other hand, such a court case would have been a profoundly political event, constituting an attack on the leaders of the Kivung community (as the first orator had pointed out). Bapka could not be sure that, as in similar court cases brought about because of the refusal of Kivung members to pay government taxes, the political wing of the Pomio Kivung would not intervene on the side of the local Kivung representatives. Therefore, Bapka had arranged with the Mali politician, Stanis (then Minister for Lands in the Provincial Government and a formidable ally), that the two of them would, if necessary, lodge the legal complaint together. All the same, this course of action was far from ideal because Bapka's home was in Dadul and to launch a legal attack construed as being against the Kivung would have strained Bapka's relations with his neighbours and local kinsmen in the long term.

The second criticism in which the resentment of outsiders to the splinter group was focused, was the removal of certain children from school, on Baninge's orders, so they might join in the vigils at Maranagi. Once again, I will not describe all the cases but illustrate the point with a single example.

Sabau was the (adolescent) eldest daughter of the widow Lagi, who had close kinsmen in Sunam (a father and siblings). Sabau lived with these relatives during term time, when she attended the community school near to Sunam. Although Lagi, as a long-term Kivung member in Dadul, did not publicly approve of Sabau living in Sunam, a haunt of Satan, it was understood that Sabau's maternal uncles and grandfather had considerable rights in the girl and her willing attendance at school in Sunam could not easily be prevented. When Baninge sent Lagi to Sunam, in order to collect Sabau and bring her to Dadul in preparation for the migration to Maranagi, Lagi probably felt that she had little choice but to obey. Moreover, she was apparently concerned with her daughter's salvation and had even tried (in vain) to persuade her father to join Baninge's followers.

From Sabau's viewpoint, the incident was ill-timed. This is because she was due to take her final (sixth) grade examination within a few days of her removal from Sunam. The matter might not have seemed quite so important if Sabau had not been a particularly talented pupil and, in the views of her teachers, a suitable candidate for a place at high school. When it was discovered that Sabau had been 'abducted' by the 'cargo cult fanatics' and her academic future ruined, the people at Sunam and the teaching staff at her school were very bitter. Sabau's father was concerned because he had invested significant resources in Sabau over the years (e.g. by paying her school fees and providing her subsistence in Sunam). Sabau's teachers vented their disappointment on Sabau's grandfather in the first instance because he was her guardian and therefore, supposedly, responsible for her sudden disappearance. He claimed that if he was summoned to court over this matter then, in order to protect himself and Lagi (who was 'only obeying the Kivung leaders'), he would rightfully re-direct the prosecution to the Dadul–Maranagi 'cargo cult' (or its representatives). Once again, a political court case was indicated.

There was, however, little to gain for any of the parties in taking the matter to court. Sabau had missed her examination and that was that. The only goal of importance to Sabau's relatives in Sunam and to her teachers was to ensure that she recommence her sixth year, if possible, in the absence of a large-scale political confrontation. Eventually, Sabau's maternal aunt (herself a teacher in New Ireland) took the girl away to complete her primary schooling out of range of the turbulent home environment. But this outcome was achieved at Christmas 1988 and during the intervening months following the vigils at Maranagi, Kivung members were undoubtedly concerned that a court case would ensue from the removal of Sabau from school (or from the abduction of some other child in a similar fashion).

A third criticism, expressing the resentment of outsiders to the Dadul–Maranagi group, focused on the provocative letters. In general, the recipients of these letters (and especially the groups which they represented in various ways) were offended by the prideful and disdainful outlook of the Dadul–Maranagi group. Since the creation of disharmony or conflict between village units was recognized in the community court system to be a violation of law, the Dadul–Maranagi group seemed vulnerable to prosecution on these grounds. In practice, the threat of court action (mooted in Sunam and Arabum) was intended more as a means of deterring further splinter-group activity than as a means of punishing the activities of the recent past.

Finally, the Dadul–Maranagi group was criticized for its explicit opposition to Christianity. This criticism was most vigorously expressed in Arabum and Reigel since these were the two main villages which, together with Dadul and Maranagi, constituted the Catholic parish of the region (Sunam was under the aegis of the United Church, formerly Methodist). The people at Arabum, in particular, were anxious to encourage the deterioration of relations between the Dadul–Maranagi group and the Sacred Heart Mission. When the priest mounted his patrols during and after the period of the vigils, he was informed at Arabum that he would be in personal peril if he attempted to hold the service at Maranagi. He was told that the Kivung group had appointed a new (native) priest of its own and no longer required his services. Although such information was false, the priest was apparently ready to accept it uncritically and part of the reason for this was probably that he had strong personal and religious objections to the Kivung, accentuated by his communications with a vehemently anti-Kivung priest who had been assigned to the region before Dadul's population was converted to (nominal) Catholicism. The current priest did not (or perhaps was not in a position to) take damaging action against the Dadul–Maranagi group, but his intensified alienation from the Kivung helped to sustain a sense of the moral victory of Christian villages over the Kivung group whereas, formerly, many Christians had been afraid that their religious affiliations might prove to have been ill-advised (i.e. if the Kivung miracle finally occurred).

The continuation of vigils and the development of new collective rituals could now only occur within strict constraints (of which a major one, discussed below, was the pressure to re-establish agricultural production). Yet the threat of prosecutions provided an equally serious constraint, because Baninge and Tanotka knew that legal action could only possibly be averted now by the renunciation of their roles as divine leaders. Moreover, if the leaders had run the risk of legal action by, for example, ordering more vigils it was by no means certain that the population would have obeyed them.

Developments in Dadul and Maranagi at this time were also influenced by Pomio Kivung leaders. One of the movement's political representatives (Francis Koimanrea) visited Dadul between 27 and 30 October 1988 at the request of Sunam's leader and the Minister for Lands (Stanis Joanis). During this visit, Francis was said (by reliable sources) to have issued five instructions to the Dadul–Maranagi group.

First, Francis (allegedly) ordered the controversial couplings in the mass marriage to be dissolved and warned that local people outside the Kivung (e.g. Bapka and members of Stanis's hamlet) would keep the youths under observation to ensure that they did not maintain conjugal relations. The sanction for disobedience would be legal action (as threatened by Bapka and Stanis). Secondly, Francis (allegedly) ordered the people of Dadul (those listed as residents on the government census) never again to migrate to Maranagi as a collective unit. If such a migration ever occurred in the future then the migrants would be arrested and imprisoned. But this particular sanction was not seriously entertained by Dadul's leaders, who believed that all people were guaranteed freedom of movement under Papua New Guinea's constitution. Yet the women were impressed by Francis's (alleged) statement that if the men chose to migrate (and therefore run the risk of imprisonment) then they should leave their women and children behind, lest they too were arrested. The fact that the women seemed to support this idea showed that they were unwilling to participate in further vigils at Maranagi. Thirdly, Francis (allegedly) ordered the destruction of the ancestral round-house at Maranagi, maintaining that a police patrol would soon be mounted to check that it had been dismantled (or that a government officer stationed at Arabum would be sent to supervise the demolition). Fourthly, Francis (allegedly) ordered that Baninge and Tanotka renounce their claims to divine authority and the people withdraw their support for these local leaders. Finally, Francis (allegedly) demanded that the idea of a splinter group be abandoned so that Dadul and Maranagi would rejoin the wider Pomio Kivung unit, owing allegiance only to Kolman.

Although a number of these instructions were associated with legal sanctions, Francis also apparently focused on the ideological legitimacy of his orders. He said that the activities of the splinter group had caused an environment of social discord and conflict and that this could only serve to anger God and the Village Government, ultimately postponing the miracle. Moreover, Francis evidently declared that many ideas put forward by the splinter group had not been supported by Kolman. Some of Francis's statements led Dadul's orators and other officials to doubt Baninge's integrity, for it now seemed that he had fabricated a number of Kolman's statements regarding the legitimacy of the Dadul–Maranagi splinter group.

The criticisms and threats which I have described helped to shape the ritual life in Dadul between October 1988 and February 1989. In the first place, they more or less ruled out the repetition or creation of splinter-group activities. Such activities could not be organized without leadership, and Baninge (like other potential instigators) was reluctant to lead anybody for the time being because of the risk of prosecution. Moreover, many people were increasingly anxious to repair their damaged relations with outsiders, whose disdain and ridicule was manifest but who, above all, seemed to pose a physical threat and were therefore studiously avoided. Although these circumstances ruled out splinter-group activities, they did not prohibit the maintenance of mainstream rituals, the performance of which was both feasible and generally desirable.

Basic temple rituals and community meetings, for example, were feasible in the sense that they could occur in the absence of leaders (people could enact these rituals without needing to be directed). The established, habit-forming ritual cycles were easily set in motion. Most people desired the familiar Kivung rituals because their enactment demonstrated to critics that Pomio Kivung doctrines had not been disproven or undermined by the non-occurrence of the miracle, at any rate not in the minds of cult followers.

The dissolution of the controversial marriages and the return of Sabau and other children to school did not meet with any opposition in Dadul.

Baninge's staunchest allies, however, said that their belief in Tanotka's original possession had not been undermined and that, although Satan had obstructed them all, Wutka would eventually find a 'path around the obstacle' and enlighten them as to the 'true' way forward. It was suggested that this would occur much later (possibly years later). In other words, the leaders did not admit defeat but nor did they propose any short-term revival of their sacred task.

Meanwhile, the whole population of Dadul was faced with the inescapable need to re-establish production. Since physical survival depended on the performance of this task, it was in that sense the primary concern of every grown person, taking precedence over issues of ideology and even the threats of prosecution, violence, and external disdain.

The Inadequacy of the Food Supply

The problem of meeting domestic subsistence requirements after the period of the vigils stemmed from the long-term inadequacy of production, the general depletion of domestic finance, and the raids on Dadul's gardens by outsiders. Baninge was under pressure from many quarters in Dadul to prosecute the thieves at Sunam's court and obtain compensation for the crops they had stolen. But Baninge was reluctant to confront the people of Sunam and excused himself on the (moral) grounds that he did not approve of the Community Government legal apparatus. Inevitably, the satisfaction of widespread financial need relied mainly on the sale of cocoa.

On average, the well-established households in Dadul each had between 300 and 400 cocoa trees. This produced a potential average weekly income of about K15 per household. In the past, such potential had rarely been realized by each domestic unit, and a large amount of cocoa was allowed to rot on the trees. But after the period of the vigils cocoa sales were maximized and the income which this generated was spent on subsistence goods (mainly rice and tinned fish) to meet the shortfall in local garden produce.

In addition to the more efficient cocoa harvests, considerable labour power was invested in the clearing and planting of food gardens. The pressure to produce was now mounted on a collective basis. The organizational framework for collective task forces was provided by mainstream Kivung institutions in that it fell to the orators in the twice-weekly community meetings to appoint the times and locations for collective clearing and planting projects to assist targeted households. The allocation of assistance to specific households was explicitly based upon need but since need was fairly evenly distributed, households received (more or less) equal benefit from the arrangement. This ensured the willing participation of the community as a whole. Needless to say, collective task groups brought a large amount of land under cultivation.

Not only production but also distribution was organized on a collective basis at this time. Until about February 1989 domestic units did not begin to reap the harvests of intensified production. This is why it was so essential for subsistence needs to be subsidized by the sale of cocoa. But Dadul's households did not have cocoa blocks of equal size. At the extremes were one mature household with only 50 bearing trees and another (Baninge's) with about 700 bearing trees. The former household could not meet its subsistence requirements independently while the latter produced harvests in excess of its immediate subsistence needs. Therefore, the orators organized a programme for the redistribution of wealth over a period of months, and this arrangement succeeded because it accorded prestige to people like Baninge (in the altruistic role of provider or 'father') while being an explicitly temporary violation of domestic autonomy (i.e. an emergency measure).

Confrontation

Attempts on the part of the people of Dadul to avoid contact with the inhabitants of surrounding villages could not be sustained indefinitely. Between October 1988 and February 1989 avoidance posed absurd difficulties. Sick people from Dadul requiring care at the government health centre near Sunam would be continuously on the alert and would make elaborate attempts to hide themselves if Sunam relatives approached. Usually, Dadul's sick used the aid post at Arabum which exposed them to some ridicule (and poorer medical treatment) but was the lesser of two evils. Without a doubt, it was direct contact with the people of Sunam which was most profoundly feared in Dadul. This was because the people of Sunam were the only close relatives of the Dadul population who were outside the Kivung, and this kinship connection provided Sunam's adult population with a justification to castigate and even to assault the members of Dadul. Moreover, the Sunam villagers had greater cause for offence than any other group, principally because the provocative letters which they had received were the most outrageous.

Nevertheless, a couple of truces did occur during the cold war between Dadul and Sunam. First, as early as November 1988, Lagi (as I have explained) was obliged to visit her father in Sunam in order to avert a legal battle over the removal of her daughter (Sabau) from school. Lagi was subjected to severe humiliation in Sunam as her kinsmen screamed abuse at her, lectured her, and reduced her to protracted weeping. But this rigmarole having been performed, Lagi's kinsmen gave her food and the psychological wounds were healed. In addition, one of the youths from the Dadul–Maranagi group whose marriage had been dissolved was sent to Sunam as a messenger of goodwill, to assist with preparations for an Uramot fire dance (see Chapter 1) to celebrate Christmas. This demonstrated the wish to reinstitute normal co-operative relations between the villages. By mid-January 1989 tempers in Sunam had cooled considerably. Threats of violence had given way to a set of Kivung jokes until finally even these lost their appeal for the adults and the theme was mainly breached in the teasing of wayward children (e.g. with the threat that they would be 'sent to Maranagi' if they did not mend their ways). The elders in Sunam took the unanimous view that good relations with Dadul must be reinstituted as soon as possible. They agreed that they would not be too severe with the people of Dadul when they finally confronted them (for fear that they would excite such profound shame that the Dadul villagers would never be able to face them again). But the ball was in the Dadul court. When the people of Dadul showed that they were ready for a confrontation, the Sunam villagers would agree to meet them.

By the end of January 1989 Baninge gave in to the pressure to prosecute the thieves who had raided Dadul's gardens. Nobody else in Dadul possessed the oratory skills and personal confidence to represent the grievances of the whole community. At the same time, Baninge considered that it was now relatively safe to set foot in Sunam. Moreover, it was obvious that this display of willingness to use the non-Kivung legal apparatus voluntarily was itself a conciliatory move, and would be appreciated as such by the people of Sunam.

Baninge and Tanotka jointly set up the court case at Sunam and in the course of their visit they held a brief discussion with the representative of Sunam. The latter asked them why they had sent the provocative letters and Baninge replied that they were both innocent of involvement in this matter and that the letters were written and sent by the first orator without their knowledge (or anybody else's). In other words, Baninge argued that the letters were not a political issue (concerning Dadul–Sunam relations) but a kinship matter (between the first orator and his Sunam relatives). Nevertheless, it was agreed that a meeting in Dadul should be held on Sunday, 5 February 1989 so that the people of both villages could confront each other and resolve the issue at last.

It was also agreed that, prior to the Sunday meeting (on Thursday, 2 February), there would be discussion of a pressing land issue in Dadul. It was implicit that this would present an opportunity for the people of Dadul and Sunam to gather together to discuss an issue on which their interests converged (as members of the inland Mali land-owning group). It would therefore enable the people of Dadul and Sunam to mingle, and the former to overcome their embarrassment in relation to the latter.

The village of Dadul and the bush which surrounded it was located on Uramot customary land. Before the Second World War, however, this land was passed over to the inland Mali in perpetuity (see Chapter 1). In recent years, the Uramot community at Riet had suffered severe land shortage. This had less to do with population growth than with the increasing alienation of Uramot land to foreign settlers. The pressure on land in Riet had led the younger men there to urge a re-evaluation of the pre-war contract with the inland Mali. They argued that, because of Kivung 'cargo cult' beliefs, the land around Dadul was absurdly under-exploited and that these areas of virgin forest should be made available to the original land owners. The more radical Riet villagers even wanted the right to buy out the land under cultivation in Dadul to pay compensation for the bush houses in the village clearing, and to drive out Dadul's population altogether (i.e. back onto Mali customary land).

The meeting in Dadul on Thursday, 2 February was attended by the representatives of Riet who stood (in an important sense) against the united villages of Dadul and Sunam who refused to forego their rights as set out in the original pre-war agreement. The Riet elders guaranteed security of tenure to the Mali, but there was a general feeling that when these elders died the new representatives of Riet might be less concili-atory. Moreover, there was a contemporary dispute over the precise loca-tion of the boundary between Dadul's land and the Uramot land available to the Riet villagers. A relevant factor was that the people from Sunam as well as Dadul had crops in the region of the boundary and had recently been involved in a controversial land sale (to Tolai buyers) involving some of these crops. Part of the dilemma was establishing to whom (and in what proportion) the money from this sale legitimately accrued. In this regard, the Dadul and Sunam parties in the dispute might have seemed, on the face of it, to be a unity.

If, however, the meeting served a useful purpose in relaxing the tension between the people of Dadul and Sunam, it did not straightforwardly unite them over the land issue. One reason for this was that the Sunam family involved in the boundary land sale issued from a mixed (Mali– Uramot) marriage, and although the family claimed land rights matrilineally (through the Mali mother), as was proper, the Uramot father (deceased) had a living brother in Riet who claimed to be the classificatory 'father' of the Sunam family. Therefore, it was far from clear where the interests of the Sunam people lay in the whole controversy. There was a strong undercurrent of feeling in Dadul that the Sunam villagers as a whole could no longer regard themselves as Mali since they had turned their backs on ancestral ways and become honorary Tolai. Therefore, it was surreptitiously mooted that if ever the Sunam villagers lost their right to reside in Sunam (which was possible, in view of their debts to the Agricultural Bank who could appropriate land titles as collateral for the original loans) they would not be permitted (by the Dadul–Maranagi group) to settle on Mali customary land. In spite of these tensions in the background, though, the atmosphere had been relatively relaxed in readiness for the Sunday meeting.

Before proceeding further, it is necessary to give an account of the two offensive letters which had contributed so much to the rift between Dadul and Sunam. The first letter was very short, and stated simply that the author (Dadul's first orator) renounced his bonds of kinship with the people of Sunam. The letter was accompanied by a pile of clothes which the author had received as gifts, over the years, from his various relatives in Sunam. The intentions behind this act were quite complex, but the general implication was that the first orator rejected his kinship ties in Sunam which, in any case, inhered in shallow material reciprocity (represented by the clothes) as against the spiritual kinship which characterized the relations with ancestors in Dadul.

The second letter was much longer. It was addressed to the leader of Sunam and signed in name by Dadul's first orator. It read as follows (translated from Pidgin):

Greetings. I alone communicate with you because I have something to tell you briefly. 1. I express my joy and thanks to you and all your people and send my pity to all of you in Sunam. I thank you for your criticisms of, and insults to, us and all the other statements you have made about us. [This was a reference to Sunam's ideological opposition to Kivung beliefs.] 2. I express my joy in relation to the time in the past when you and ToBana [a Tolai political and Christian leader] prosecuted me and my people, and I thank you sincerely for this. [This was a reference to a meeting, rather than a legal prosecution, which had taken place some years before in Sunam's court house, at which pressure was placed on the people of Dadul to pay their community government taxes.] 3. Now I will speak thus: who among you recognizes God's pity? For what purpose did Jesus Christ die? What follows from His death? What is the point of Christmas? What is the point of Easter? [These questions were intended to suggest that Kivung members alone knew the true meaning of Christian ideas and that the highlights of the Christian ritual calendar, which were scarcely acknowledged in the Kivung, were celebrated to disguise religious truths rather than to illuminate them.] 4. My final statement to you all is this: I pity you and my pity is like the great Warangoi River which flows even in the dry season. And so I tell you again that the pity in God's eyes is infinite. [An ironic statement, since the author believed that God's pity would soon be exhausted.] We all know that this is a Christian country, not a land of violence and larceny and anger. [This was explicit saracasm.] But you should all consider this statement: you must eat your fill, seek inebriation, wander as you please, and seek commercial success to your heart's desire. That is all. 5. My harsh words are directed at all of you, all the leaders, adults, and children, to all of you along with your intimate friends [sarcastic] such as the magistrates and councillors of the community government for whose unstinting support [sarcastic] I offer thanks. I express my joy to you for your patient ears and your concern with my views. [These sarcastic statements were singled out in Sunam as grounds for prosecution since the author was effectively accusing the government of unconstitutional behaviour in the form of discrimination against a group of its constituents.] I am particularly sorry for you [Sunam's representative] and pity your decision to leave the Kivung [during the climactic period of the late 1970s]. I offer sincere thanks to you and all the people who left the Kivung [and went to Sunam] with you. I am joyful and thankful. When exactly do you think the pity of Jesus Christ will be exhausted? Sit and think about this. Do not fight. All the same, stealing and anger are rife. Which church do you think will bring about the last Easter celebrations, and call a halt to the life we have all known on earth? Do you imagine that the Catholics or the United Church or the Seventh-day Adventists or some other Church will produce the Second Coming? [The implication was that only the Kivung can bring about a miracle.] That is all. I suggest you read carefully my last statements and my final display of pity. Thank you.

The meeting in Dadul on Sunday, 5 February was opened by a statement from the leader of Sunam who said that relations between Dadul and Sunam had been severed for a number of months and the aim of the meeting was to reunite the two villages. Another Sunam elder asked if the people of the two villages were kinsmen or enemies. After repetitions of this question in various ways from the people of Sunam, Dadul's first orator announced that his letters had not reflected the views of the people of Dadul but had come from him alone, without any other person's approval or support. Presently, the orator's wife (who had many close kinsmen in Sunam) publicly castigated him for having taken this unilateral action, which had undermined the relations of two whole villages. Her husband responded apologetically but with some humour (revealing that there was an element of play-acting in his expression of contrition). Presently, the second of the two letters was produced and its contents discussed section by section. The orator gave outlandish (and often humorous) explanations for many of his broader statements relating to the morals of the Sunam villagers. He made it plain that he did not wish to stand by his statements. Where explicit retractions were essential, the orator was quick to apologize and accept the (token) reprimands of fellow Kivung members, such as Baninge and Tanotka.

The meeting remained superficially light-hearted until the first orator began (obliquely) to defend what he saw as the overall intention of his letter which was to draw attention to the low morals of the Sunam villagers. This excited some fairly heated exchanges about the relative merits of Christianity and the Pomio Kivung. Finally, the leader of Sunam said that this whole argument proved that the orator's letters reflected the views of all the people in Dadul. The latter cried out in unison that they had known nothing of the letters until after they were sent. The first orator added that he should never have written the letters and that if he had merely made his points face to face, the rift would not have occurred. This enabled the Sunam leader to point out that his people had themselves been too virtuous to write a reply and had decided on the righteous course which was to come to Dadul on this day and resolve the matter face to face. The unanimous conclusion was that both communities would henceforth strive for the harmonious and co-operative relations which they had enjoyed in the past.

It is interesting to note that both sides had met with the intention of producing a certain kind of reconciliation, yet the people of Sunam had required a moral victory. The kind of reconciliation which was sought, was one based upon superficial rather than genuine amity. After the Sunam people went home, the Kivung members declared that they would maintain bodily kinship with non-Kivung relatives, through small material exchanges and visits, but would not acknowledge spiritual kinship (i.e. the sort expressed in offerings to the ancestors). In the latter sense, the people of Sunam were declared to be outside the Mali ethnic group. Meanwhile, back in Sunam, it was acknowledged that the rift with Dadul had only been papered over rather than genuinely resolved, but this did not matter because (for many years) that had been the normal state of affairs. In pursuit of this superficial reconciliation, the people of Sunam had been obliged to temper their desire for a moral victory. Sunam's representative later explained to me that he had been careful not to be too relentless in his questions about the contents of the letters, lest the people of Dadul give up the pretence of contrition and widen the rift. Yet the complaints of the Sunam group had to be met with a display of sorrow, otherwise the Sunam people might have stormed away in anger. The net result was that the people of Dadul were humiliated up to a point, but no further.

The Death of Ribari

On 1 March 1989 Ribari died at Maranagi. Ribari was an old man who normally lived in Dadul. It was he who had given his permission for the slaughter of his enormous pig prior to the migration to Maranagi. Ribari's kinsmen in Sunam (and particularly his son) had acknowledged rights in the disposal of the pig, and its consumption at Maranagi overlooked these rights. News of Ribari's death reached Sunam almost at once, and was greeted with considerable resentment. Ribari's kinsmen in Sunam asserted that if they had been informed of the deterioration in Ribari's condition some days before his death, they could have gone to Maranagi, carried him down the mountain on a stretcher, and delivered him to the government health centre at Sunam to recover. They argued that if Ribari had not been at Maranagi in the first place, but had returned to his home in Dadul, then they could have cared for him during his illness (as they had done in the past). Indeed, for some years they had been trying to persuade Ribari to give up the Kivung and come to live in Sunam where they had proper medical facilities (including access to powerful Tolai medicine men). Therefore, Ribari died because he had been isolated in Maranagi. He had gone to Maranagi because of the climactic events in the Kivung but, most importantly, he had remained there (arguably) because he was ashamed to confront his Sunam kinsmen following his wrongful disposal of the pig. This was the last and crucial step in the reasoning which prevailed in Sunam. It meant that Ribari died because of the Kivung.

Ribari's kinsmen in Sunam were convinced that he had refused to return to his home in Dadul because of his shame regarding the pig episode. It was asserted that this had not really been Ribari's fault because, whilst Ribari knew that his children and grandchildren in Sunam had rights in the pig, he had been deceived into believing that the Period of the Companies would soon shower him with wealth, the better to endow his descendants in Sunam. The crucial point is that Ribari's death provided his kinsmen in Sunam with a powerful argument for their moral superiority over the Kivung members in Dadul: the former displayed Christian virtues such as forgiveness (of Ribari, the pig killer) and charity (for Ribari, the aged invalid) whereas the Dadul–Maranagi group displayed Satanic wickedness in deceiving Ribari (the vulnerable dupe) and causing his death. Under other circumstances, Ribari's death would not have been politically significant. As it was, the people of Sunam exploited the situation to the full.

In the first place, Ribari's relatives in Sunam registered their bitterness by refusing to attend the funeral. Secondly, Ribari's stronger male kinsmen went as a mob to Dadul and publicly felled his coconut and betel palms and took their fruits so that the Kivung members could not accrue benefit from them (in the case of betel, only by its sale). They left the evidence of this act of aggression strewn across the path through Dadul. But their primary *coup* was the need for yet another meeting at which to settle the matter, and demonstrate the moral superiority of the people of Sunam (once again the injured party).

The Cash-Cropping Drive

The problems confronting the people of Dadul in March 1989 were rather different from those which had prevailed towards the end of 1988. At that time food shortages and legal threats had preoccupied the population, with the approach to problems in the group's external relations being essentially evasive in character. By March 1989, however, gardens were bearing fruit once more and material survival was no longer endangered. Moreover, the threat of legal action over the September and October events of 1988 had been averted, and the approach to external criticism had shifted to one of (relatively) innocuous confrontation. What remained was an undercurrent of frustration, especially in Dadul, over the fact that their neighbours in Sunam, Arabum, and Reigel appeared to have won a substantial moral victory over them, and over the Pomio Kivung movement generally.

Many of those who had participated enthusiastically in the splinter group experienced no discernible disillusionment with regard to basic Kivung ideas. For them, the non-occurrence of the miracle was convincingly explained as the result of a temporary victory of evil over good. The forces of evil were said to operate at an incorporeal level, in the obstruction of Wutka and other ancestors who sought to break the fence dividing the living and the dead, but Satan was also believed to exert his will over earthly agents, including the state and mission whose representatives criticized, opposed, and effectively prevented the proper completion of splinter group rituals. Far from undermining commitment to Kivung ideology, the climactic rituals at Maranagi had rejuvenated that commitment in important ways (as I argued in the last chapter). The most frustrating and disappointing result of splinter-group activities was not the invalidation of Kivung ideology but a recognition among the people of Dadul and Maranagi that they had become objects of disdain, ridicule, and derision in the outside world. An important aim of the splinter group had been to achieve exactly the opposite effect—namely to demonstrate the foolishness of siding with the state and missions, and to cultivate a deep regret among opponents that they had not joined or remained within the Pomio Kivung. These aspirations were explicitly communicated in the provocative letters of the splinter group, and the loss of face ensuing from the non-occurrence (or postponement) of the miracle presented an acute psychological burden.

One of the arguments put forward by opponents of the Kivung with particular vigour was that cash cropping, rather than ritual, provided the only reliable method of producing economic development. This was expressed in the dictum: 'something does not arise from nothing' (*samting i no kamap nating*). Yet the people of Dadul noted the hypocrisy of those who espoused this argument. The very people in Sunam who advocated commitment to cocoa production persistently underproduced and, according to the people of Dadul, habitually squandered their money on sensual pleasures (particularly alcohol). Meanwhile, it was said that the people of Riet, who wanted to reclaim the land on which Dadul was situated, were likewise subsistence-oriented and in reality wanted additional land in order to sell (or to recompense other land sales). In the eyes of the people of Dadul, this behaviour was motivated by the desire for alcohol and was ironically an attempt to obtain something (e.g. vodka) from nothing (i.e. unworked land). It was thus mooted in Dadul that if they could beat the villages of Sunam and Riet at their own game, through the implementation of a successful cash-cropping drive, then the basis for self-congratulation in such villages would be removed and the loss of face experienced by splinter-group members would be effectively counteracted.

The idea of starting a cash-cropping drive in Dadul was thus proposed as a cynical ploy to undermine the arguments of Kivung opponents, much as the conversion to Catholicism a few years earlier had been. It was argued that the cash-cropping drive in Dadul should be organized and financed at the community level, and directed towards the collective investment of profits (to finance a fermentary in Dadul) and the co-ordinated expansion of cocoa production. The orators in Dadul con-trasted this scenario with the selfish hedonism of Sunam and Riet critics who (allegedly) raised cash crops through the independent and self-interested action of households (and particularly the heavy drinkers within them). The idea of a cash-cropping drive was in no way intended to vindicate external criticisms but, rather, to turn them back on themselves. The people of Dadul would still be Kivung members, but their claims to moral superiority would no longer be refutable on the grounds that Kivung members seek to obtain something from nothing.

There was another respect in which the proposed cash-cropping drive constituted a defensive tactic in a climate of external criticism. This drive was intended to promote the exploitation of land which many Riet villa-gers wanted to reclaim. By replacing virgin forest with cocoa trees, the people of Dadul hoped to prevent the appropriation or sale of this land by outsiders and also to make the aim of buying out the Dadul community financially impossible. This was seen as a defensive move in relation to Sunam critics as well, who said that the people of Dadul had practically invited conflict with the Uramot land owners through being too lazy to exploit the resources which accrued to Dadul in the pre-war agreement.

By May 1989 the cash-cropping drive was substantially underway. It took the form of a 'cash-cropping association', of which Baninge became established as 'president'. The two men who had been (and still were) assistants to Baninge in various ritual contexts in the Kivung were selected as the 'vice-president' and 'treasurer' respectively, and Dadul's first orator was selected as the 'secretary'. A special office was constructed for the activities of these officials. The mechanism for the organization of collective work parties was rooted in Kivung institutions (the key roles accruing to the three orators in the twice-weekly meetings). It is interest-ing to note that a large portion of the capital used for the purchase and transportation of hybrid cocoa plants was raised through the sale of a piece of land on the contested Riet-Dadul boundary, in contravention of the agreement reached at the February meeting which forbade any fur-ther land sales until the boundary had been officially fixed. This sale had only been possible because the cash-cropping drive was now organized and undertaken at the level of the community and the land sale was consequently unopposed by Dadul's elders and Kivung officials.

The Aftermath and Religious Experience

The dramatic events I have described in these last three chapters form part of a broader historical pattern in the Pomio Kivung. Most communities which are under the umbrella of the movement have, at one time or another (often a number of times), radically modified or replaced conventional, mainstream ritual in order to engage in climactic activities intended to herald the returning ancestors. Tovalele (1977: 127) records eight outbursts of such activity among the Maenge between 1964 and 1972. The frequency with which they occur among the Mali Baining appears to be lower. I collected accounts of a period, around 1977, when Dadul attracted a large number of visitors (including people from Sunam), who had heard that the ancestors were at last to return. The greatly expanded community at Dadul fervently prepared for three days of darkness, and conducted mass baptisms and all-night vigils. When the eschaton failed to occur, the non-residents of Dadul became discontented and were in turn blamed by the original community for obstructing the miracle through degeneracy and scepticism. In the face of growing external criticism, however, the vigils were abandoned and an attempt was made by the Dadul community to rebut accusations that they hoped to obtain money for nothing (i.e. cargo for ritual) by means of a drive to produce cash crops. The evidence of this drive is still around in Dadul in the form of a large number of polyclonal cocoa trees. Other outbursts of climactic millenarian activity were reported in the mid-1970s and early 1980s (oral testimony, in Sunam), suggesting that these activities occur roughly every five years on the average.

Although the disruption of the 1988 splinter group was rapidly repaired, and the basic patterns of social life in Dadul were restored more or less as if the episode had never occurred, the vigils had inevitably affected people's attitudes in profound and enduring ways. During the first half of 1989, it was very apparent that many people in Dadul felt an intense resentment towards the outside world. Whenever there was any mention of people, groups, or agencies external to the Pomio Kivung, whether at meetings or in informal conversations, the people of Dadul expressed extreme contempt, especially through the use of sarcasm and disdainful facial expressions. Negative attitudes towards outsiders had been apparent before the splinter group became established, but they were expressed less frequently, with less intensity, and by fewer people. Following the immediate aftermath of the vigils, however, racial hatred (directed especially towards Tolai, Highlands, and Sepik groups) was

expressed widely and continually in Dadul. This bitterness towards outsiders was by no means confined to opponents of the splinter group but
seemed to encompass anybody who was not a Kivung member. Moreover, even certain groups within the Pomio Kivung came in for criticism,
in so far as the extent of their commitment to the movement was questioned. The only community with whom the people of Dadul expressed
unconditional solidarity was Maranagi. Thus, one effect of splinter-group
rituals had been to create an intense bond between Dadul and Maranagi
which, given the impressive and memorable nature of the metaphor of
the ring, provided a potentially enduring basis for political identity. The
special closeness of Dadul and Maranagi had long been recognized in
terms of historical and genealogical connections, but the splinter-group
rituals had transformed this link into a much more prominent and
emotive issue.

In Dadul and Maranagi people's attitudes towards mainstream Kivung
institutions had also been changed. The images and feelings evoked by
repetitive mainstream rituals had a different character. They were not
merely thought about in terms of the logical strings of ideas reiterated in
community meetings, but in terms of their connotations with the climactic and, at times, traumatic revelations of the splinter group. For example, basic ideas about ancestors, salvation, and evil now had a more
emotive character, being associated respectively with disembodied ancestral voices (in reports), the mysterious metaphors of the ring and the post
(e.g. in ring ceremonies and vigils), and the dramatic struggle with Satan
(e.g. in the violent exorcism of Lagawop). Obviously, each person's memories would be unique, and the connotations evoked by orthodox rituals
would vary, but everyone who had participated in the splinter group was
bound to be haunted by the images, feelings, and sensations of the climactic period, set to reverberate for years to come with the doctrines and
rituals of the mainstream movement. That these are the enduring effects
of Melanesian cult outbursts, rather than disillusionment or cynicism, is
supported by the fact that climactic millenarian rituals have a tendency to
re-emerge every few years in Dadul, and follow similar patterns of intermittent recurrence in other regions (e.g. Gesch 1990, Lawrence 1971). It
is partly because these religious experiences are stimulating, moving, and
compelling that people are willing to repeat them, and the humdrum
routines of social life are periodically superseded.

7

Religious Persuasion

FOR the Mali Baining, the attractiveness of the Pomio Kivung movement during the early 1970s had to do with the fact that its ideas were intellectually persuasive. On the one hand, they provided comprehensive and logically integrated answers to pressing questions and, on the other, they were rooted in various indigenous cultural assumptions. In these respects, the Pomio Kivung had the edge over competing ideological systems—for example Christianity, which did not address or sufficiently clarify issues of paramount interest, and which was (often inexplicably) intolerant of indigenous religious practices.

One of the ways in which traditional assumptions were exploited in the Pomio Kivung was through Koriam's apotheosis, which, as I show in this chapter, was to some extent prefigured in indigenous cosmology. Koriam's assumption of absolute authority in religious matters enabled him to insist upon an extensive body of incontrovertible dogma, transmitted in public speeches, his own and those of trusted leaders empowered to relay his pronouncements. Since the central ideas of the Pomio Kivung were codified in language, Koriam and his standard-bearers, supervisors, and orators, were able to transport the movement far and wide through direct proselytization. The uniformity and continuity of such an elaborate ideology as that of the Pomio Kivung necessitated a regime of frequent transmission. In the absence of widespread literacy, continual sermonizing was the only way of ensuring that supporters maintained a comprehensive understanding of authoritative doctrines. The resulting system of orthodox orations and rituals was highly routinized, and this meant that innovation was readily detected and penalized. But although the Pomio Kivung proved capable of reproducing fixed ideology and structures of authority, it provided a rather dull and repetitive experience of religion. Thus, routinized activity was not sufficient in itself to generate intense and emotional support indefinitely. This aspect of Kivung religion is typically cultivated in periodic outbursts of climactic ritual, when the millennium is thought to be imminent. Although such outbursts in any given community only occasionally and temporarily interrupt the repetitive performance of conventional Kivung rituals, people's memories of climactic periods enrich and deepen their experience of orthodox practices and, in the long run, help to sustain commitment to the mainstream Pomio Kivung movement.

This penultimate chapter explores in more detail the various cultural assumptions which lend plausibility to Pomio Kivung ideology, and the engagement of thoughts and feelings in the course of transmission that transform plausibility into persuasiveness. Nevertheless, the Pomio Kivung does not enjoy universal support within its catchment area. While most people concede that the Pomio Kivung has the capacity to bring back the dead, levels of interest in the goals of the movement, and evaluations of the sacrifices which membership entails, are subject to variation. Thus, not all Mali Baining people support the Pomio Kivung (or support it to the same degree) and some actively oppose it. I therefore examine the main variables affecting degrees of support or opposition.

The Pursuit of Wisdom

In the course of my fieldwork in Dadul, I conducted extended interviews with all the adults who had reached maturity prior to the spread of the Pomio Kivung, in which I tried continually to draw out their former attitudes to the Tolai and to the Australian colonists, and their motives for joining Koriam's movement. My initial discussions of this topic with senior members of the community produced unexpected results. In the first place, my informants denied that their attitudes towards the colonial authorities had been hostile, or that they had entertained hopes of driving them away. On the contrary, people said that they had envisaged the Australians as a potential source of many desirable things (moral and spiritual, as well as material) and, if anything, were fearful that the Australians might suddenly depart. In the second place, former attitudes towards the Tolai were described as having been suspicious but not decidedly negative. The reason for my initial surprise was that I had expected these interviews to confirm my assumption that, because the Pomio Kivung promised political autonomy for the Pomio–Baining peoples and damnation for Western missionaries and for the Tolai generally, that the popularity of the movement derived from pre-existing hatred towards external, dominating powers. Such an assumption informed Worsley's interpretation of Melanesian cults, which he claimed were:

the product of the ambivalent attitudes and feelings of men torn between hatred of the White people who had destroyed the old way of life and who now dominated them by force, and the desire to obtain for themselves the possessions of these very Whites.[1]

These biases sometimes heavily coloured my line of questioning, as the following extract from a conversation with one of the orators in Dadul illustrates:

WHITEHOUSE. I have read that some *kiap* [colonial patrol officers] caused problems. Were you fearful at that time to say outright what you thought of them? Were you afraid that they would send you to prison?

ORATOR. Each village had a *luluai* [an appointed indigenous leader] and they were really the ones in charge. The patrol officers only helped to make sure that we behaved morally. And there were the police too—they were better than the police of today.

WHITEHOUSE. But what did you think about the fact that these whites were in a dominant position? Did you feel angry and wish that you could find a way to drive them off your land? Or did you consider that they had a right to boss you around because you were vulnerable and had little power over the situation?

ORATOR. We never saw it like that. It was only when the Pomio Kivung arrived that we began to see things differently.

This line of questioning proved in all my interviews to contribute little to an understanding of people's motives for joining the Pomio Kivung (or, more precisely, their contemporary memories of their reasons for joining). The way that interviewees voluntarily represented their motives was nevertheless strongly patterned. Most informants said that they had originally joined the movement because they had been persuaded by Koriam's moral arguments, extending principles that they already believed to be plausible and integrating them into a more comprehensive and persuasive ideology. Moreover, it was frequently said that a strong attraction of the movement was that it answered questions about new developments which had previously been profoundly mystifying. For example, people often mentioned the fact that the Pomio Kivung silenced speculation about the implications of Tolai incursion. In the late 1960s Tolai settlers at Sunam (from whom most of those at Dadul had fled: see Chapter 1) visited Dadul from time to time to make friends with the villagers. The people of Dadul were uncertain as to whether they should welcome or repudiate these overtures, but were aware that the relatives they had left behind in Sunam were beginning to regard close association with the Tolai as a prerequisite of future development and prosperity.

The Pomio Kivung greatly clarified this situation for its supporters by advocating avoidance of interactions with the Tolai whose aim was to use their friendship with the Baining to gain access to their land, and to spread various morally contaminating ideas.[2]

Among the many issues raised and answered in the Pomio Kivung was the matter of national independence. Before the movement spread to the Mali Baining, there was widespread and growing concern about the anticipated departure of the whiteman. There was considerable uncertainty about the implications of independence, and it was no doubt feared by some as a kind of negative, apocalyptic event (see Chapter 1). The Pomio Kivung gave credence to such pessimism, in asserting that the removal of colonial institutions would leave the Baining peoples vulnerable to naked domination by the Tolai, who would no longer be constrained by the lawcourts from using physical coercion and sorcery to seize Baining land and drive the present inhabitants into extinction. But the Pomio Kivung simultaneously offered protection from the very threat which it identified, by providing powerful political leadership capable of defending Pomio-Baining interests in the new order, until such time as the miracle of returning ancestors rendered such precautions unnecessary.

At the same time as developing a new and attractive vision of political authority, dignity, and wealth for the Pomio-Baining peoples, the Pomio Kivung provided an explanation for the present lack of these things, encompassing problems which the Mali Baining were already posing but were unable to answer. Lindstrom (1990) argues that such motives should figure more highly in anthropological interpretations of Melanesian cargo cults. As he puts it: 'the major concern of some movements is the achievement of wisdom in general . . . rather than some plane load of material goods' (1990: 251). Lindstrom therefore highlights the fact that leaders of the John Frum Movement on Tanna claimed to have specialist knowledge in fields as diverse as geography, telecommunications technology, and linguistics. Koriam likewise laid claim to expertise in Western fields of influence, such as state politics and administration, and Christianity. He was able to understand and assess the relative merits of these impressively complex fields of knowledge, and to devise a programme for dealing with such agencies in a way which served the interests of his followers. The 'proofs' of Koriam's superior discernment lay not merely in the attribution of divine authority but in the logical force of his arguments and the soundness of the assumptions from which they proceeded. I have attempted to convey a sense of this in my summary of the institutions and doctrines of the Pomio Kivung, which show a high degree of logical integration. Koriam siezed upon some of the most credible elements of traditional religion and of Christianity, and advocated rejection of the rest. He proscribed certain ideas and practices, not on mysterious or arbitrary grounds (as the missions and Administration had appeared to do), but because they directly conflicted with his Laws and cosmological visions. Thus, the confusing complexity of Christian doctrine was pared down to its valid essentials, and the remainder was condemned as mystification. Correct attitudes towards the diverse opportunities afforded by colonial arrangements were likewise spelled out; Koriam offered clear and practical policies in relation to participation in cash cropping, Western education, health care, and government, and he gave reasons for his policies which followed logically from the basic tenets of the movement.

Pomio Kivung members still continue to stress the role of their ideology in clarifying and answering the complex issues ensuing from colonization. Prevalent metaphors used to describe the former experience of confusion are a 'maze of paths' and a 'mass of branches'. Koriam showed people the 'correct path' and 'cut away obscuring branches' to reveal the 'straight trunk' of the tree (the same metaphor as applied to Tanotka's role in the splinter group). Having made the decision to join the Pomio Kivung, supporters described a sense of enlightenment but, above all, a feeling of relief at having regained the clarity of thought which preceeded colonization, the self-esteem and confidence which comes with comprehension of one's environment, and a clear programme for dealing with it. These benefits were emphasized continually by Pomio Kivung supporters during my fieldwork, both when attempting to explain to me the value of their activities and when reflecting among themselves on the tragic existence of non-members, whom they frequently described as 'lost' or 'confused'.

Old Religions, New Religions

Another critical factor in the persuasiveness of the Pomio Kivung package was that it was firmly rooted in indigenous cosmology, restoring confidence and pride in local *kastam* and exploiting some of the most compelling and plausible assumptions of traditional religion. Prior to the arrival of the Pomio Kivung, two of the most absorbing questions being posed by the Mali Baining were: where did the wealth and technology of the whiteman come from, and how could indigenous peoples gain access to it? Many of my informants recalled a mixture of intense interest and confusion in relation to these questions. The Mali Baining had encountered a number of competing answers but none of them was regarded as authoritative. Stories concerning the origins of Western cargo often took the form of rumours, perceived as emanating from distant prophets, but since nobody had actually seen the source of authority in these cases the ideas remained speculative. What lent credence to such rumours, and encouraged them to circulate, was that they were consistent with at least one irrefutable assumption: that Western cargo had a transcendental source. What was lacking was an authoritative account of the nature of this source and of the means of tapping it.

Since the Mali Baining had no uniquely plausible explanation for the possessions of the whiteman, a variety of tentative hypotheses ebbed and flowed. Meanwhile, people experienced feelings of covetousness in varying degrees; some developed a longing for certain Western goods and entertained fantasies of stealing them, occasionally seizing an opportunity to do so. From time to time, an exceptionally promising theory would be expounded by one prophet or another, but the authority of exponents would subsequently be undermined, and consequently the plausibility of his vision would evaporate. The hopes of some Mali Baining individuals were most strongly aroused by the so-called 'Melki Movement' of the late 1960s and early 1970s, affecting mainly Uramot Baining villages. The movement was centred in Gaulim, under the leadership of Melki Tomot, although it spread as far as the Uramot village of Riet, a mere half-hour's walk from Dadul. Some people from the latter village became involved in the Melki Movement for a time, well before the Pomio Kivung spread to their area.

In some ways, Melki's ideas foreshadowed Koriam's as far as the Mali Baining were concerned (although the direction of any influence would probably have been from Koriam to Melki). A common element of both movements was the anticipation of returning ancestors who would transmit vast amounts of knowledge to cult followers by a kind of telepathy. Similarities also existed in attitudes towards the missions. Melki was famous for his reinterpretations of the Minister's sermons in Gaulim every Sunday, which he conveyed to large gatherings after the service in church. Like the Maenge cultists, and many others in Papua and New Guinea before them, Melki maintained that the missionaries were willing to transmit only part of the message necessary for the acquisition of cargo. Moreover, like Koriam, Melki advocated a form of worship as the means of producing the desired miracle. The Pomio Kivung, as I have explained, drew heavily on a combination of indigenous ideas about reciprocity and solidarity with the ancestors, and ideas spread by the mission, construed as originating in the revelations of Koriam. Melki was more willing to attribute the sources of his inspiration to Western influence, and advocated the extensive use of Christian prayer, the wearing of European clothes, and the 'worship' of Queen Elizabeth II (Dargie 1969).

Some of the things which made Pomio Kivung ideology persuasive when it finally spread to the Mali Baining were the same sorts of things that lent credence to the Melki Movement and other cults and rumours of cults in the region. These were collective memories relating to a period before the lifetimes of those who decided to follow Koriam. The Pomio Kivung, however, exploited these memories far more effectively than any ideology which had gone before. At the heart of these memories was the idea that all material abundance, prosperity, and fertility have a transcendental source. The pre-contact rituals of the Mali Baining were concerned primarily with the health and fertility of humans, game, and crops. Many of the details of their former religious system are no longer known, because the rituals which sustained them were prohibited by missionaries, and because the temple sacra were confiscated (and allegedly shipped to Germany). But memories are preserved of the basic underlying assumptions of the traditional religion and are still transmitted on various occasions: when magical formulae are pronounced over hunting equipment; when an elder is called upon to recite one of the ancient myths; when loneliness induces the men to sing traditional songs; when a fire dance is performed in celebration of some communal achievement or Christian holiday, at which time the ancient forces of fertility are set loose in the night, dangerous to encounter in ignorance, yet at one time a source of vital control over fertility and general welfare for those initiated into their mysteries. Nevertheless, there is a profound sense of entropy in these rites, as if most of the efficacious content has been lost. What has remained is a residue of conviction that the physical matter of 'this world' is created and transformed through esoteric knowledge which the mission promised but failed to transmit. The betrayal of the mission is all the more serious because the early exponents of Christianity insisted on the elimination of traditional religious practices, which it turns out were in fact comparatively efficacious. It is hardly surprising that, having prevented 'genuine' religious knowledge from being passed down, the missionaries are now accused of deliberately obstructing the path to salvation.

Accordingly, all cults affecting the Mali Baining during the colonial era, including Melki's and Koriam's ideas, gave expression to deeply held convictions about the origins of material abundance. Where the Pomio Kivung represented a considerable advance was in the way that it embodied transcendental authority in a living man, with whom converts could have direct contact. This was likewise a fulfilment and culmination of traditional religious ideas, but what makes it uniquely important is that it provided a basis for ideological stability, for the ongoing affirmation of a particular programme by an unchanging authority.

Among the Mali Baining, early rumours concerning the origins of Western cargo failed to cohere into a stable, standardized form because there was no way of assessing the relative merits of competing and conflicting speculations. Even Melki's pronouncements lacked absolute authority because (according to people's recollections in Dadul) he was not a divinity but a man. To be sure, he was a special man, in so far as he enjoyed privileged insights into the will of the divine and he was also perceived as a good man, in so far as he was driven by a moral imperative to share his revelations for the sake of collective advancement. As such, like many of the leaders of small cults, Melki might be described as a prophet (see Firth 1970: 31–3). This meant that his statements were fallible interpretations of things he discerned, or thought he discerned. If, as frequently happened, Melki's prophesies failed to occur, his interpretations and even the prophesies on which they were based could be questioned. This made for instability and disintegration in the institutional system of the Melki Movement, and ultimately contributed to its demise. By contrast, Koriam's apotheosis set the stage for uniform, incontrovertible conventions and long-term continuity. He was not merely an interpreter of the divine will but a vehicle for it. Support for Koriam's movement therefore entailed acceptance of the absolute authority of his statements and of the institutional arrangements which he advocated. People either supported the Pomio Kivung or they did not. If they did, then they were obliged to abide by its rules, and not to propose alternatives. In practice, those who attempted to change the movement from within ran the risk of excommunication, or managed to achieve only local support on a temporary basis. Koriam occupied a position of authority which few could emulate and none with comparable success. For committed supporters of the Pomio Kivung, the failures of Koriam's prophesies (see Tovalele 1977: 127–8) had to be attributed to some cause other than Koriam's fallibility (for example, satanic intervention or the inability of followers to carry out instructions). These factors help to explain the long-term continuity of Pomio Kivung institutions, in contrast with the ebbing and flowing of comparable ideologies and rumours in the region.

The existence of links between apotheosis of the leader and the scale and longevity of cargo movements has long been recognized in Papua

New Guinea. For example, Yali's expansionary and long-lived organization was founded on the incontrovertibility of the leader's doctrines
(Morauta 1972: 436). Yali was much more like a divine king than a
prophet and, indeed, was popularly described as the 'King of New Guinea'
(Morauta 1972: 433). This process of apotheosis in Melanesian cargo
cults frequently constitutes a fulfilment of indigenous mythology, in which
heroic figures confer benefits on loyal supporters on the basis of religious
revelations, as is suggested by Lacey's (1990) discussion of the role played
by images of 'myth-heroes' in the construction of Melanesian religious
leaders (see also Errington and Gewertz 1985).

One of the things which great leaders and myth-heroes have in common is a capacity to move among transcendental beings as one of them
without danger, whereas ordinary people have to approach the divine
with extreme caution (for example, see Barth 1975: 219). As an embodiment of ancestral authority, Koriam was attributed the ability to confer
other-worldly benefits without endangering the living, and as a sort of
representative of their interests. This idea coincided neatly with Koriam's
political success and his association on equal terms with the whiteman.
The idea that there is a link between access to the halls of power in the
Western governmental structure and access to transcendental authority
has been noted by other commentators (see, for example, Trompf 1990*a*:
65; Morauta 1974: 102).

Many Mali Baining people regarded the claims about Koriam's divinity as plausible, because they were persuasively supported by local mythology and the underlying logic of traditional ritual. Yet the Pomio
Kivung was probably the first post-war movement in the region fully to
exploit these collective memories, and to utilize them in an enduring
political programme.

Leadership, Spread, and Endurance

The fact of Koriam's apotheosis is not sufficient to explain the enduring
nature of the Pomio Kivung. Koriam had a clear advantage over Melki
and other prophets in so far as his theological pronouncements were regarded as incontrovertible. But Tanotka and Baninge were recently accorded divine authority and their leadership was by no means enduring.
The critical difference resides in the uses to which divine status was put.

During the climactic era of the Dadul–Maranagi splinter group,
Baninge's and Tanotka's divinity was expressed primarily through the
imagery of the ring and the post, cultivated through collective ritual

performances. The goal of their initial programme of dynamic leadership and proselytization had been the establishment of moving and climactic rituals, in which the actions of the whole community, rather than the words of leading individuals, carried the burden of transmitting religious revelations. Since this was the ultimate destination of splinter-group activity, it was confined to a relatively small population and had a short life span.

Koriam's aim, by contrast, had been to establish an expansionary and enduring movement. If the Pomio Kivung had been based around mass gatherings, it would have disintegrated rapidly as people ran out of food and other basic necessities. Koriam somehow had to come to the people, rather than they to him, if the movement was to be constructed on solid and enduring foundations. A particularly effective way in which a few individuals can spread a movement across dispersed populations is through words, whether in the form of sacred texts or orations (or both). In the predominantly non-literate region in which the Pomio Kivung spread, speech became the privileged medium of transmission, and this had a series of political implications.

Since Koriam codified his religious programme in language, he placed considerable emphasis on logical persuasion and the force of argument. But although his evangelical techniques were capable of stimulating religious conversion at the time of transmission, a problem with elaborately constructed ideology is that it is not intrinsically memorable, and is likely to be modified or even substantially forgotten after the leader has moved on to address fresh audiences. As a result, Koriam advocated a highly routinized religious organization, by means of which his authoritative statements would be continuously transported and transmitted by a hierarchy of close disciples, supervisors, and local orators (see Chapters 2 and 3; see also Koimanrea and Bailoenakia 1983: 175). The rituals of the movement were likewise standardized and routinized, so that considerable institutional uniformity and stability were achieved. One effect of frequent repetition was that any departure from convention was readily apparent, and correspondingly easy to eliminate. The ideal pattern which emerged was one in which a large number of Kivung communities, dispersed across a substantial territory, independently operationalized the same set of ideas and rituals, which were subject to the authority of a single leader, who disseminated his policies from a central seat of power.

The emphasis on oratory and routinization had obvious advantages. The reasoned arguments of sermonizers were, as I have shown, capable of answering a widespread need for 'understanding' in ways that were intrinsically plausible and persuasive, and frequent repetition meanwhile contributed to the standardization of religious dogma, greatly reducing the risk of innovation and regional variation within the movement. Nevertheless, there are limits to the persuasiveness of oratory. This is suggested by the fact that routine practices are occasionally superseded by climactic rituals, which convey religious understandings most poignantly through non-verbal communication.

A central argument of this book has been that the mainstream institutions of the Pomio Kivung, however plausible they may be, are not in themselves sufficient to account for the enduring *popularity* of the movement. Repetitive speeches and rituals constitute a viable method of sustaining an intellectual understanding of the religious ideology, and when the movement first spread to the Mali Baining the revelatory character of this understanding was probably sufficient to generate commitment to the main goals of the Pomio Kivung: political autonomy, wealth, knowledge, and salvation. But the habitual reproduction of Kivung institutions for years at a time inevitably reduces the intensity of religious experience, and perhaps produces impatience for the millennium to occur. The main stimulus for renewed commitment to the mainstream movement is, paradoxically, provided by temporary attempts to break away from it and to produce the millennium through the isolated performance of climactic rituals. This was the main thesis of Chapters 4 to 6, in which I argued that splinter-group rituals imbue the guiding themes of Kivung ideology with mystical, compelling, and emotive connotations, which verbalized doctrine alone cannot successfully cultivate.

Periodic millenarian outbursts transform and deepen people's appreciations of the meaning and value of salvation. Although mainstream institutions are intellectually or logically persuasive, they are not productive of an intense yearning for the millennium. Climactic rituals, by contrast, cultivate compelling and moving images of eschatological themes (through concrete symbols such as the ring or the post), combining the revelation of these images with an experience and expression of solidarity, awe, suffering, mystery, and suspense. This gamut of emotions and sensations becomes associated in the minds of cultists with the central project of the movement. Splinter-group activities are intrinsically temporary and commitment to the mainstream Pomio Kivung is typically restored. Nevertheless, the intensity of climactic rituals, and the simplicity and power of their iconic imagery, render them highly memorable, so that they haunt and reverberate with the humdrum repetitions of mainstream religion for years to come.

Variable Commitment and Abstention

To say that Pomio Kivung ideology is highly persuasive is not the same as saying that there is (or ever was) uniformity in people's motives for participating. In this part of the chapter I examine four main areas of variation in levels of commitment to the Pomio Kivung. The first area concerns the stated goals of the movement. Some people experience a strong yearning for the attainment of these goals, whereas others experience a relatively weak interest in them. This is not so much a matter of epistemology, of the plausibility of miraculous transformation, but a question of variable interest in its achievement. Secondly, some people enjoy greater immediate fulfilment from participating in the movement than others. This is related to the different kinds of involvement available within the community, and especially the tendency to accord more satisfying and responsible positions to men, and lower status roles to women and children. The third factor concerns the sanctions which can be applied to defectors from the movement, which vary in their severity at different times and for different people. Fourthly, the disadvantages of Kivung membership are evaluated according to individual circumstances and predilections. Some people experience the constraints on behaviour implied by Kivung membership to be unbearably onerous, whereas others do not acknowledge or feel oppressed by loss of freedom. Moreover, involvement in the movement may imply greater or lesser material sacrifices for different people.

The stated goals of the Pomio Kivung are numerous and complex. It is likely that some people are most impressed by the idea of salvation as an eternal state of harmony and plenty (the Period of the Government), whereas others are more intensely excited by the prospect of political and economic ascendancy over their adversaries (the Period of the Companies). Of course, there are many other components to Kivung eschatology, encompassing a variety of personal aspirations. But since the movement presents followers with an integrated ideological package, people are under a moral pressure to give more or less equal weight to all the religious themes (in so far as each carries the endorsement of the ancestors) and are reluctant to prioritize their individual interests. Nevertheless, there are readily discernible differences between genuine enthusiasts and mere conformists. This may be illustrated with a brief comparison of two teenage boys, Toma and Sega, the sons respectively of Dadul's first and second orators.

I sometimes wandered around with the boys on their visits to gardens or forays in the bush, and on these occasions the contrasting personalities and attitudes of Toma and Sega were clearly apparent. Toma was observant of, and sensitive to, the mood of his peers. Whenever some decision about the boys' activities was being debated, his suggestions were likely to be popular and uncontroversial. His sense of humour was tame but entertaining. He was unusually energetic, though not of strong build, and could be relied upon to contribute enthusiastically to any group endeavour. Above all, he was responsible in his conduct. His was the voice of caution and moral sense whenever a dangerous or wicked scheme was proposed.

In contrast, Sega was stubbornly independent, often ready to undertake a project alone or to split the group if he favoured some controversial course of action. His sense of humour tended to be bawdy, raucous, and morally suspect. He was strikingly muscular, and frequently flaunted his physical prowess in tests of strength. Yet he was not an industrious gardener, and frequently caused consternation among the senior men for his tendency to shirk obligations to work for them. He was sometimes verbally defiant of authority, and had been publicly castigated on more than one occasion for violations of the Laws, including the most heinous crime of stealing money from the receptacles kept in the Cemetery Temple.

Sega once told me that he did not care about salvation, and doubted his chances of meriting it. He never denied the existence of the Village Government, but his sense of bravado was such that he claimed not to be afraid of its judgements. He wanted to follow his own inclinations, and was resigned to eternal punishment (or so he said) when it eventually came. Sega was the youngest bachelor in Dadul to have constructed his own house and to obtain a meagre subsistence more or less independently of his father's domestic unit. He participated in Kivung activities without enthusiasm, and was sucked along with the splinter-group activities of 1988 during which time his waywardness was inconsistently dealt with— sometimes overlooked, and sometimes vehemently attacked. Not surprisingly, he left the movement and went to live in Sunam towards the end of 1988.

Toma, meanwhile, expressed unrelenting devotion to the goals of the Kivung, and once told me that he suffered sleepless nights, worrying about his spiritual condition. He made frequent donations in absolution and catharsis receptacles, and unfailingly discharged his obligations to senior relatives, and obeyed his father. He was also a reliable attendant and conscientious participant in Kivung rituals. In short, Toma was a model of piety, and there can be little doubt about the depth of his personal commitment to the goals of the movement.

A second parameter of variation, often related in practice with the first, concerns people's experience of fulfilment through participation in the Kivung. In the mainstream community system, orators obviously enjoy relatively high status and seem to derive additional satisfaction from exercising their arts of public speaking, and from their prominent role in organizing or presiding over group activities. To a lesser extent, all the witnesses and other male officials derive status from their specialist participation in the community system. Women are excluded from specialist roles and seem, in general, to find the ritual work less enjoyable and fulfilling. One woman told me that the system was unjust in this respect, and at one time she had even led a minor rebellion among the women on the grounds that, since they prepared the offerings for temples, they should be allowed to present them to the ancestors. The orators could not accept such an innovation, since it was not proposed by Koriam or Kolman, and the women had to resign themselves to the situation. In general, it may be that the sexual politics of domestic life tend to induce (or strongly encourage) the wives of Kivung members to participate in the movement, in spite of the lack of personal satisfaction available to them. There may also be lower commitment, in general, among the women to Kivung goals. But it is certainly true that the radical who proposed a more fulfilling role for women in temple rituals, was also renowned for the depth of her commitment to Kivung ideology. And there are undoubtedly other women in Dadul who, whilst deriving little satisfaction from the community system, enthusiastically anticipate the millennium which will (among other things) eliminate most forms of sexual inequality, along with the torments of childbirth and child rearing.

One of the most powerful, but for most people improbable, recommendations for involvement in the Pomio Kivung is the opportunity it sometimes affords for dramatic upward mobility. Baninge and Tanotka, for example, almost certainly derived personal satisfaction from the process of apotheosis. I have elsewhere explored Baninge's motives, revolving around the desire to cast off a poor reputation and to acquire in its place general respect and renown (see Whitehouse, forthcoming [a]). Other people also gained more responsible and fulfilling roles in the community as a result of the splinter-group activities, most notably the witnesses at the Cemetery Temple.

The third area concerns the variable impact of sanctions for abstention from the community system in Dadul. The ultimate sanction available to the community is excommunication. If somebody decides to leave the movement by physically leaving Dadul and setting up in Sunam, the effectiveness of excommunication is reduced somewhat. As I have mentioned, this was the option favoured by Sega. Coming at a time when hostility towards Dadul was at its most intense, Sega's defection was triumphantly welcomed in Sunam, and he was enthusiastically invited to stay with relatives there until he could establish independent residence. Yet there are also cases where individuals defect from the movement without leaving Dadul, or even changing their domestic circumstances. A case in point is provided by the wife of Dadul's first orator who had managed to abstain from community life for many years. Athough her original defection had caused outrage, people had gradually come to accept the situation and her relations with many of the villagers had been repaired (although she inevitably remained an outsider from that point on, and had to bear the emotional burden of being excluded from certain conversations and other potentially enjoyable activities). Thus, people can endure not only the sanctions of the community but of their own family, if the desire to abstain is very strong. This is harder for women than for men since the sway of the husband over the wife is usually greater than her influence over him. Yet the case at hand shows that even a wife, if she is determined, can do as she pleases. A less emotionally self-reliant person might have been daunted by the sanctions in prospect.

The fourth consideration is the way people evaluate the disadvantages of Kivung membership. Here again there is considerable variation. People who abstain have cited numerous disadvantages of joining the movement, including the renunciation of luxuries (implied by ascetic ideology, and the channeling of surplus money into the movement), and loss of freedoms of association and movement (implied by avoidance of the Tolai, and of fraternization with sinners generally). A motive for abstention from the movement mentioned with striking regularity is the reluctance to forego betel chewing, partly because it is addictive and partly because it is conducive to certain forms of sociability. For some individuals, considerations of this kind can outweigh the advantages of joining (or remaining within) the movement and seem to enjoy particular sway over those unmarried youths who especially value the freedom to roam and associate as they please. This is reported to have been an important factor in the reluctance of many young men to join the Pomio Kivung in the early 1970s although, since marrying, these latecomers have come to form the core of support for the Kivung in Dadul (all three orators, for example, fall into this category).

There are also rare instances of individuals who abstain from the Pomio Kivung on the grounds that membership would oblige them to forgo valuable economic resources. For example, the brother of Dadul's infamous cynic, Bapka, devoted an extraordinary amount of energy to raising cocoa. His lifestyle was not lavish, in fact quite the opposite. He was noted for his meanness with money, and it was rumoured that he would always remain a bachelor because he could not bring himself to share his resources with a family. Nobody knew what this eccentric did with his money, but presumably he buried it at a secret location (a standard joke was that death would intervene before he disinterred his stash). Nevertheless, Bapka's brother argued that participation in the Kivung would rob him of his savings and the time available to tend his cocoa. It is hard to accept this argument at face value, but there are cases of people who have apparently been dissuaded from joining the movement because of the material sacrifice this would entail. People in Sunam, for example, who might otherwise have been tempted to migrate to Dadul, were reluctant to forgo their titles to government blocks and their ownership of crops already planted there. Yet the relative sway of these considerations clearly varied from one person to another. One of the largest families in Dadul migrated there long after the Kivung was established with the explicit intention of joining the movement. In so doing, this family left behind a block in Sunam, and lost all rights over the extensive cocoa growing there.

What is clear is that there is considerable variation in people's motives for withholding, maintaining, or removing their support for the Pomio Kivung. Not only are there different grounds for supporting or abstaining from the Kivung, but also marked variations in the importance people attach to them. The decision to leave the movement, or not to join it in the first place, is probably explicable in most cases in terms of low motivation in relation to several criteria. For example, Sega not only experienced little interest in the goals of the Pomio Kivung, he also had low status in the community system, an acute sense of the disadvantages of involvement, and almost no anxiety about the sanctions for defection. The fact that he left the movement was therefore somewhat predictable. Another case in point is Lagawop, who underwent the painful and humiliating exorcism at Maranagi. Lagawop and Sega are in fact the only recent defectors from the Kivung in Dadul. They left at the same time, each taking full advantage of an assured welcome in Sunam. Consequently, Lagawop (like Sega) had little to fear in the way of secular sanctions. Unlike Sega, however, she had entertained high hopes for a better existence within the movement, both as an inspired leader and as a recipient of the anticipated cargo. Yet Lagawop's hopes of personal celebrity had been crushed and disappointed and, in the process, she had acquired the poorest reputation of any person in Dadul. Moreover, her relations with her father (Dadul's third orator, a widower) had been strained as a result of his decision to remarry, and so she longed for release not only from the community but from these unhappy domestic circumstances. Her case was, in the end, more tragic than Sega's since her yearning for salvation had been far more earnest and sincere and I suspect that her conscience was deeply troubled by the move.

Opposition

Those who abstain from the Pomio Kivung can either adopt an attitude of indifference to the movement or can explicitly oppose it. Indifference is typical among those who abstain from all kinds of community life in general. The cases of Bapka, his family, and the wife of the first orator in Dadul illustrate this very clearly. Yet such people live alongside supporters of the Pomio Kivung and do not publicly criticize them, unless they have some (fleeting) personal grievance (see Chapter 6). Sustained opposition to the Pomio Kivung, on the other hand, typically implies involvement in some kind of 'Westernized' community system, in which development associations, the Church, and the state, play a prominent and influential role. This situation prevails in certain coastal Mali villages as well as inland. But I have more intimate knowledge of the case of Sunam.

The crucial point to make about opposition to the Pomio Kivung in Sunam is that it is not widely motivated by cynicism with regard to the efficacy of cargo cult rituals. Even the staunchest supporters of Mataungan ideology in Sunam used to travel to Dadul every so often, when the miracle was rumoured to be imminent. On such occasions, they would participate in Pomio Kivung rituals, just to be on the safe side. During the period of my fieldwork, long after these sporadic attempts to keep a foot in both camps had ceased to occur, the most confirmed opponents of the Pomio Kivung still admitted in private that they believed the rituals of the movement to be potentially efficacious. Thus, the oft-quoted slogan in Sunam, *samting i no kamap nating* ('something does not arise from nothing'), is more ideologically correct than psychologically convincing. Since the people of Sunam are not really hard-nosed cynics, their motives for opposing the Pomio Kivung have to be identified on other grounds.

Sunam village could never have formed a viable Kivung community. Being sited on government land, surrounded by Tolai settlements, a stone's throw from permanent church and government buildings, Sunam has long been a tiny and tenuous outpost of Mali Baining culture. The very location of Sunam meant, in terms of Kivung ideology, that its inhabitants would be subject to continuous contamination by foreign things. Unlike Dadul or Maranagi, Sunam could not hope to isolate itself from interventions of the state, nor limit its contact with the Tolai. In order to join the Pomio Kivung, many of Sunam's residents moved to Dadul or other Kivung communities, and those who remained behind could only participate in the movement on an occasional basis, by temporarily evacuating Sunam. For the most part, however, their decision to favour land titles and cash crops over the spiritual values of the Kivung, meant that the people of Sunam were extensively criticized by their relatives in Dadul. Sunam villagers were frequently dismissed as selfish and hedonistic, guided by a love of money, luxuries, and promiscuity. At times, these accusations may have appeared in Sunam as fair comment, since their occasional involvement in Kivung rituals showed that they acknowledged the plausibility of Koriam's ideas without, on balance, being swayed by them to join the Pomio Kivung permanently. It seems most likely that these circumstances were conducive to low self-esteem in Sunam, and thus provided a powerful motive to adopt ideologies which counter-attacked the Pomio Kivung, representing its institutions as evil. Thus, the Pomio Kivung is most effectively opposed in Sunam, not on the grounds that it cannot work, but on the grounds that it is immoral.

This is the same strategy which proved to be successful in the missionization of Papua New Guinea. Traditional practices (just like Kivung rituals) were not deemed to be inefficacious but, on the contrary, diabolical and therefore powerful in an undesirable way. Opposition to the Pomio Kivung, like support for it, has thus been cultivated along the lines of well-established themes. Indeed, these are themes which pre-date missionization, and reverberate with memories of traditional conceptions of destructive supernatural forces, unleashed on humanity through illegitimate tampering with the sacred realm. Accordingly, it is not so much that Pomio Kivung ritual is logically criticized, as that the whole edifice is contaminated by the notion of evil: 'evil' houses for feeding the dead, 'evil' goings-on in the cemetery, and 'evil' meetings of conspirators and agitators. These are the negative images conjured up by opponents and these, rather than sustained logical critique, provide the most enduring and pervasive bases for opposition. Such anti-Kivung ideologies have been provided in Sunam by the United Church, the instruments of modernity (e.g. development associations and the state), and by Mataunganism (see Chapter 1).

Notes

1. Worsley 1957: 44; but note that many other writers seeking to interpret 'cargo cults' in sociological terms have commented on the limitations of this kind of simplistic assertion (e.g. Brunton 1971: 126, and Trompf 1990*b*: 75).
2. The ancestors of Pomio Kivung members look favourably on the preservation of each group's traditional culture (barring practices deemed to be sinful). Tolai culture is, of course, alien to all Pomio Kivung members and so Pomio-Baining people who use Tolai magic, grass baskets, and shell money, are seen as contaminated, and are roundly condemned (see Chapter 2).

8

Codification, Transmission, and Politics

THE purpose of this final chapter is to draw together the main strands
of my argument, and relate them to broader theoretical problems in the
anthropology of religion. I begin by summarizing the characteristic features of religious life in the mainstream Pomio Kivung (discussed in
Chapters 2 to 3) and the localized splinter group (discussed in Chapters
4 to 6). Mainstream ideology is codified in the form of verbalized doctrine
and exegesis, and this is related to the frequency of transmission, styles of
cognition, and the sociological features of centralization, hierarchy, and
expansionism. I refer to this constellation of interconnected variables as
the 'doctrinal mode of religiosity'. Splinter-group ideology is primarily
codified in the form of non-verbal iconic imagery, and this is related to
the periodicity of transmission, the evocation of affective episodic memories, and the formation of localized, solidary communities. This contrasting concatenation of features may be dubbed the 'imagistic mode of
religiosity'.

This approach to the material sheds new light on the debate about the
relationship between millenarism and nationalism. The popular view in
anthropology, history, and general sociology, that millenarian movements
give rise to nationalist ones, is inapplicable to cults operating in the
imagistic mode. The relationship between millenarism and nationalism
has more to do with styles of codification and transmission than with
similarities in their ideological themes.

There is then the question of how my distinction between doctrinal
and imagistic modes of action in the Pomio Kivung articulates with a
range of existing dichotomous representations of religious phenomena. In
particular, my arguments bear comparison with those of I. M. Lewis,
Ruth Benedict, Victor Turner, Richard Werbner, Ernest Gellner, Jack
Goody, Fredrik Barth, and Max Weber. These writers have all grappled
with precisely the same dichotomy elucidated in the present study. Within
religious traditions all around the world, scholars have documented a
divergence between two basic modes of religiosity. Many have sought to
fathom the distinctive qualities and wider sociological implications of

each. But none of these scholars has been able to construct a satisfactory picture because parts of the jig-saw puzzle were missing. Some theorists have assembled more bits than others, but all of them have lacked one very important part of the design, and that is the way in which religion is handled cognitively. Political, religious, and economic institutions cannot be said to affect each other without first affecting people's minds. I claim to be able to piece together a more comprehensive picture of religion than has hitherto been possible, by making use of some crucial recent findings in cognitive psychology. This leads in the end to a dissolution of the boundaries between intellectualist, psychological, and sociological perspectives on religion.

Modes of Religiosity

In Chapters 4 to 6 I described the brief history of a breakaway cult, in the course of which there was a gradual shift of emphasis away from verbalized doctrine and exegetical commentary, and towards the cultivation of analogic imagery in climactic ritual. I argued that the psychological impact of ring ceremonies, vigils, nocturnal dances, the *awan*, etc., resided in a combination of distinctive cognitive, affective, and sensory experiences. The privations and degradations of confinement in the round-house, the suppressed eroticism of the first ring ceremony, the stirring rhythms and haunting melodies of the nocturnal choirs, the drama, fear, and aggression inspired by the *awan*—these are just some of the intense feelings and sensations aroused by the splinter group. Pervading all these experiences was an awareness of their collective nature, a sense of undergoing something unusual and profoundly significant as a solidary group. This received a suitable focus ideologically in the image of the ring, whether it was formed of house posts, human bodies, or beer bottles planted in the ground. From a simple concrete metaphor sprang a plethora of evocative experiences—the solemn gatherings in a circle, the dancing around a post, the *awanga* charging in a circle, and the congregation in the round-house, etc. The ring was more than a symbol of the community, it became a physical instantiation of it. Or, to put this another way, the ring of people favoured by the Village Government was not just an abstract conception, but a physically experienced reality.

In attempting to understand how this experience was handled cognitively, brief reference must be made once again to psychological studies of the relationship between emotion, revelation, and memory. For a long time, it was thought that emotional arousal beyond a certain point automatically impaired cognitive processing and therefore memory (Yerkes and Dodson 1908, Loftus 1980). This basic thesis is apparent in Western folk-psychology, manifested for example in legal assessments of the reliability of eyewitness testimony, greatly influenced by psychoanalytic and other clinical findings on repressed traumas and anxieties. Nevertheless, a large and growing body of research shows that certain aspects of emotionally arousing events are very well retained over time (an excellent summary of the literature is provided by Christiansen 1992).

One especially pertinent response to these findings is the theory of 'flashbulb memory' (Brown and Kulik 1982, Winograd and Killinger 1983). According to this theory, a particular neural mechanism is activated in response to events which are surprising, salient, and emotionally arousing. In the Papua New Guinea context flashbulb memory has been described in connection with moments of intense religious revelation (Herdt 1989: 115, Whitehouse 1993). Flashbulb memories do not seem to decay, and may actually become more vivid over the years (e.g. Scrivner and Safer 1988). This seems to me to be borne out by Worsley's description of people's memories of the Vailala Madness (1957: 91–2):

the cult-activities were remembered as true happenings, not frauds. The leaders had received messages via the flagpoles . . . Informants 'remembered' hearing a warning hum in the poles . . . The steamer of the dead, moreover, actually had appeared. . . . noises were heard as it disappeared without ever having actually been seen. Others remembered obscurely seeing her large red funnel and three masts, and many saw her lights. . . . as time passed, the era of the Madness became more wonderful in memory.

Worsley appeared to attribute this phenomenon to retrospective fabrication, although some members of the Dadul–Maranagi group seemed genuinely to perceive what they took to be supernatural signs (see Chapter 5). What is more important is that the unusual events which everybody perceived (from nakedness at the first ring ceremony to the violent excorcism of Lagawop) were accompanied by high emotion (fear, shame, anticipation, etc.) and peculiar sensations (nausea, music, pungent odours, etc.). One of the marked features of memories encoded in these sorts of conditions, whether or not they have the character of flashbulb memories, is that people are very likely to remember central details, such as who else was there at the time. In the context of the Dadul–Maranagi group this is crucially important. Not only did the gatherings, based around ring symbolism, create and express solidarity among particular people co-ordinated in time and space, but it impressed on memory the unity of a particular community of people.

This state of affairs contrasts very starkly with the experience of routinized ritual in the mainstream movement. As I described in Chapter 3, mainstream rituals are performed with great frequency (mainly in daily, twice-weekly, and weekly cycles), and are not remembered as separate events but in the form of 'scripts'. In the terminology proposed by Tulving (1972), splinter-group rituals are encoded in 'episodic' (or autobiographical) memory, whereas mainstream rituals are encoded in 'semantic' memory. The emphasis on ritual scripts in the mainstream tradition, combined with the fact that participants in the rituals come and go (see Chapter 3), has profound implications for the way in which people cognize their religious community. It is not a 'real' community, as in the case of the Dadul–Maranagi group, but an 'imagined' community (cf. Anderson 1983) in the sense that it encompasses a blur of unspecifiable and 'imagined' persons. Solidarity in this model is based on presumed similarities—everybody in the Pomio Kivung is presumed to perform the same rituals and to be pulling in the same direction. But this is only a conceptual community, not one which physically presents itself to the senses. It has all the makings of a national grouping, unlike the splinter-group community which was a local cult *par excellence*.

These are merely aspects of a wider divergence between contrasting regimes. I have also focused on the fact that verbalized doctrines are easier to transport than non-verbally transmitted ideas (Chapter 2). I have explored some of the implications for leadership, where revelations are imparted by orators or sermonizers (Chapter 7) and where inspiration is direct, personal, and unmediated (Chapter 5). I tried to draw out some of the numerous implications of frequency of transmission and styles of codification when it comes to issues of uniformity, stability, and centralization (Chapter 3). I will not seek to reiterate the foregoing arguments in detail, but merely to depict some of the main contrasts between divergent regimes in a schematic form (Table 5).

The features which cluster together within the mainstream movement are the main characteristics of what may be called the doctrinal mode of religiosity. By contrast, the features which I have highlighted in connection with the splinter group exemplify the imagistic mode of religiosity. These terms, 'doctrinal' and 'imagistic', are imperfect, since I wish to refer to whole sets of contrasting variables rather than merely to differences between two of them. Nevertheless, contrasts in the style of codification are more basic than other kinds of differences, lying as they do at

TABLE 5. *Modes of religiosity*

Variable	Doctrinal Mode	Imagistic Mode
1. Style of codification	Verbalized doctrine and exegesis	Iconic imagery
2. Frequency of transmission	Repetitive (routinized)	Periodic (at most every few years)
3. Cognitive processing	Generalized schemas (semantic memory)	Unique schemas (episodic memory)
4. Political ethos	Universalistic (imagined community)	Particularistic (face to face community)
5. Solidarity/cohesion	Diffuse	Intense
6. Revelatory potential	Intellectual persuasion	Emotional and sensual stimulation
7. Ideological coherence	Ideas linked by implicational logic	Ideas linked by loose connotations
8. Moral character	Strict discipline	Indulgence, license
9. Spread by	Proselytization	Group action only
10. Scale and structure	Large-scale, centralized	Small-scale, localized
11. Leadership type	Enduring, dynamic	Passive figureheads
12. Distribution of institutions	Uniform beliefs and practices	Variable beliefs and practices
13. Diachronic features	Rigidity (permanent 'breaking away')	Flexibility (incremental change/ radical innovation)

the roots of a series of causal chains which encompass all the variables listed in Table 5.

I have argued that if the chosen style of codification is language (1), then transmission must be frequent (2), otherwise the cultural material cannot be reproduced. If transmission is frequent or routinized then materials tend to be organized in semantic memory, in the form of generalized schemas (3). This helps to produce imagined communities, and a universalistic orientation (4). Social cohesion in such communities is comparatively diffuse (5), and this is linked to the emotionless way in which revelations are cultivated (6), and the ideology constructed (7). Going back to the style of doctrinal codification (1), this inspires revelation through intellectual persuasion (6), which necessitates logical coherence (7). Continuity in the practices routinely performed from one day to the next requires highly disciplined behaviour which is readily (and, in practice, ubiquitously) construed as a moral virtue (8). Meanwhile, doctrinal codification (1) also facilitates proselytization by patrolling individuals

(9), which in turn implies wide dissemination (10). The fact that religious truths emanate from the mouths of proselytizing leaders means that leadership is dynamic (11). But it also means that local orators and sermonizers can be designated to convey the leaders' words to grass roots supporters, leading to centralization (10), uniformity in beliefs and practices (12), and doctrinal rigidity (13). Clearly, all these variables are linked in a variety of ways, most of which have been explored in the course of the book. But the connections I have just skimmed over are sufficient to show that the style of codification is the most basic of these variables, giving rise to the more encompassing implicational links between them.

Complementary patterns of interconnections can be discerned with respect to the imagistic mode of religiosity. If the chosen style of codification is non-verbal imagery (1), then the ideology is held together by loose connotations rather than logic (7). There is nothing intrinsically persuasive or compelling about iconic imagery *per se*, so its revelatory potential has to be realized through emotional and sensual stimulation (6) and cognitive shocks, producing unique schemas in episodic memory (3). The emotionality and uniqueness of such experiences implies a departure from normal routines and constraints; thus, the behaviour in question appears to involve unusual license and indulgence (8). It follows from all these points that transmission must be infrequent (2). Affective episodic memories in the imagistic mode give rise to a particular political ethos (4), to intense solidarity or social cohesion (5), and therefore to ideological diversity among the discrete groups operating in this mode (12). Iconic imagery engendered in collective ritual can only be spread through group action (9), which severely restricts the scale of individual cults (10). Since the group rather than an inspired individual is the vehicle for transmission, it is hard for leaders to exercise a dynamic influence over cult activities (12). A general diachronic feature of the imagistic mode is that the ideology is flexible (13). Religious representations may be highly variable, and interference in one sector of the imagery does not automatically affect the religious system as a whole. Partly for this reason, change tends to be either incremental or radically innovative. I elaborate on this point below in my discussion of Max Weber's theoretical insights.

The contrast between doctrinal and imagistic modes of religiosity is apparent in all Melanesian cargo cults, and often one mode dominates a cult at the expense of the other. A common feature of localized cults (albeit absent from the splinter group in Dadul and Maranagi) is an experience of collective paroxysms or 'shaking-fits' which are typically experienced as both traumatic and inspiring. These practices are usually combined with dancing and feasting. Such cults rarely possess a body of doctrines, and sometimes participants are unable to provide even the barest exegetical accounts of their activities, or an explanation as to how they began. Revelations are cultivated primarily through personal inspiration, and tend to cluster around a few concrete metaphors. For example, in the Eastern Central Highlands cults (Berndt 1952/53), images of the pole and cane-torch figured highly (presumably as a conduit to heaven and enlightenment respectively). In the cases of the Letub cult of the Madang area (Inselmann 1944) and the Taro cult (Williams 1928), dissemination mainly took the form of contagion, whereby shaking fits were spread virus-like from one group to another. No verbalized ideology accompanied this process of transmission, so people down the line were not aware how or where the cult started. Each local community affected in this way tended to adapt the rituals, thereby marking itself off from neighbouring groups. Thus, even though certain basic practices spread widely (especially in the case of the Taro cult) they did nothing to promote unification, but in fact produced a fragmentary pattern of competing local communities (see Whitehouse 1994).

Conversely, it is possible to have large-scale movements, dominated by the doctrinal mode, which lack these sorts of features. The Paliau movement on Manus placed very great emphasis on verbally codified doctrines, and its leader was 'an orator of exceptional calibre' (Otto 1992: 440). Like Koriam, Paliau spread his message over considerable distances and he established channels 'through which new thinking could be disseminated by instructors and group-leaders (*pesmen*), whose duty it was to instruct the people' (Steinbauer 1979: 69). Figures like Paliau, Koriam, and Yali operated strikingly similar regimes, over which they exercised absolute authority as conduits for the divine will. Their support cut across traditional divisions (e.g. Morauta 1972: 434–6, Otto 1992: 445–6), creating a common identity among peoples who were not in direct contact. Yet these sorts of movements always come up against certain disadvantages of routinization. Steinbauer (1979: 69) describes how, under Paliau's influence, 'life became austere and regulated almost like a military establishment' and 'the movement lacked spontaneity' (1979: 71). The way is therefore open, in such movements, for the periodic resurfacing of localized, climactic cults, dominated by the imagistic mode of religiosity. The political effects of such cults are markedly different but not, as I have tried to show, necessarily incompatible with the reproduction of routinized religions.

The Relationship between Millenarism and Nationalism

There has been a general tendency among anthropologists to regard cargo cults and secular movements as stages in an evolutionary model. This is seen for example in Peter Worsley's claim that cargo cults are 'typical only of a certain phase in the political and economic development of [Melanesia]' and that 'future nationalist developments will probably be less and less under the aegis of millenarian cult leadership' (1957: 255). Although many cargo cults, both past and present, cannot be attributed millenarian features, Worsley's underlying intention was to distinguish between activist and passivist forms of religion (1957: 12): activism implying the expectation of imminent supernatural intervention, and passivism implying that such intervention was a remote prospect to be hoped for in the distant future or the next life. Passivist religion was like having no religion in at least one sense—that it fostered a practical orientation to solving worldly problems. Rather than performing rituals, the indigenous peoples of Papua New Guinea would band together in pursuit of more realistic means of obtaining cargo, and the political and economic autonomy which this represented.

Worsley's use of the label 'millenarism' as a shorthand for activist religion is to be explained in terms of his commitment to a strong tradition among social scientists, and especially European historians, of envisaging millenarism as the ideological and organizational progenitor of nationalism and other secular political movements. The progressivist hypothesis classically takes two forms (Smith 1979: 16): the 'triple progression thesis' which sees millenarism, nationalism, and socialism as three discrete evolutionary phases, and the 'secular heir thesis' which sees nationalism as the natural successor of millenarism because of the ideological similarities and historical connections between the two. Although Worsley's Marxist agenda (see also Lanternari 1963, and Bodrogi 1951) led to an interpretation of New Guinea cults in terms of the formation of class consciousness, most scholars (although see Cochrane 1970: 150–2, and May 1982: 445) subscribe to the conservative variant and thus interpret cargo cults as proto-nationalist, without invoking the framework of historical materialism (e.g. Lawrence 1971, Morauta 1974, Guiart 1951, Mead 1964, Belshaw 1950, Hogbin 1958, Rowley 1965, Brown 1966, etc.).

A crucial question I want to address is whether this general conception of the role of indigenous movements in Melanesian history, one which has enjoyed virtual hegemony in the anthropological literature for a very long time, is broadly correct. The short answer is that it is only broadly correct with respect to cults dominated by the doctrinal mode of religiosity. Such cults are characterized not by their ideological themes, but by the way their ideas are extensively codified and transmitted in language, and by the implications of this for political scale and structure. The prevailing view seems to me incorrect with respect to cults in which the imagistic mode of religiosity predominates. This is probably the most common situation among New Guinea cargo cults. Such cults are distinguished by an emphasis on non-verbal codification and infrequent transmission.

The mainstream Pomio Kivung movement, in which the doctrinal mode of religiosity prevails, sits reasonably comfortably with the progressivist hypothesis. It has long promoted forms of pragmatic intervention, with notable success. Although the Pomio Kivung emerged against a background of activist fervour (Panoff 1969, Trompf 1990*a*), it was rapidly transformed into a massive administrative and electoral machine, commanding support across several language groups, and with strong representation at all levels of government. As these changes took place, supporters of the movement did not abandon or even temper their expectations of supernatural intervention (principally the return of the dead and the arrival of cargo), but these expectations were combined with attempts to introduce measures to improve the political and economic conditions of Pomio Kivung members in the here and now. On the political front, the Pomio Kivung has campaigned, by parliamentary means, for various forms of self-government for its members and, on the economic front, it has sought to attract outside investment and to promote internal capital formation as an alternative to dependence on cash-crop exports.

In spite of the fact that the Pomio Kivung operates as a political party within an existing constitutional system, the movement simultaneously advocates withdrawal from the state.[1] It sustains its own system of taxation and legal apparatus, and members avoid dealings with provincial or community courts, agricultural officers, tax collectors, and other government personnel. They live to all intents and purposes within a mini-province of their own, for which they continue to seek statutory recognition through the movement's representatives in central government.[2] Less realistic hopes for a Pomio Kivung nation-state are commonplace among members. This general pattern has been well documented in relation to other routinized movements in Papua New Guinea, including Yali's in Madang (Lawrence 1971) and Paliau's on Manus (Otto 1992: 443).

Although these aspirations appear unrealistic at present, some commentators (see Spriggs 1991) have observed that if the recent secession of Bougainville is recognized by the Papua New Guinea state, then other movements which have long been demanding independence may also attempt to secede, and (if so) the Pomio Kivung might well be among them. Indeed, the boundaries of the would-be Pomio Kivung state have already been mapped out and are known to most followers of the movement.

Alongside the political and economic goals of the Pomio Kivung, expectations of supernatural intervention flourish. Although autonomy from the existing provincial government is pursued by parliamentary means, it is also construed by members as an inevitable result of the eventual return of their ancestors, who are believed to congregate in a sort of ghostly assembly (the Village Government) that will one day materialize on earth. The movement's internal legal apparatus upholds laws received from the ancestors via the movement's leader, and their observance is not simply a matter of achieving a peaceful and harmonious society as an end in itself, nor of the expectation of rewards in the afterlife. Rather, it is intended to expedite the return of the dead in 'this world', an event which most followers expect to witness within their own lifetimes. Meanwhile, the taxes collected within the Pomio Kivung, although occasionally used to finance projects in the here and now, are pooled in a large collective fund which will be used to buy shares in the manufacturing companies that are to be established by the returning ancestors. It will be recalled that the first phase of the millennium in Pomio Kivung eschatology, described as the Period of the Companies, constitutes the overt cargoist theme of the movement.

It is clear, therefore, that the presence of secular and nationalist political aspirations does not necessarily displace cargo cult ideas. Indeed, the notion that cargo (and all that it represents) can ultimately be obtained by supernatural means is not so much the precursor of nationalist ideas in Papua New Guinea as a potentially complementary theme, and one which may well persist indefinitely. But what needs to be stressed above all, given the biases of the existing literature, is that cargoism is not in itself the historical dynamo behind the emergence of large-scale indigenous movements. On the contrary, the idea that material abundance has an other-worldly source which can be tapped through ritual resides just as firmly at the heart of fragmentary regimes, such as the Dadul–Maranagi splinter-group, which have nothing to do with nationalism.

The imagistic mode of religiosity is a source of profound religious

experience and local solidarity, but it does not have anything to offer to
nationalist aspirations. By contrast, the larger movements dominated by
the doctrinal mode of religiosity often give rise to nationalist struggles,
although there is no reason to suppose that, in the process, nationalism
must colonize and displace millenarian expectations. Localized cults dominated by the imagistic mode can occur in isolation from unifying movements. But they can also coincide with them, perhaps enhancing their
long-term popularity (as in the Pomio Kivung). The emphasis in the
literature on Melanesian cults has tended to focus primarily on ideological similarities and differences, producing a plethora of labels for movements which have yet to demonstrate explanatory power (e.g. millenarian,
salvation, soteriological, nationalist, adjustment, nativistic, cargo, revolutionary, activist, passivist, separatist, synchretic, etc.). I have chosen, as
my primary focus, aspects of cognition, affect, dissemination, structure,
and scale within two regimes whose ideological themes are very similar
(and, in this case, directly related). This has led to the conclusion that it
is not the vision of a better way of life that determines the political nature
of Melanesian movements, it is the way this vision is codified and
transmitted.

Dichotomous Representations of Religious Phenomena

It is clear from the literature in religious anthropology that the existence
of divergent modes of religiosity has long been recognized. This recognition has given rise to a variety of dichotomous representations of religious
phenomena, many of which highlight features that I have been exploring
in this study. But there are two things which make my theory of doctrinal
and imagistic modes exceptional. The first is that it is more comprehensive in its coverage of previously identified parameters of variation than
any single existing discussion. The second is that my theory links these
variables, for the first time, to recent findings in cognitive psychology.

In his study *Ecstatic Religion* (1971), I. M. Lewis put forward a distinction between 'central' and 'peripheral' cults which brought into focus
very nicely the contrasts between sober, rule-governed, orthodox practices in central or mainstream religion, and the more emotional, innovative styles of religiosity among relatively deprived peoples on the periphery
of society. Unfortunately, however, Lewis did not focus on the divergent
sociological possibilities that ensue from alternative styles of codification,
transmission, cognition, and innovation. Rather, Lewis confined himself

to what he saw as the 'functions' of ecstatic religion (both social and psychiatric).

Another, rather earlier, attempt to get to grips with the phenomenon was Ruth Benedict's theory of Appolonian and Dionysian modes of religiosity. Drawing on Nietzche's studies of Greek tragedy, Benedict declared that 'the desire of the Dionysian, in personal experience or in ritual, is to press through it towards a certain psychological state, to achieve excess' (1935: 56). By contrast, the Appolonian is inclined to eschew extreme psychological states and to remain within the confines of daily routine and tradition. Benedict's contribution was useful in so far as it highlighted a basic difference of orientation among religious people: the one excessive and the other moderate. This is essentially a point about the moral character and revelatory potential of divergent modes of religiosity (see Table 5). But, again, Benedict did not develop her argument very far, and it tended to degenerate into an overly simplistic opposition between individualism (a Dionysian trait) and something resembling mechanical solidarity (a characteristically Appolonian aspiration).

Nevertheless, a clutch of studies has advanced much further in attempting to get to the heart of the phenomenon of divergent modes of religiosity. An excellent example is Victor Turner's well-known discussion of 'Pilgrimages as Social Processes' (1974). In this essay, Turner distinguished between what he called 'fertility rituals' and 'political rituals', giving rise to a discussion which parallels in numerous ways my conception of doctrinal and imagistic modes of religiosity.

I have stressed the fact that the splinter group in Dadul and Maranagi, founded as it was around the imagistic mode, was an inherently localized phenomenon. This is likewise the kind of thing which Turner had in mind when he talked of 'political cults', founded around 'politico-jural rituals focused on localized subsystems of social groups and structural positions' (1974: 197). Turner described 'political ritual' as a 'domain of exclusivity', focusing religious activity on localized objects of worship. He envisaged an emphasis on 'selfish and sectional interests' (1974: 185) and on the boundedness of social groups arising from this mode of ritual action. Moreover, Turner argued that political rituals engendered particularistic relationships—a notion of social bonds negotiated between particular persons rather than systematized between categories of persons. These are all features that are encapsulated in my notion of an imagistic mode of religiosity.

The relevance of Turner's line of thought becomes more fully apparent when we consider the converse of political rituals, which he referred to as 'fertility rituals'. The latter, according to Turner, were expansionary and outward-looking in character. In contrast with political rituals, fertility rituals were 'concerned with the unity and continuity of wider, more diffuse communities' (1974: 197). Turner characterized this mode of ritual action as a 'domain of inclusivity', leading to the formation of ties across a diversity of groups rather than consolidating localized bonds within them. All these points obviously apply more generally to the doctrinal mode of religiosity.

There are, however, two serious limitations of Turner's approach. The first of these stems from the fact that Turner tied his numerous dichotomies to what he clearly regarded as a more fundamental one between 'structure' and '*communitas*'. Political ritual, according to Turner, was an embodiment of structure, by which he meant 'the bonds between members of tightly knit, multifunctional groups' (1974: 201). The functionalist conception of structure, which seems to have remained with Turner from his early career, is of course at variance with my notion of the imagistic mode of religiosity. Far from implying a synchronic conception of social relations, my analysis of the splinter group in Dadul and Maranagi is a processual one (and presented as such). Moreover, although I have argued that splinter groups happen to serve the interests of the continued reproduction of the wider Pomio Kivung movement, I see this as an unintended consequence of innovative behaviour, rather than as a functional mechanism.

Turner's conception of fertility ritual, meanwhile, revolved around his concept of *communitas* and here too we part company. Turner's concept of *communitas* was an extension of the notion of universalism wherein particular identities and roles give way to anonymous membership of social categories. At one point Turner described *communitas* as a 'simplification' and 'homogenization' of social structure (1974: 201). Following this line of thought, *communitas* emerged as a mysterious (not to say mystical) conception, something defined in opposition to structure, as 'anti-structure', but never in its own right. At certain points in his discussion of *communitas*, I think Turner was struggling with an aspect of cognition markedly different from that entailed in what he called political ritual, and yet which ultimately eluded him. In the context of my imagistic–doctrinal dichotomy, the contrast in cognitive processes which I think Turner sometimes had in mind, comes rather more clearly into focus.

In the imagistic mode rituals are encoded, by and large, in autobiographical memory in which particular participants feature. Accurate memories need not be assumed, since what really matters is the form of cognitive processing rather than the particular content of people's recollections. Whether people accurately recall who was present at a ritual organized in the imagistic mode is not important. What counts is that people are inclined to think that they ought to be able to remember, and often claim to be able to do so. I have suggested that particularly surprising, salient, and emotionally arousing rituals may give rise to 'flashbulb memories' which indeed produce extraordinarily accurate and widespread recall of such information. But the relevant point is that this mode of religiosity produces memories of particular persons and social relations, rather than of anonymous members of social categories.

By contrast, the doctrinal mode of religiosity engenders a rather different cognitive process. In the case of the collective temple rituals of the mainstream Pomio Kivung, for example, these are performed on a regular basis by teams of participants which change their composition over time. If you ask somebody who was there when a particular temple ritual was performed some time ago, they will not even attempt to recall the event in autobiographical memory. If they consider the question to be answerable at all, it will be with reference to *semantic* memory—who was likely to have been in the village at that time, and therefore a probable participant in the ritual. The solution is inferred or deduced (if at all) rather than specifically recalled. The way in which routinized rituals are handled cognitively is in the form of universal scripts or schemas for *ideal* performances, rather than as unique schemas for *actual* performances. It follows that the figures who populate these semantic scripts are indeed anonymous members of social categories rather than particular persons. In this way, the distinction between particularism and universalism with which Turner grappled, may be seen to be rooted in everyday aspects of cognition rather than in some more mysterious mental process.

Thus, certain aspects of Turner's distinction between political and fertility ritual, in the context of what he called 'ancestral cults' and 'earth cults', are in fact subsumed under my imagistic–doctrinal dichotomy. But in so far as Turner's arguments are founded on an opposition between a functionalist conception of structure and a mystical conception of *communitas*, we are bound to diverge. There remains, however, a second and equally important difference between the general thrust of my argument, and that of Victor Turner. This second divergence concerns the relationship between analytical dichotomies and the social institutions they are intended to illuminate.

Richard Werbner has discussed in some depth the merits of Turner's dichotomy between political ritual and fertility ritual, attaching particular emphasis to the notion that one operates in a localized domain, whereas the other is concerned with homogenizing a regional tradition. This of course is also a central aspect of my imagistic–doctrinal dichotomy. Yet Werbner was distrustful of the simplicity of dichotomous thinking. He wrote (1977: xiii; emphasis in original):

> The great utility of this [i.e. Turner's] contrast is its illumination of extreme cases. Like other ideal typologies, however, it tends to represent as mutually exclusive alternatives—the halves of parallel dichotomies—what are, in fact, *aspects* which combine in a surprising variety of ways within a range of actual cases.

I sympathize with this criticism and indeed would hope that my argument is immune to it. My point is not that a given religion or ritual is either imagistic or doctrinal, but rather that it can operate in either mode. In so far as I am proposing 'ideal types', these are abstract constellations of variables rather than types of either religion or ritual. In other words, particular religions and rituals may utilize one or other, or both, modes of religiosity.

To illustrate this point in concrete terms, it is useful to consider collective monetary donations in the Pomio Kivung, performed to obtain absolution and catharsis. These are specific types of named rituals: the absolution ritual is known as *Baim Lo* or *Stretim Lo* ('paying for/correcting [violations of] the Law') and the catharsis ritual is known as *Rausim Sem* ('casting out shame'). In a doctrinal mode, this ritual has no communicative content built into it. The action of placing money in a receptacle derives its meaning from verbalized exegesis, arising from Kivung doctrines concerning sin and atonement. But when this ritual was performed by members of the splinter group, it operated in an imagistic mode, and the transmission of meaning became more substantially an artefact of the actions themselves. Thus, the donors of money formed a naked human ring around the receptacle, such that their bodies connoted the outer posts of a round-house and the receptacle itself connoted the central, supporting post, which in turn resonated with emergent notions of the local leaders and Ten Laws post. In theological terms the rituals of catharsis and absolution were unquestionably the same rituals, but they were now operating in an altogether different way. The exegetical level was unimpaired, yet an alternative style of codification and transmission had been triggered, and a shift of emphasis from the doctrinal to the imagistic mode had been effected. Thus, if Turner's dichotomy is fundamentally about types of cults and types of rituals, mine is intended to distinguish types of *religiosity* which can mingle in both, albeit with contrasting cognitive and sociological implications.

Richard Werbner's own analysis bears very directly on the doctrinal–imagistic dichotomy. Here it assumes the guise of an opposition between 'regional' and 'non-regional' cults. Werbner defined 'regional cults' as 'cults of the middle range—more far reaching than any parochial cult of the little community, yet less inclusive in belief and membership than a world religion in its most universal form' (1977: ix). It is clear that the mainstream Pomio Kivung is, in Werbner's terms, a 'regional cult', whereas the splinter group of Dadul and Maranagi would be a 'cult of the little community', or what Werbner proceeded to call a 'non-regional cult'.

Yet, as Werbner's critique of Turner implied, the former eschewed dichotomous representations of cults and wanted to envisage regional cults as simultaneously non-regional in some domain of operation. In many ways Werbner appeared to follow Turner in his notion of what was entailed in these two domains, but believed that they operated in an 'unstable combination' (1977: xiv). The fundamental question which Werbner posed was 'what impact do regional and non-regional cults have on each other, and how do they wax and wane in relation to each other?' (1977: xi). If the terms 'regional' and 'non-regional' were substituted for 'doctrinal' and 'imagistic' (and it would not be entirely misleading to do so), then clearly Werbner was asking the same questions to which this present study addresses itself. And yet the force of Werbner's argument is reduced by his commitment to two theoretical assumptions, which I do not share.

The first is that the non-regional level of operation is amenable to symbolist and functionalist interpretations. Although firmly rejecting this approach in the analysis of regional cults, Werbner appeared to follow Turner in his basic orientation to the 'cult of the little community'. Werbner wrote (1977: xviii):

The 'community of the god' is a conception of boundedness, within the exclusive domain in Turner's terms. Membership in the ritual congregation is on a closed basis; its members share rights in resources, recognition of their vital interdependence, or the concern with the maintenance of the group. The correspondence theory suggests that the cult's spiritual subjects . . . and material objects . . . stand for something else: there is a symbolic representation . . . of particular interests. . . . It fits with Turner's understanding of the exclusive domain, also, that the 'community of the god' has its own shrines, the foci of segments, in central locations valued for communal control of crucial resources. After all, the contrary—the peripherality of shrines—would express and foster the tendency towards universalism, openness, and emancipation from the community.

As in my comments on Turner, with whom Werbner appears to be in agreement on this point, I should emphasize that the 'cult of the little community' discussed in this book (i.e. the splinter group of Dadul and Maranagi) was in no sense a functional response either to the demands of the wider movement or to common interests manifested at some other (i.e. non-religious) level of social reality.

A second assumption of Werbner's, which I do not share, results from his reaction (or, arguably, over-reaction) to Turner's apparent interest in religious typologies. Werbner, as I have pointed out, did not accept the notion that cults must be either universalistic or particularistic, or either inclusive or exclusive, or either outward-looking or localized, etc. Rather, he saw these as alternative dynamics that were mutually compatible in given cults. But Werbner seemed to go further than this—further, in fact, than may be necessary—by suggesting that *all* regional cults simultaneously operate in the local dynamic of an 'exclusive domain'.

Werbner distinguished between two main types of regional cults, a strategy hastily rationalized in view of his professed aversion to religious typologies. These two types were 'élitest' and 'egalitarian'. The Pomio Kivung would, of course, be an élitest regional cult, by virtue of its stable, centralized hierarchy and elaborate machinery for regulating behaviour among its ethnically diverse supporters. Werbner hypothesized systematic differences in the relations between non-regional and regional domains of operation within élitest and egalitarian cults, but he assumed that both domains were a ubiquitous feature of such cults. Here, once again, we diverge because, in so far as these domains correspond to doctrinal and imagistic modes of religiosity, I take the coincidence of both in a particular cult to be a matter of empirical investigation. They happen to coincide in the Pomio Kivung but, as I have observed, they do not coincide in all Melanesian movements. This is a crucial point if the sociological trajectories of these cults are to be correctly interpreted.

Ernest Gellner has proposed another dichotomous representation of religious and ritual action, which ties in with my imagistic–doctrinal dichotomy. In his famous article, entitled 'A Pendulum Swing Theory of Islam' (1969), Gellner distinguished between two 'syndromes' of characteristics in Muslim religious life, which he labelled 'P' and 'C'. The 'P' syndrome has much in common with what I call the doctrinal mode of religiosity. For example, the 'P' syndrome is characterized by reliance on *words* as the principal medium for transmission; the emotionality and sensuality of ritual action is 'minimized'; syndrome 'P' is uniformly distributed across a wide area and relatively stable over time; its ethos is 'universalistic' and its followers are 'anonymous' (1969: 130–5).

Gellner explicitly contrasted this state of affairs with syndrome 'C', which correspondingly has much in common with my notion of an 'imagistic' mode of religiosity. The 'C' syndrome is characterized by reliance on 'perceptual symbols and images' rather than words, as the principal medium for transmission; emotionality and sensual 'excesses' are a typical feature of syndrome 'C'; it is fragmented, heterodox, and unstable; its ethos is 'personalistic', and it produces localized solidarity, emphasizing 'both spatial and temporal boundaries' (1969: 130–6).

Gellner's dichotomy between syndromes 'P' and 'C' was clearly intended to shed light on the same divergence, explored in this study, between doctrinal and imagistic modes of religiosity. Gellner's explicit goal was to effect a kind of synthesis between Ibn Kaldun's model of political rotation in the Muslim state, and David Hume's model of an oscillation in religious phenomena.

Gellner's argument ran as follows. Syndrome 'P' (what I am calling the doctrinal mode of religiosity) predominates in the political centres (the towns), whereas syndrome 'C' (roughly my imagistic mode) prevails on the rural periphery. It is in the nature of syndrome 'P' that levels of cohesion are low, whereas syndrome 'C' promotes intense solidarity. Thus, 'the organization and ethos of the towns make them inimical to social cohesion and military prowess' (1969: 132), whereas the cohesion arising from the mode of ritual action prevailing in the countryside produces formidable political units. Due to the prevalence of syndrome 'C' (the imagistic mode) among the rural tribes, one of them is sooner or later able to move in on the town and replace the urban dynasty. But over time the new dynasty of rural origin is weakened: it comes to be dominated by syndrome 'P' (the doctrinal mode) and therefore loses its cohesiveness. Eventually, it is in turn replaced by another rural tribe whose syndrome 'C' characteristics are intact. Hence, we have in prospect a 'pendulum swing theory'.

A limitation with Gellner's approach arises from its macroscopic bent, viewing the historical process in exclusively abstract sociological terms. Gellner maintained that tribal 'unification is only achieved by religious means' (1969: 137) but whatever it is about syndrome 'C' that promotes cohesion was not specifically examined. Here, Gellner seems to be in the same boat as Turner and Werbner, who likewise associated the parochial cult with intense, localized solidarity by invoking the general formula of symbolist theory (wherein, crudely, 'the group equals god'). And yet, the reproduction of social cohesion, pregnant with sociological possibilities, has to be understood in the first place in *psychological* terms.

This is where my notion of an imagistic mode of religiosity is rather different from Gellner's notion of syndrome 'C'. The concern with 'perceptual symbols and images' as opposed to words, and with the emotionality of ritual action, has to be *shown* to be connected to sociological variables such as military prowess—the connection cannot be simply assumed or intuited. What is suggested by the notion of an imagistic mode of religiosity is that emotion and codification are linked with political potentialities, *via* specific processes of cognition and transmission.

The political potentialities apparently realized in the Muslim state are consistent with the model I have formulated, but clearly do not apply in the case of the Pomio Kivung. That is, although the splinter group in Dadul and Maranagi aspired to the goal of replacing the 'ruling' élite of the movement in Malmal, it never took pragmatic steps in that direction. The Pomio Kivung leadership is not reproduced by means of a political rotation. In fact, altogether different potentialities of the parochial cults on the periphery seem to be realized. In particular, I have suggested that these sporadic activities (possessing many of the characteristics of what Gellner called syndrome 'C') happen to safeguard rather than threaten the hegemony of the Pomio Kivung leadership.

Gellner associated syndrome 'P' with literacy. If only implicitly, the uniformity and stability of urban Islam was attributed to writing (1969: 131). Such an argument is entirely plausible but it leads to a serious oversimplification of the relationship between syndromes 'P' and 'C'. The latter was interpreted negatively, as a style of religiosity which has to make up for the absence of textual revelation, through 'the provision of audio-visual aids for the illiterate devotees' (1969: 134). My own view is that the style of codification engendered in scriptural revelation can *also* be activated in non-literate conditions. Conversely, the style of codification engendered in the imagistic mode cannot be transmitted in language, whether written or oral; it is part of an alternative mode of religiosity, describable in positive terms, which can, in principle, be activated in literate as well as non-literate societies. Here, the crucial corpus of writing to which I must address myself, is that provided by Jack Goody.

In a variety of publications (e.g. 1968, 1977, 1986) Goody has argued for a fundamental dichotomy between literate and non-literate societies, and the 'cultural genetics' which they engender. This in turn gave rise to a dichotomous representation of religious phenomena, conveyed in its essentials by the following passage (Goody 1986: 9–10):

In the literate churches, the dogma and services are rigid. . . . If change takes place, it often takes the form of a break-away movement . . . the process is deliberately reformist, even revolutionary, rather than the process of incorporation that tends to mark the oral situation.

In various ways, this contrast between oral and literate religions is of relevance to my imagistic–doctrinal dichotomy. The institutions and doctrines of the mainstream Pomio Kivung are characteristically rigid, producing marked uniformity and stability over space and time. In other words, some of the features which I associate with routinization are also among the features which Goody (and Gellner, above) have associated with literate traditions. What is it then that the social practices of routinization and literacy have in common, giving rise to parallel processes of cultural genetics?

I have attempted to provide an answer to this question in a recent article in *Man* (1992*b*), where I described a series of equivalencies between styles of codification in literate religions and in the non-literate but doctrinal mode of the Pomio Kivung movement. The main feature which (as Goody points out in numerous contexts) obviously helps to fix literate religious representations, and insulate them from innovation, is the fact that the written word is itself fixed. In the crudest terms, a commandment written on paper cannot be unconsciously revised, nor can revisionists ignore the palpable evidence which conservatives can physically brandish in their faces. This, Goody would argue, contrasts starkly with the oral situation where there is no material evidence to challenge revisionist ambitions. Where the principal repository for religious representations is memory, one might suppose that there is far greater scope for unrecognized, or at any rate unchallengeable, innovation. Religions would change gradually, perhaps even imperceptibly, and innovators would not be obliged to break away and go it alone. This, however, is to oversimplify the nature of memory as a cognitive faculty and as a sociological *tour de force*.

As I argued in Chapter 3, innovation within the mainstream Pomio Kivung (notwithstanding the orality of its followers) is a very tricky business. A major reason for this, in essence, is that most of the representations of the mainstream movement are fixed in people's minds, as surely as if they were fixed on paper. This state of affairs is a direct concomitant of routinization. The Ten Laws are repeated in five-week cycles, at least fifteen minutes of speech being publicly devoted to an elucidation of each of the Laws. Other religious representations are likewise repeated at length in public on a very regular basis (see Chapter 2). People have highly convergent schemas for these representations and instantly recognize deviations from them. Not only are deviations recognized but they are explicitly forbidden, requiring ratification by the Pomio Kivung leadership in Malmal. In these general conditions, it is inconceivable that major innovations could occur unnoticed or without a sound basis for conservative opposition.

Social memory (by which I mean, of course, convergent individual memories) is capable of fixing representations in much the same way as a written text. Moreover, the fact that these representations are codified in language means that they *could* be sustained in the form of a literate tradition were it not for the fact that rural New Guinea is largely non-literate. This suffices to explain the correspondences between my model of routinization in the doctrinal mode and Goody's conception of the literate churches.

The situation of 'gradual change' which Goody unfortunately attributed to oral conditions in general, is applicable to religions operating in the imagistic mode. This is not, however, largely because people forget their own cultural materials and have to invent new ones. I think it has more to do with the way these materials are codified. I have elsewhere pointed out that analogic imagery is somewhat self-contained, in the sense that interference in one iconic process does not automatically require modifications of surrounding imagery (see Whitehouse 1992*b*: 789–92). By contrast, logically integrated doctrines codified in language cannot be disrupted in one sector without affecting the ideology more generally. Thus, the features of divergent 'cultural genetics' which Goody attached to a literate–oral dichotomy can in fact be more precisely located in my doctrinal–imagistic dichotomy.

Yet another model which has striking relevance for the one elaborated in this book was recently put forward by Fredrik Barth (1990). Barth's model was inspired by the contrasting ways in which Balinese Gurus and Melanesian initiators manage religious knowledge. What is especially pertinent about Barth's line of argument is that it focused on alternative styles of transmission and codification. The Guru transmits religious ideas in the medium of language (primarily the spoken word), whereas the initiator cultivates revelations in a non-verbal medium (primarily through ritual action). Barth also made the crucial point that verbalized ideas are more transportable than analogic imagery engendered in collective ritual performances (1990: 646–7). Nevertheless, the force of Barth's argument was reduced by a naïve view of cultural transmission.

Barth associated the transmission of Gurus' ideas with a particular emphasis on the relation between givers and receivers of knowledge, and he proceeded to explore the sociological implications of this emphasis. For example, his analogy with material exchange encouraged him to envisage the Guru–pupil relationship as one of nurturance in a parent–child model. Conversely, the initiator was seen as being engaged in exchange with spiritual agencies, in a kind of sacrifice. According to this view, novices undergoing initiation, in contrast with the pupils of a Balinese Guru, should not be regarded as the main recipients of transmission.

But even if this serves to highlight certain ideological contrasts between some Balinese representations and some Melanesian ones, the theoretical merits of the argument (regarding transmission) are hard to see. The thrust of Barth's argument is expressed in his assertion that whereas Gurus 'provide' knowledge, initiators 'withhold' it (1990: 641–2). This implies that a Guru's representations, codified in language, are somehow more substantially transmitted than an initiator's non-verbal analogic imagery. The problem with couching the contrast in these quantitative terms (i.e. 'more' transmission versus 'less') is that these alternative bodies of cultural materials are not in fact measurable on a common scale (if indeed they are measurable at all). New Guinea initiations *do* serve to transmit a complex body of religious knowledge (otherwise, of course, they would not survive through the generations). In an earlier work Barth (1987) developed an interesting theory of how inter-generational transmission occurs in New Guinea initiation systems, albeit one with which I partially disagree (Whitehouse 1992*b*). Thus, whatever the ideological purpose of initiation might be, it actually fails to withhold knowledge from novices and, on the contrary, positively transmits a wealth of it.

In any case, the realities of cultural transmission are probably not as much at variance with the ideologies of initiators as this notion of withholding might imply. In many cases, novices are explicitly the pupils of their initiators, in much the same way as the followers of Balinese Gurus. The principal difference lies in the *mode* of transmission: initiators demonstrate (i.e. transmit their wisdom through actions) whereas Gurus explicate (i.e. transmit their wisdom by word of mouth). This difference in the mode of transmission may be put to a variety of theologically stipulated purposes, but these are not concomitants of the mode itself, as Barth seems to suppose. The prayer of a pious Catholic is codified in language but it is primarily a transaction with the 'other world' rather than with a human audience. This, of course, is the converse of the Guru principle, although the style of codification and transmission may be precisely the same. Thus, the connection which Barth observes between styles of codification and the directionality and quantity of transmission is theoretically unwarranted.

In concluding my survey of dichotomous representations of religious life, I must give space to one which precedes all the others, and in some way has probably inspired them all. This is Max Weber's portrayal of routinization and charisma. Weber's conception of 'charismatic authority' contains much that is of relevance to an understanding of the imagistic mode of religiosity. For example, Weber's notion of charismatic 'inspiration' served to highlight the emotionality of this type of religious experience and its resistance to verbal formulation or expression. Weber once observed that religious experience, in its 'highest, mystical form . . . cannot be adequately reproduced by means of our lingual and conceptual apparatus'. And he went on to observe of the Baptist sects of the seventeenth century 'how unbelievably intense, measured by the present standards, the dogmatic interests even of the laymen were' (1930: 233).

There are numerous other ways in which the notions of charismatic and imagistic modes of religiosity overlap. Weber associated the charismatic style with social cohesion 'based on an emotional form of communal relationship' (1947: 360). Like the other theorists discussed above, Weber merely intuited rather than laid bare the nature of the connection between the imagistic mode of religiosity and the promotion of social cohesion. But at a time when psychological theories were rudimentary, Weber can hardly be criticized on this account with the same vigour.

Weber also acknowledged an intermittent or periodic pattern of recurrence in the charismatic mode of religiosity. Weber observed that this mode occurs 'specifically outside the realm of everyday routine' (1947: 361). At this point in his argument, Weber was primarily concerned with showing that charismatic authority is innovative rather than 'institutionalized'. This is not something which I regard as an absolutely necessary feature of the imagistic mode, although it is a typical one, and for good reason. The splinter group in Dadul and Maranagi departed from the routine institutional framework of the mainstream movement in an innovative fashion. That is, it did not simply reproduce the climactic rituals and ideas of former splinter groups in the region. Nevertheless, New Guinea initiation rites, in which the imagistic mode is also predominant, probably have greater continuity over time. This is feasible because novices undergo the rites once in a lifetime (at least, as 'objects' of the performance). If novices were to undergo the same initiation rites more than once, it would hardly be conducive to intense religious experience and revelation to reproduce substantially the form and content of the earlier rites. In practice, where there are several grades in an initiation system, each fresh wave of rituals that the novices must undergo will be different from the last. But either way, this does not require innovation because only some of the participants must experience a novel set of revelations. In the cargo cult, it is normally rather different. Everybody, in an important sense, is a novice; there is no initiated set that can reproduce what its members have already experienced. Necessity is in this case the mother of invention and, in practice, innovation is a normal feature of such cults.

The major weakness in Weber's model arises from his attachment to the idea of charisma as the most basic, identifying feature of what I call the imagistic mode of religiosity. Weber used the term charisma to refer to a personal attribute of leaders rather than to a mode of religiosity. And, as Bendix points out 'Weber made it clear that charisma has been a recurrent phenomenon because persons endowed with this gift of grace . . . have asserted their leadership under all historical conditions' (1960: 326). This, I think, is Weber's argument at its weakest. To say that a leader is charismatic is to say something about his or her followers, rather than simply about the leader. This is a point cogently elaborated by Peter Worsley in the revised edition of his famous study of Melanesian cargo cults (1968).

Weber's preoccupation with charismatic leadership is problematic in other ways. In particular, the kind of leadership which Weber had in mind is not in fact an intrinsic feature of the imagistic mode, but simply one of many catalysts that can give rise to it. As soon as the imagistic mode is in full swing, dynamic leadership becomes virtually impossible. This is a point which I elaborated at great length in Chapters 4 and 5, when I described the rise and zenith of splinter-group leaders. In the case of the Dadul–Maranagi group charismatic leadership was a trigger for largely non-verbal forms of expression. When these forms were substantially in place, in the guise of collective ritual performances founded around analogic imagery, the dynamism of the splinter-group leaders was seriously curtailed. Tanotka's and Baninge's leadership was then expressed, not so much by their public oratory, as by the image of a central object enclosed by a wall of house-posts or naked human bodies. Once the leadership had been objectified in this way, it could not communicate anything in or of itself, and the burden of transmission was shifted onto the ritual architecture or choreography itself, which was a collective responsibility. This never happens in cults which are founded around the doctrinal mode of religiosity. Koriam, and latterly Kolman, retained their charismatic and dynamic influence over the mainstream Pomio Kivung, although the movement could, hypothetically, be reproduced in the absence of such figures. It would then look very much like the Christian churches, which manage in the absence of a Christ incarnate. It is a different matter for cults operating in the imagistic mode. Charismatic leadership is not an optional extra, except in the early phases of its construction; it is an irrelevance to the basically non-verbal, analogic mode of cultural transmission.

The point to emphasize, however, is that Weber's model of the divergence between charismatic and routinized modes of religiosity has many features in common with my imagistic-doctrinal dichotomy. The charismatic mode entailed high levels of emotional and sensual arousal, whereas routinization was the expression of rational authority, and of intellectual, rather than affective, concerns. Consequently, Weber associated charismatic authority with intense social cohesion, and routinization with more diffuse solidarity. This dichotomy was in turn linked up to Weber's recognition of a divergence in the diachronic features of innovation and stability respectively. For Weber, charismatic regimes were intermittent phenomena. He famously postulated an oscillation between occasional bursts of charismatic religiosity and periods of stability, or what he referred to as 'routinized' orders. Weber's model of these processes has seeped into the anthropological imagination, as the foregoing discussion of comparable models suggests. Clearly, these dichotomous representations have been stimulated in large part by empirical discoveries, all around the world, of contrasting modes of religiosity. But many of us are indebted, however indirectly, to Weber's early formulation of this divergence.

The Interpretation of Religion

Within social anthropology there are three main types of perspective on religion. These can be glossed as intellectualist, psychological, and sociological. The most straightforward of these approaches, perhaps, is the intellectualist one. In its essentials, this is the argument that religion provides answers to cosmological problems. In so far as these religious solutions are compelling, they answer a basic intellectual desire for comprehension. The intellectualist tradition in anthropology, commonly traced to nineteenth-century origins in the work of Spencer, Tylor, and Frazer, continues to attract 'modern' scholars (e.g. Horton 1967, Jarvie and Agassi 1970, Lindstrom 1990, etc.).

On the whole, theories in the intellectualist tradition do not encompass sociological arguments, although they can easily be regarded as complementing them (e.g. Gluckman 1963: 100–37). By contrast, psychological theories often incorporate an intellectualist bent. Gell, for example, observes that Juillerat's recent psychoanalytic interpretation of a New Guinea ritual, adopts an intellectualist stance (Gell 1992: 136). This is hardly surprising since the intellectualist perspective is based on certain psychological presuppositions. A hard line is sometimes taken by sociologically oriented anthropologists, who reject these presuppositions outright (e.g. Brunton 1980). What is very rare is a mode of interpretation which draws on all three approaches simultaneously, welding them together into a unified theoretical framework. The absence of such a synthesis has been particularly marked in the context of dichotomous representations of religious phenomena.

I share the presuppositions of intellectualists that religion has an explanatory role in human affairs. But unlike many Victorian scholars, who envisaged religion as a kind of 'failed science', I do not presume that the problems with which religion grapples necessarily inhere in everyday human experience. What makes the religious life intellectually compelling is its capacity to trigger 'revelations': particularly salient or valued experiences of insight, comprehension, or enlightenment. This is not achieved in religious action simply by seizing upon some mysterious phenomenon and inventing an unfalsifiable and unnecessarily extravagant explanation for it. What is more characteristic of revelatory experience is the realization that what one thought to be true, as well as what one failed to comprehend, is not at all as one might expect. Transcendental truths may be persuasive because they fill in gaps in one's comprehension, but alternatively because they eliminate recognized possibilities, even ones that have formerly been taken for granted. Two of the basic ways in which this can be done have been explored above.

First, revelation can take the form of logical persuasion by means of the force of argument, codified in language. The power of this form of revelation is temporary, however, because that which comes as a surprise initially rapidly becomes familiar and therefore unsurprising. In other words, the psychological impact of revelation through logical argumentation is subject to decay. Secondly, revelation can take the form of cognitive shocks embedded not so much in logic as in something akin to ecstatic states. For example, Baktaman novices discover in the course of their initiation that their everyday assumptions about certain animals are entirely false. A species of marsupial which, in everyday life, is classed as vermin 'is elevated [in ritual] to a sacramental category all of its own: privileged food monopolized by the ancestor' (Barth 1975: 82). The reversal of taken-for-granted assumptions is underpinned by the poignancy and emotionality of the circumstances in which it is transmitted. Novices do not attempt to insert religious revelations into a logically integrated framework, such as one typically finds in routinized and literate traditions. Rather, these revelations are cognized as more or less independent concrete metaphors, which are linked (if at all) by thematic association rather than by logical (e.g. causal, implicational) connections. These revelations have a lasting impact, partly because of the high level of emotional and sensual stimulation at encoding. As episodic memories, they have their analogue in Western experiences of 'conversion' or 'divine inspiration', rather than in persuasion from the pulpit.

What makes a set of representations 'revelatory', whether they are logically or iconically codified, is their capacity to overturn old presumptions and to replace them with superior, authoritative ones. Acknowledging this important facet of religious experience requires both an intellectualist and psychological approach. But the intellectualist component should not restrict itself to the religious resolution of problems engendered in everyday experience. The everyday assumption, among the Baktaman, that a particular marsupial constitutes disgusting vermin, is in no way problematic. It is not a mystery crying out for resolution. Likewise, where verbally codified revelations spread, they need not address themselves exclusively to existing queries. For example, the Baining followers of the Pomio Kivung were astonished to discover that betel-nut was polluting, and that its repulsiveness extended to (and originated in) menstruation. In the past, neither betel-chewing nor menstruation had been perceived by the Baining as problems requiring some religious solution. But there is no reason to suppose that this reduced the revelatory power of Koriam's pronouncements on these subjects. By the same token, it is undoubtedly true (and of considerable importance) that religion can also provide answers to questions prefigured in everyday discourse (see Chapter 7). The intellectualist perspective commonly confines itself to the latter scenario, to the exclusion of the former, but in this study I invoke the perspective to encompass both.

The same psychological arguments which underpin my intellectualist orientation give rise to the main sociological arguments of this book. I have explicitly linked the scale, structure, ethos, and longevity of cults to the cognitive operations entailed in their transmission. Like Turner, Werbner, Gellner, Weber, and others, I perceive connections between one mode of religiosity and social cohesion, and between another mode of religiosity and universalism/expansionism. But, unlike these other writers, I have sought to identify the psychological dynamics which give rise to these divergent sociological patterns. Much more research needs to be conducted along these lines but, as Sperber (1985: 78–9) points out:

[it is no longer adequate to formulate] causal explanations of cultural facts . . . at a fairly abstract level, ignoring thereby the micro-mechanisms of cognition and communication. This is certainly what anthropologists and sociologists have tried to do, linking, for instance, economic infrastructure and religion. However good it might be, any such explanation would be incomplete. For economic infrastructure to affect religion, it must affect human minds.

It is precisely this line of reasoning which gives rise to a dissolution of the boundaries between intellectualist, psychological, and sociological approaches to the interpretation of religion. The great challenge lies in providing a more comprehensive and plausible theory of cultural transmission. Within 'new religions' transmission is often particularly varied and intense, and what Sperber calls the 'micro-mechanisms of cognition and communication' may be especially amenable to observation. The principal aim of this book has been to sketch just such a view, however impressionistically, from 'inside the cult'.

Notes

1. In May's terms (1982: 1–2), the Pomio Kivung would therefore be described as a 'micronationalist movement'.
2. One of the leading campaigners for a separate Pomio-Baining province has been Alois Koki, the acknowledged leader of the Pomio Kivung political wing since the death of Koriam. During the 1970s, Alois was often to be heard on the radio, criticizing the East New Britain Provincial Government for its alleged neglect of ethnic groups outside the Tolai-occupied Gazelle. Attempts on the part of the ENBP Government to allay such criticism have a long history, but the first really substantial attempt to rectify iniquities in the province began with the commissioning of a 'Pomio-Bainings Area Study', undertaken by the British consultancy outfit, Atkins International, in 1985. On the strength of this report, Alois Koki persuaded the Prime Minister of the day (Wingti) to allocate a budget of K5.37 million to development projects in the Pomio-Baining area over a five-year period (1988–93). These projects

were co-ordinated by a so-called 'Pomio-Baining Area Authority', whose expenditure was to be met by the national government budget, supplemented to the tune of 20 per cent from provincial coffers. Although the 'Technical Committee' which divided up the cake was dominated by Tolai provincial politicians (notably the Premier and Minister for Finance), the Area Authority operated in a constitutional 'grey area', since the only authorities accorded statutory recognition were community governments. The period leading up to the establishment of the Pomio-Baining Area Authority was marked by a weakening of Pomio Kivung calls for a separate province. But the early stages of the project have been beset with problems. Wastage of funds, adverse weather conditions, political wrangles, and other difficulties greatly reduced the effectiveness of the authority in its first two years, and it remains to be seen whether Pomio Kivung demands for political autonomy will soon be renewed.

BIBLIOGRAPHY

ANDERSON, B. (1983), *Imagined Communities*, London: Veso.

BARTH, F. (1975), *Ritual and Knowledge among the Baktaman of New Guinea*, New Haven, Conn.: Yale University Press.

——(1987), *Cosmologies in the Making: A Generative Approach to Cultural Variation in Inner New Guinea*, Cambridge: Cambridge University Press.

——(1990), 'The Guru and the Conjurer: Transactions in Knowledge and the Shaping of Culture in Southeast Asia and Melanesia', *Man*, NS 25: 640–53.

BATESON, G. (1931/2), 'Further Notes on a Snake Dance of the Baining', *Oceania*, 2: 232–44.

BELSHAW, C. S. (1950), 'The Significance of Modern Cults in Melanesian Development', *Australian Outlook*, 4: 116–25.

BENDIX, R. (1960), *Max Weber: An Intellectual Portrait*, London: Doubleday.

BENEDICT, R. (1935), *Patterns of Culture*, London: Routledge & Kegan Paul.

BERNDT, R. M. (1952/3), 'A Cargo Movement in the East Central Highlands of New Guinea', *Oceania*, 23: 40–65, 137–58.

BODROGI, T. (1951), 'Colonization and Religious Movements in Melanesia', *Academia Scientiarum Hungaricae-Acta Ethnographica*, 2: 259–92.

BORO, R. W. H. (1951), 'Patrol to the Central Bainings', *Patrol Report No. 2, 1951/2*, Kokopo Sub-district.

BROWN, G. (1908), *Pioneer-Missionary and Explorer: An Autobiography*, London: Hodder & Stoughton.

BROWN, P. (1966), 'Social Change and Social Movements' in E. K. Fisk (ed.), *New Guinea on the Threshold*, Canberra: Australian National University Press.

BROWN, R. and KULIK, J. (1982), 'Flashbulb Memory' in U. Neisser (ed.), *Memory Observed: Remembering in Natural Contexts*, San Francisco: W. H. Freeman.

BRUNTON, R. (1971), 'Cargo Cults and Systems of Exchange in Melanesia', *Mankind*, 8: 115–28.

——(1980), 'Misconstrued Order in Melanesian Religion', *Man*, NS 17: 239–58.

CALVERT, K. (1976), 'Cargo Cult Mentality and Development in the New Hebrides Today' in A. Mamak and G. McCall (eds.), *Paradise Postponed: Essays on Research and Development in the South Pacific*, Rushcutters Bay: Pergamon Press.

CHRISTIANSEN, S. A. (1992), 'Emotional Stress and Eyewitness Memory: A Critical Review', *Psychological Bulletin*, 112: 284–309.

COCHRANE, G. (1970), *Big Men and Cargo Cults*, Oxford: Clarendon Press.

CONNERTON, P. (1989), *How Societies Remember*, Cambridge: Cambridge University Press.

CORBIN, G. A. (1979), 'The Art of the Baining: New Britain' in S. M. Mead (ed.), *Exploring the Visual Art of Oceania: Australia, Melanesia, Micronesia, and Polynesia*, Honolulu: University Press of Hawaii.

COUNTS, D. E. A. (1971), 'Cargo or Council: Two Approaches to Development in North-West New Britain', *Oceania*, 41: 288–97.

COUNTS, D. E. A. and COUNTS, D. (1976), 'Apprehension in the Backwaters', *Oceania*, 46: 283–305.

DARGIE, R. E. (1969), 'Patrol to the Central Bainings', *Patrol Report No. 15, 1968/9*, Kokopo Sub-district.

EPSTEIN, A. L. (1969), *Matupit; Land, Politics, and Change among the Tolai of New Britain*, Canberra: Australian National University Press.

——(1978), *Ethos and Identity*, London: Tavistock.

EPSTEIN, T. S. (1968), *Capitalism, Primitive and Modern: Some Aspects of Tolai Economic Growth*, East Lansing: Michigan University Press.

——(1969), 'The Mataungan Affair: The First Radical Mass Political Movement', *New Guinea and Australia, The Pacific and South-East Asia*, 4: 8–14.

ERRINGTON, F. and GEWERTZ, D. (1985), 'The Chief of the Chambri: Social Change and Cultural Permeability among a New Guinea people', *American Ethnologist*, 12: 442–54.

FAJANS, J. (1985), *They Make Themselves: Life Cycle, Domestic Cycle and Ritual among the Baining*, Ph.D. thesis, Stanford University.

FAYLE, R. J. (1959), 'Patrol to the Central Bainings', *Patrol Report No. 6, 1958/9*, Kokopo Sub-district.

FINGLETON, J. S. (1985), *Changing Land Tenure in Melanesia: The Tolai Experience*, Ph.D. thesis, Australian National University.

FIRTH, R. (1970), *Rank and Religion in Tikopia: A Study in Polynesian Paganism and Conversion to Christianity*, London: George Allen & Unwin.

FORGE, A. (1966), 'Art and Environment in the Sepik' in *Proceedings of the Royal Anthropological Institute of Great Britain and Ireland for 1965*, 23–31.

GELL, A. (1975), *Metamorphosis of the Cassowaries: Umeda Society, Language, and Ritual*, London: Athlone Press.

——(1992), 'Under the Sign of the Cassowary' in B. Juillerat (1992) (ed.).

GELLNER, E. (1969), 'A Pendulum Swing Theory of Islam' in R. Robertson (ed.), *Sociology of Religion: Selected Readings*, Harmondsworth: Penguin Education.

GERRITSON, R. (1975), 'Aspects of the Political Evolution of Rural Papua New Guinea: Towards a Political Economy of the Terminal Peasantry', unpub. paper, Australian National University.

GESCH, P. (1990), 'The Cultivation of Surprise and Excess: The Encounter of Cultures in the Sepik of Papua New Guinea' in G. W. Trompf (1990) (ed.).

GLUCKMAN, M. (1963), *Order and Rebellion in Tribal Africa*, London: Cohen and West.

GOODY, J. (1968), 'Introduction' in J. Goody (ed.), *Literacy in Traditional Societies*, Cambridge: Cambridge University Press.

GOODY, J. (1977), *The Domestication of the Savage Mind*, Cambridge: Cambridge University Press.

——(1986), *The Logic of Writing and the Organization of Society*, Cambridge: Cambridge University Press.

GROSART, I. (1982), 'Nationalism and Micronationalism: The Tolai Case' in R. J. May (1982) (ed.).

GUIART, J. (1951), 'Forerunners of Melanesian Nationalism', *Oceania*, 22: 81–90.

HARRISON, S. J. (1990), *Stealing People's Names: History and Politics in a Sepik River Cosmology*, Cambridge: Cambridge University Press.

HERDT, G. (1989), 'Spirit Familiars in the Religious Imagination of Sambia Shamans' in G. H. Herdt and M. Stephen (eds.), *The Religious Imagination in New Guinea*, New Brunswick, NJ: Rutgers University Press.

HESSE, K. (1982), *Baining Life and Lore*, Port Moresby: Institute of Papua New Guinea Studies.

HIRSCH, E. (1990), 'From Bones to Betelnuts: Processes of Ritual Transformation and the Development of "National Culture" in Papua New Guinea', *Man*, NS 25: 18–34.

HOGBIN, H. I. (1958), *Social Change*, London: Watts.

HORTON, R. (1967), 'African Traditional Thought and Western Science', *Africa*, 37: 50–71, 37: 155–87.

INSELMANN, R. (1944), *Letub: The Cult of the Secret of Wealth*, M.A. thesis, Kennedy School of Missions.

JARVIE, I. C. and AGASSI, J. (1970), 'The Problem of Rationality of Magic' in B. R. Wilson (ed.), *Rationality*, Oxford: Blackwell.

JUILLERAT, B. (1992) (ed.), *Shooting the Sun: Ritual and Meaning in West Sepik*, Washington: Smithsonian Institution Press.

KLEMENSEN, A. (1965), *Strange Island: the Noona Dan in the South Seas*, London: Souvenir Press.

KOIMANREA, F. and BAILOENAKIA, P. (1983), 'The Pomio Kivung Movement', *Religious Movements in Melanesia Today*, 1/2, Goroka: The Melanesian Institute.

LACEY, R. (1990), 'Journeys of Transformation: The Discovery and Disclosure of Cosmic Secrets in Melanesia' in G. W. Trompf (ed.).

LANG, K. J. (1950), 'Patrol to the Central Bainings', *Patrol Report No. 3, 1949/50*, Kokopo Sub-district.

LANTERNARI, V. (1962), 'Messianism: Its Historical Origin and Morphology', *History of Religions*, 2: 52–72.

——(1963), *The Religions of the Oppressed*, London: MacGibbon & Kee.

LAWRENCE, P. (1971), *Road Belong Cargo: A Study of the Cargo Movement in the Southern Madang District, New Guinea*, Prospect Heights, Ill.: Waveland Press.

LEWIS, I. M. (1971), *Ecstatic Religion: A Study of Shamanism and Spirit Possession*, London: Routledge.

LINDSTROM, L. (1990), 'Knowledge of Cargo, Knowledge of Cult: Truth and Power on Tanna, Vanuatu' in G. W. Trompf (1990) (ed.).

LOFTUS, E. M. (1980), *Memory*, Reading, Mass.: Addison-Wesley.

MAY, R. J. (1975), 'The View from Huron: The Peli Association of the East Sepik District', New Guinea Research Discussion Paper No. 8, unpub. paper.

——(ed.) (1982), *Micronationalist Movements in Papua New Guinea*, Canberra: Australian National University Press.

McDOWELL, N. (1988), 'A Note on Cargo Cults and Cultural Constructions of Change', *Pacific Studies*, 11: 121–34.

MEAD, M. (1964), *Continuities in Cultural Evolution*, New Haven, Conn.: Yale University Press.

MORAUTA, L. (1972), 'The Politics of Cargo Cults in the Madang Area', *Man*, NS 7: 430–47.

——(1974), *Beyond the Village: Local Politics in Madang, Papua New Guinea*, London: Athlone Press.

NEUMANN, K. (1992), *Not the Way It Really Was: Constructing the Tolai Past*, Honolulu: University of Hawaii Press.

O'HANLON, M. (1992), 'Unstable Images and Second Skins: Artefacts, Exegesis, and Assessments in the New Guinea Highlands', *Man*, NS 27: 587–608.

OTTO, T. (1992), 'The Paliau Movement in Manus and the Objectification of Tradition', *History and Anthropology*, 5: 427–54.

PANOFF, M. (1969), 'Inter-Tribal Relations of the Maenge People of New Britain', *New Guinea Research Bulletin*, 30: 1–62.

PARKER, J. and PARKER, D. (1974), 'A Tentative Phonology of Baining (Kakat Dialect)', *Phonologies of Four Papua New Guinea Languages*, Ukarumpa: Summer Institute of Linguistics.

——(1988), 'Du Mythe à la propagande: un cas Melanesien', *L'Homme*, 28: 252–62.

POOL, J. (1984), 'Objet Insaisissable ou Anthropologie sans Objet?', *Journal de la Société des Oceanistes: Musée de l'Homme*, 79: 219–33.

ROWLEY, C. D. (1965), *The New Guinea Villager: A Retrospect from 1964*, Melbourne: F. W. Cheshire.

SAHLINS, M. (1972), *Stone Age Economics*, London: Tavistock.

SALISBURY, R. F. (1970), *Vunamami: Economic Transformation in a Traditional Society*, Berkeley, Calif.: University of California Press.

SCHOLEM, G. (1946), *Major Trends in Jewish Mysticism*, New York: Schocken Books.

SCRIVNER, E. and SAFER, M. A. (1988), 'Eyewitnesses show Hypermnesia for Details about a Violent Event', *Journal of Applied Psychology*, 73: 371–7.

SHANK, R. C. (1982*a*), *Dynamic Memory*, Cambridge: Cambridge University Press.

——(1982*b*), 'Reminding and Memory Organization' in W. G. Lehnert and

M. H. Ringle (eds.), *Strategies for Natural Language Processing*, Hillsdale: Lawrence Erlbaum Associates.

SMITH, A. D. S. (1979), *Nationalism in the Twentieth Century*, Oxford: Martin Robertson.

SPERBER, D. (1985), 'Anthropology and Psychology: Towards an Epidemiology of Representations', *Man*, NS 20: 73–89.

SPRIGGS, M. (1982), 'Bougainville, December 1989 – January 1990: A Personal History' in R. J. May and M. Spriggs (eds.), *The Bougainville Crisis*, Bathurst: Crawford House Press.

——(1991), 'Bougainville talks may offer chance for peace' *The Canberra Times*, 23 August.

STEINBAUER, F. (1979), *Melanesian Cargo Cults: New Salvation Movements in the South Pacific*, London: George Prior.

STRATHERN, M. (1988), *The Gender of the Gift: Problems with Women and Problems with Society in Melanesia*, Berkeley, Calif.: University of California Press.

TALMON, Y. (1966), 'Millenarian Movements', *European Journal of Sociology*, 7: 159–200.

THRUPP, S. L. (1962) (ed.), *Millennial Dreams in Action*, The Hague: Mouton.

TOVALELE, P. (1977), 'The Pomio Cargo Cult—East New Britain' in R. Adams (ed.), *Socio-Economic Change—Papua New Guinea*, Lae: University of Technology.

TROMPF, G. W. (1984), 'What Has Happened to Melanesian "Cargo Cults"?', *Religious Movements in Melanesia Today*, 3/4, Goroka: The Melanesian Institute.

——(1990*a*), 'Keeping the Lo under a Melanesian Messiah: An Analysis of the Pomio Kivung, East New Britain' in J. Barker (ed.), *Christianity in Oceania: Ethnographic Perspectives*, Lanham, Md.: University Press of America.

——(1990*b*), 'The Cargo and the Millennium on Both Sides of the Pacific' in G. W. Trompf (1990) (ed.).

——(1990) (ed.), *Cargo Cults and Millenarian Movements: Transoceanic Comparisons of New Religious Movements*, Berlin: Mouton de Gruyter.

TULVING, E. (1972), 'Episodic and Semantic Memory' in E. Tulving and W. Donaldson (eds.), *Organization of Memory*, New York: Academic Press.

TURNER, V. W. (1974), *Dramas, Fields, and Metaphors: Symbolic Action in Human Society*, Ithaca, NY: Cornell University Press.

WAGNER, R. (1986), *Asiwinarong: Ethos, Image, and Social Power among the Usen Barok of New Ireland*, Princeton: Princeton University Press.

WEBER, M. (1930), *The Protestant Ethic and the Spirit of Capitalism*, London: George Allen and Unwin.

——(1947), *The Theory of Social and Economic Organization*, Oxford: Oxford University Press.

WEINER, J. F. (1991), *The Empty Place: Poetry, Space, and Being among the Foi of Papua New Guinea*, Bloomington: Indiana University Press.

WERBNER, R. P. (1977), *Regional Cults*, London: Academic Press.

WHITEHOUSE, H. (1989), 'The Oscillating Equilibrium of Production among the Mali Baining', *Research in Melanesia*, 13: 34–53.

——(1990), 'A Cyclical Model of Structural Transformation among the Mali Baining', *Cambridge Anthropology*, 15: 70–84.

——(1992*a*), 'Leaders and Logics, Persons and Polities' in *History and Anthropology*, 6: 103–24.

——(1992*b*), 'Memorable Religions: Transmission, Codification, and Change in Divergent Melanesian Contexts', *Man*, NS 27: 777–97.

——(1993), 'Religions of Fear and Religions of Routine', unpub. paper, University of Oxford.

——(1994), 'Strong Words and Forceful Winds: Religious Experience and Political Process in Melanesia', *Oceania*, 65: 40–58.

——(Forthcoming *a*), 'From Possession to Apotheosis: Transformation and Disguise in the Leadership of a Cargo Movement', in R. Feinberg and K. A. Watson-Gegeo (eds.), *Leadership and Change in the Western Pacific*, London: Athlone Press.

——(Forthcoming *b*), 'Music and Religious Experience in Papua New Guinea' in *Encyclopedia of World Music*, New York: Garland Publishing.

WILLIAMS, F. E. (1928), *Orokaiva Magic*, London: Humphrey Milford.

WINOGRAD, E. and KILLINGER, W. A. (1983), 'Relating Age at Encoding in Early Childhood to Adult Recall: Development of Flashbulb Memories', *Journal of Experimental Psychology: General*, 112: 413–22.

WORSLEY, P. (1957), *The Trumpet Shall Sound: A Study of 'Cargo' Cults in Melanesia*, London: MacGibbon & Kee.

——(1968), *The Trumpet Shall Sound: A Study of 'Cargo' Cults in Melanesia*, 2nd, augmented ed., New York: Schocken.

YERKES, R. M. and DODSON, J. D. (1908), 'The Relation of Strength of Stimulus to Rapidity of Habit-Information', *Journal of Comparative Neurology of Psychology*, 18: 459–82.

GLOSSARY

Mali Baining terms

angarega: bullroarer (see Fig. 2).
awan: celebratory daytime dance.
awanga: costumed figures appearing at the *awan* (see Figs. 1 and 12).
ilotka: costumed figures normally appearing at the *mendas* (see Fig. 17).
mendas: night-time dance, celebrating the completion of initiation rites.

Pidgin terms

aipas: unenlightened, blind.
baim lo: receive absolution.
gavman: government.
Glas Bilong Rausim Sem: catharsis receptacle.
Glas Bilong Sek/Glas Beilong Stretim Lo: absolution receptacle.
Haus Bilong Bernard: Bernard's Temple.
Haus Famili: Family Temple.
Haus Kivung: Meeting House.
Haus Matmat: Cemetery temple.
Kalibus: Hell (also 'gaol').
komiti: appointed official ('orator', in the Kivung context).
kastam: traditions, customs.
kuskus: clerk, record-keeper ('witness', in the Kivung context).
loea: lawyer.
marimari: atonement (also 'pity').
masalai: spirits.
pekato: sin.
ripot: reports (messages) from the ancestors, received in temples.
Setan: Satan, the Devil.
Taim Bilong Gavman: Period of the Government.
Taim Bilong Kampani: Period of the Companies.
Tenpela Lo: the Ten Laws.
tubuan (sometimes *tumbuan*): masked dancers.
Vilij Gavman (formerly *Kaunsel Tumbuna*): Village Government, a body composed of God and the morally pure ancestors.

INDEX

absolution: and codification 207–8; and finance 50, 142; and purification 64 n., 77, 80, 82, 112, 140; and ritual 55–6, 66, 78, 112, 126; and salvation 130, 143; and temple ritual 69–70, 75, 76, 77, 80

Adam and Eve 1, 56–7, 79, 113; *see also* original sin

Agassi, J. 218

ancestors: bringing wealth and power 2–3, 35, 39, 41, 43, 94, 143, 144, *see also* cargo cult, millenarism, Period of the Companies; relations with 52–4, 77–8, 89, 133; welcoming back 5, 115, *see also* vigils; and white skin 6–7, 35, 43, 47, 54, 93, 96–7, 115, 117–18, 130, 143–4; *see also* Adam and Eve, Aringawuk, bosses, Gwasinga, Kivung, splinter group, Village Government, Wutka

Anderson, B. 86, 196

Arabum: and evil 115, 147; history 25, 26; location 9, 20; marching through 136; and the mission 158; people 24, 26; and Sawai 133, 145; school 132

Aringawuk 93–5, 103, 105, 106, 123, 146, 153

atonement 53–4, 78, 207

Australian Administration: and Koriam 50, 51; and land 25, 27–9; and Mataunganism 29–33, 38–9; and native officials 59, 75; protection by 61, 176–7

awan 7, 15–16, 20, 23, 102–3, 123–5, 151

awanga 15–18, 20, 103, 124–5, 126, 128 n., 137, 151

Baining: dances 13–15; relations with Tolai 1–2, 12, 31–2, 36; traditional social organization 23; *see also* Kairak, Kaket, Mali Baining, Simbali, Uramot

Bailoenakia, P. 42, 45, 47–8, 59, 62 n., 183

Baninge 5: his apotheosis 116–20, 143; his background 90; and confrontation 161; and defiance 131–7, 153; and dreams 103–5, 109–12; and finance 122, 141–2, 143, 145; his installation 119; and

proselytism 133–4; and reports 99–101, 138; and ritual 105–8, 117–19, 129–31, 137–54; and Tanotka's possession 90–5; and waning authority 156, 159, 160; his withdrawal 143–4, 146, 147, 153, 216

Bapka 133, 134, 141, 155–7, 189, 190

Barth, F. 14, 51, 128, 152, 182, 193, 213–15, 219

Bateson, G. 8, 13, 14, 19

Belshaw, C. 200

Bendix, R. 216

Benedict, R. 193, 204

Bernard 41, 48, 53, 54, 59, 80, 102

Bernard's Temple: description of 74–5; and doctrine 78; and reports 139, 140; ritual 53, 66, 75, 81

Berndt, R. M. 128, 199

betel-nut: and addiction 188; and anti-Tolai sentiment 2, 60; felling of palms 169; and national culture 60; and original sin 56–7; and revelation 219; sale of 169; and sectarianism 21, 62; and the splinter group 134

blasphemy 63 n., 64 n.

Bodrogi, T. 200

Boro, R. W. H. 27

bosses 68, 75, 78, 98, 110–12, 146

Bougainville 202

Brown, G. 22

Brown, P. 200

Brown, R. 195

Brunton, R. 192 n., 218

bullroarer (*angarega*) 16, 17, 19, 124–5

Calvert, K. 39

cargo cult: and commerce 39; and criticism 7, 157, 164; and dual leadership 128 n.; and innovation 216; and Kivung 1, 41, 47, 50; and Mali history 179–80; and nationalism 200–3; and routinization 87; and traditional religion 180–2

cash cropping: and contested land 171; history of 27, 28, 34, 172; and reciprocity 36–8, 39; and splinter group 121–2, 161–2, 169–71